MW00830735

Pop Culture, Politics, and the News

JOURNALISM AND POLITICAL COMMUNICATION UNBOUND

Series editors: Daniel Kreiss, University of North Carolina at Chapel Hill, and Nikki Usher, University of Illinois at Urbana-Champaign

Journalism and Political Communication Unbound seeks to be a high-profile book series that reaches far beyond the academy to an interested public of policymakers, journalists, public intellectuals, and citizens eager to make sense of contemporary politics and media. "Unbound" in the series title has multiple meanings: it refers to the unbinding of borders between the fields of communication, political communication, and journalism, as well as related disciplines such as political science, sociology, and science and technology studies; it highlights the ways traditional frameworks for scholarship have disintegrated in the wake of changing digital technologies and new social, political, economic, and cultural dynamics; and it reflects the unbinding of media in a hybrid world of flows across mediums.

Other books in the series:

Journalism Research That Matters
Valérie Bélair-Gagnon and Nikki Usher

Reckoning: Journalism's Limits and Possibilities
Candis Callison and Mary Lynn Young

Imagined Audiences: How Journalists Perceive and Pursue the Public
Jacob L. Nelson

Democracy Lives in Darkness: How and Why People Keep Their Politics a Secret
Emily Van Duyn

Pop Culture, Politics, and the News

Entertainment Journalism in the Polarized Media Landscape

JOEL PENNEY

OXFORD
UNIVERSITY PRESS

Oxford University Press is a department of the University of Oxford. It furthers
the University's objective of excellence in research, scholarship, and education
by publishing worldwide. Oxford is a registered trade mark of Oxford University
Press in the UK and certain other countries.

Published in the United States of America by Oxford University Press
198 Madison Avenue, New York, NY 10016, United States of America.

© Oxford University Press 2022

All rights reserved. No part of this publication may be reproduced, stored in
a retrieval system, or transmitted, in any form or by any means, without the
prior permission in writing of Oxford University Press, or as expressly permitted
by law, by license, or under terms agreed with the appropriate reproduction
rights organization. Inquiries concerning reproduction outside the scope of the
above should be sent to the Rights Department, Oxford University Press, at the
address above.

You must not circulate this work in any other form
and you must impose this same condition on any acquirer.

Library of Congress Control Number: 2022938349
ISBN 978–0–19–755759–4 (pbk.)
ISBN 978–0–19–755758–7 (hbk.)

DOI: 10.1093/oso/9780197557587.001.0001

1 3 5 7 9 8 6 4 2

Paperback printed by Marquis, Canada
Hardback printed by Bridgeport National Bindery, Inc., United States of America

To Jiayang

Contents

Acknowledgments

First and foremost, I would like to thank Nikki Usher and Daniel Kreiss, editors of the Journalism and Political Communication Unbound series, for making this book possible. What began as a friendly "Hey, what are you working on?" transformed over time into an enormously beneficial mentorship and friendship, the results of which we hold now in our hands. Thank you for your guidance, your advice, your tough questions, and, above all, your enthusiastic support.

This book would also not have been possible without the immensely valuable help of Angela Chnapko at Oxford University Press. As we worked together again, the process could not have been more enjoyable. You always make it look easy when it is most certainly anything but.

I am also deeply grateful for the mentorship and support of Andrew Chadwick, editor of my first book at Oxford University Press and provider of my "big break," as it were. As I have said before elsewhere and will keep saying, thank you for believing in me and my work.

On the subject of mentors, I must extend the deepest gratitude to my dissertation advisor, Barbie Zelizer. It may have taken me a long time to come around to becoming a journalism scholar proper, but there's no way that I could have pulled it off without your wisdom and endless inspiration.

Recently, I learned of the passing of Elihu Katz, another one of my esteemed professors at the University of Pennsylvania's Annenberg School. I consider myself beyond fortunate to have studied firsthand with one of the pioneers and intellectual heavyweights of the communication studies field, who is and will always be greatly missed. This one's for you, Dr. Katz.

Big, big thank yous also go out to the entire Annenberg faculty, who helped launch my scholarly career and gave me the confidence to pursue the big questions that preoccupy my mind as well as the tools to effectively probe them. There are too many to thank here individually, but I would single out Michael X. Delli Carpini, who has helped make examining the relationship between entertainment and politics an absolute delight.

I am deeply grateful for the support of the faculty and staff at Montclair State University's School of Communication and Media, my academic home now for more than a decade. Special thanks to our director, Keith Strudler, for creating such a vibrant and encouraging professional environment, as well as the great Harry Haines, who helped bring me there in the first place and has been an outstanding colleague ever since. There is truly no shortage of great colleagues at Montclair State, and thank yous also go out to, among others, Chris McKinley, Hugh Curnutt, Yi Luo, Todd Kelshaw, Christine Lemesianou, Marylou Naumoff, Bond Benton, Tara Conley, Vanessa Greenwood, Tara George, Kelly Whiteside, Roberta Friedman, Tony Pemberton, David Sanders, Tom Franklin, and the irreplaceable Stephanie Wood.

Beyond the Red Hawk community, I am greatly thankful for the support and friendship of many remarkable colleagues across the communication, media, and political science fields. That list is too long to ever complete but most certainly includes Brooke Erin Duffy, Michael Serazio, Lee Shaker, Matt Carlson, Aymar Jean Christian, Jennifer Stromer-Galley, Jonathan Corpus Ong, Thierry Giasson, Neta Kligler-Vilenchik, Lynn Schofield Clark, Larry Gross, Emilija Gagrcin, David Karpf, Philip N. Howard, and, last but not least, Abraham Khan, who helped out with some valuable sports journalism references for this book.

I would also like to extend the deepest of thanks to the dozens of entertainment journalism professionals and news audience members who volunteered to participate in the interview research for this book. In the middle of a pandemic, you dropped it all to help out with an academic study, and I know that could not have been easy. Without your time and effort and willingness to share, this project would simply not have been possible.

On a personal note, I would never have been able to weather the pandemic and keep trudging on without the support of fabulous friends like Peter Micek and Isedua Oribhabor, Michael Sherman, Gina Yates, Mark Siegmund, Gilbert Galindo and Marcel Pena, Ryan McGavin, An Phan, Yaowei Yeo and Michael Weatherbee, Chris Sherman, Jon Monteverde, and Brett Bumgarner. Thanks for the great times and good vibes.

My deepest thanks and my heart go out, always and forever, to my wonderful, loving family: Jacqueline and Dean, David and Adriana, Hilary and Fran, Fiona and Brynn, Darren and Micole, Eric and Jenn, Margeaux, Sandy, the Surkin family, Celia and the Flynns, John and Kim, Chris and Jane and Alby, and Grandma Sue. I also want to pay special tribute to two incredible people we lost during the pandemic, John Sullivan and Florence Surkin, whom we remember with abundant love. We keep on remembering Marvin and Flora Birnbaum and Norman Penney, my late grandparents and eternal inspirations.

Finally, I want to thank my husband, Jiayang—for your love, your support, your kindness, and your remarkable ability to put up with me and bring me joy. Over the course of writing this book, we moved in together, got married, and survived a global pandemic—pretty eventful, huh? Here's to a life of happiness ahead and, I hope, some very long-awaited vacations!

Introduction

News about an actor's firing from a TV sitcom after tweeting a racist joke or an uproar over a pop star appropriating African American culture in a music video. News about a Hollywood film franchise hiring its first female director after years of employing only men. News about a drama series' stereotypical portrayal of a gay character or another's groundbreaking inclusion of a transgender lead. Headlines mocking celebrities for grandstanding about progressive causes at awards show podiums. Exposés of male Hollywood power players abusing actresses behind the scenes. Reviews of a new superhero film that examine its progressive racial symbolism or those looking at another's lack of inclusion of performers of color. Columns lambasting the entertainment industry for "cancel culture" and "wokeness" or columns defending it for holding public figures in pop culture accountable for racism, sexism, and homophobia. If you scanned the digital news landscape on any given day, you would likely encounter stories such as these. Typically categorized as "entertainment" or "culture" by various outlets, these news reports and commentaries nonetheless address some of the most contentious, hot-button social and political issues of our time.

Yet up to this point, the work of news professionals covering the world of Hollywood and celebrity has rarely been given serious attention in discussions of political journalism and political communication. Instead, it has been largely written off as trivial and disposable "soft news," with little to offer in terms of substance or public value. This book, by contrast, explores how entertainment journalism has taken on a key role in contemporary political discourse. Through news formats such as the editorial "think piece," review-based arts and cultural criticism, investigative reports on celebrities' off-screen behavior, and daily coverage of "social media outrage cycles," the field of entertainment journalism has come to occupy a prominent position in today's public political conversation. This is especially the case for "culture war" battles over the identity politics of race, gender, and sexuality and their symbolic representation in the media, which journalists not only cover but also frequently participate in as advocates and agents of agenda-setting.

Pop Culture, Politics, and the News. Joel Penney, Oxford University Press. © Oxford University Press 2022.
DOI: 10.1093/oso/9780197557587.003.0001

From controversies over Hollywood's on-screen portrayals and off-screen decision-making to the latest outrage over a celebrity's public statements or private behavior, the terrain of pop culture now serves as the basis for politically oriented news and commentary across a wide range of outlets and from both left and right perspectives. However, very little is known about how this form of journalism is produced and consumed as a component of the digital news ecosystem or about its potential impact on the political interest and knowledge of its audiences, the politics of the entertainment industry it covers, and the shape of public debate more broadly. *Pop Culture, Politics and the News* fills this gap by offering a comprehensive analysis of this timely yet vastly understudied topic. Drawing on dozens of interviews with entertainment journalists who produce politically minded coverage as well as dozens of testimonials from news audience members who share it on social media, this book argues for the importance of reframing our understanding of impactful journalism and persuasive political communication at a time when issues of culture and identity have moved thoroughly to the center of US public discourse.

However, while making the case that entertainment journalism must be taken seriously as political communication even though it may sometimes appear frivolous on the surface, the book also considers the for-profit nature of this work and how the day-to-day economic pressures of the digital news landscape complicate its public value. By squaring journalists' accounts of industrial practice with critiques of hyper-commercialism, "clickbait," and the lure of social media virality, it takes stock of both the potential dangers and the potential benefits of channeling political discourse through the attention-grabbing lens of pop culture and celebrity news. In addition, it examines how audiences engage with this highly accessible and emotionally resonant form of journalism on social media and use it as a resource for political expression and conversation, raising important questions about how it may serve as a bridge to public issue engagement as well as a potential distraction from on-the-ground political concerns. As a cutting-edge, data-rich analysis of the blurring boundaries between entertainment, politics, social media activism, and partisan and advocacy journalism, *Pop Culture, Politics, and the News* offers a new road map for understanding the complex and shifting digital information landscape.

Chapter 1 begins by detailing the key theoretical frameworks of the book and their relationship to previous scholarship on cultural journalism, "soft news," and the digital information economy. It then provides a historical narrative of entertainment journalism's ongoing role in political discourse that emphasizes its development in conjunction with the post-1960s emergence of modern identity politics and subsequent battles over media representation of marginalized groups. Opening with the exemplary case study of entertainment awards show controversies in front of the camera and behind the scenes, the chapter defines the terrain of today's politically engaged pop culture journalism and situates it in a context that accounts for its recent flourishing in the digital news ecosystem as well as its relationship to the long-term trends of identity-based polarization and the hybridization of the political and cultural spheres. Through its exploration of both past and present, chapter 1 argues that pop culture discourse in the news plays an important role in communicating political viewpoints and ideological critiques to the public and therefore must be taken more seriously in journalism and media studies and not simply dismissed as a diverting reprieve from "real" public affairs content. The chapter also introduces the key tensions surrounding entertainment journalism's growing engagement with hot-button political debates that lay the groundwork for the theoretical interventions of subsequent chapters—that is, the potential for the accessible lens of pop culture and celebrity to create new points of entry into public issue discourse and expand the political engagement of its audiences, as well as the dynamics of hyper-commercialism and hyper-partisanship that have made lifestyle and opinion news formats into targets of critique and consternation.

Chapter 2 explores how reporters and critics who approach pop culture from a left-wing perspective understand their role in shaping the political conversation around Hollywood. The first of several chapters built around firsthand interviews with entertainment journalists who explicitly engage with political issues in their work, the chapter focuses on how pop culture coverage of the left seeks to advance a project of cultural, social, and political progress by publicly scrutinizing the entertainment industry for its messages, representations, and off-screen actions that are collectively understood as having a meaningful impact. The analysis centers on the voicing of feminist, antiracist, and LGBT perspectives in cultural reporting across a bevy of mainstream and specialty digital news outlets, affording widespread public circulation to viewpoints and ideas that may otherwise be confined to the far more limited discursive spaces of critical theory and cultural studies. Furthermore, the chapter explores how these journalists assess their influence on cultural producers and form an apparatus of accountability—typically in conjunction with social media activists—that creates public pressure on Hollywood to reform in alignment with shared ideological agendas. At the same time, journalists also raise concerns about how the push for pop culture progress can be taken advantage of by Hollywood decision-makers to merely secure glowing news coverage for corporate entertainment products. Furthermore, the chapter addresses how issues of tokenism and surface-level progress also vex the field of entertainment journalism itself, even as it has made parallel moves to diversify its workforce and elevate the cultural voices and political concerns of members of marginalized groups.

Chapter 3 shifts focus to how journalists working for conservative news outlets use pop culture coverage as a weapon in a broader "culture war" that attacks the perceived dominance of left-wing ideology throughout US society. In contrast to the frames of social progress and industry accountability that characterize politically oriented entertainment journalism of the left, its right-wing counterpart is animated by feelings of victimization and resentment, as commentators see themselves as fighting back against Hollywood's unfair treatment of conservative messaging and talent that dovetails with broader narratives of right-wing social and cultural grievance. Interviews with conservative entertainment journalists highlight the key influence of Andrew Breitbart, whose dictum that "politics are downstream from culture" has fueled new generations of conservative reporters and critics who seek to reclaim the battleground of pop culture as a means of securing long-term political success. Chapter 3 details the specific frames that these journalists employ in their work, focusing on the embrace of freedom-of-expression rhetoric as a tactical response to the perceived moral wrongs of "cancel culture." The interviews further reveal how these journalists often frame themselves as fighting for a depoliticized space in pop culture that eschews left-wing messaging and "woke" agendas around identity and representation, in direct contrast to the core belief among progressive cultural commentators that "all art is political." Yet, rather than acting as a monolithic bloc, the field of conservative entertainment journalism is seemingly divided between a more self-consciously nuanced approach that makes appeals to traditional journalistic standards and seeks to avoid extremism around matters of identity politics and a more aggressive far-right approach that draws upon heated "culture war" passions to martial forces of bigotry and hate.

After detailing the specific political interventions and agendas of pop culture journalists working in the left and right news spheres, chapter 4 explores how such agendas are also shaped, as well as sometimes undercut, by the demands of the for-profit digital news ecosystem. This chapter provides an in-depth look at the economics of entertainment journalism and how coverage of political controversy in pop culture aligns with the broader profit-making strategies of digital media companies and demands for online clicks and social media shares. In addition to examining commercial pressures within specific news organizations, the discussion also maps the broader field-level dynamics of entertainment journalism and how it fits within an industry that is struggling for monetization in a crowded and rapidly changing digital information environment. Furthermore, the chapter explores how individual journalists at the pop culture–politics nexus adopt specific strategies to negotiate the pressures of "clickbait" commercialism—such as pegging long-developing works of social and political criticism to the biggest blockbuster entertainment events of the day—as well as how they address critiques about quality and sincerity and accusations of cynical pandering to polarized audiences. Throughout the analysis, the chapter interrogates the seeming contradiction of the news industry's embrace of pop culture controversy to serve bottom-line needs and its simultaneous devaluing of professional roles and expertise in entertainment journalism that threaten to hold the field back from fulfilling its important public mission.

Continuing chapter 4's inside look into the practice of entertainment journalism within the commercialized and polarized digital media landscape, chapter 5 examines how these journalists use social media monitoring and feedback to aid in their professional work while also contending with the heated and often vicious online responses they receive from a deeply fractured public. The chapter begins by exploring how entertainment reporters and critics track social media for story ideas and mine user tweets and posts for content and trend analysis, with particular attention to the "social media outrage cycles" that fuel pop culture controversies and catalyze coverage in digital news outlets. The discussion then turns to entertainment journalists' accounts of how they make sense of the online responses to their work, which range from positive affirmations that can provide a tangible sense of public impact to more negative and even hateful reactions that can actively discourage future coverage. In particular, the disturbing accounts of harassment and death threats that journalists routinely receive when criticizing beloved pop culture properties on political grounds offer a sobering look into the toxic environment of many online fan communities as well the fraught landscape that journalists face when challenging impassioned segments of the audience who can now speak back directly via social media. Furthermore, the fact that pop culture news stories provoke such extreme reactions on the internet, frequently of a hyper-partisan nature, further attests to how the terrain of entertainment and celebrity has become a key battleground of contemporary political discourse.

Chapter 6 expands on chapter 5's discussion of the journalist–audience relationship by exploring firsthand interviews with members of the news audience who actively engage with politically oriented pop culture stories on social media. The chapter 6 traces how these audiences encounter this kind of journalism as part of their everyday news diet, as well as how they perceive its relative importance and how they gauge their relative interest in comparison with other types of news content. Furthermore, it probes the specific social media habits of those who interact online with this kind of news content, examining how they share it among groups of peers and how they incorporate it into acts of personal political expression and conversation—in terms of both sympathetic amplification and reactionary critique (often taking the form of "cancel culture" backlash). After mapping the different types of audiences who find their way to news at the pop culture–politics nexus, the analysis turns to how these audiences understand its relative value for learning about specific political issues and gaining exposure to new ideological perspectives and viewpoints. Although there is some evidence to suggest that pop-culture-focused audiences can use entertainment news as a bridge to political discourse that they would not otherwise access, a more common pattern appears to be that audiences who already have high levels of political interest find value in pop culture news discourse as a supplemental element of the political information environment. At the same time, however, some audience members who follow and share this news voice concerns about its capacity to distract them from more traditional public affairs content, suggesting that entertainment journalism can function as a bridge both toward and away from the sphere of political engagement.

The book concludes with chapter 7, a discussion that summarizes its key themes and integrates accounts of production and reception into a cohesive picture of entertainment journalism's complex role in contemporary politics and the business of news. While affirming that pop culture reporting and commentary can provide significant value to the public, particularly when elevating culturally situated perspectives and voices that have been historically marginalized in political news discourse, the chapter interrogates how this value is challenged by dynamics of hyper-commercialism and hyper-partisanship. Using right-wing news outlets' increasingly exaggerated claims about the dangers of "cancel culture" as a backdrop, the discussion explores how the business models of what has been termed "identity media" risk obscuring on-the-ground political realities in favor of coverage that indulges "culture war" appetites and fantasies in potentially manipulative fashion. Furthermore, the use of pop culture discourse as a tool in service of political advocacy also poses risks to the integrity of the cultural journalism field, whose members often resist being reduced to pundits or propagandists and seek to secure a space for complex cultural conversation that does not conform to simplified partisan categories. To help address these issues, the concluding chapter argues for the importance of committing institutional resources to professional roles in entertainment journalism and building closer relationships to the academic fields of media and cultural studies, as the theoretical innovations of the latter can contribute to the sophistication of the field and strengthen both its quality and its public value.

Entertainment journalism still has many barriers to overcome in terms of providing a meaningful public service to news audiences. Yet such an endeavor is increasingly necessary at a time when the cultural and political spheres are colliding in ever more unprecedented and consequential ways. One only needs to consider the election of a former reality-TV game-show host as US president to understand that pop culture matters for politics, no matter how trivial it can appear. Moreover, as entertainment industry figures increasingly embrace the roles of political advocates and agents of transformation in a landscape of blurred media and social boundaries, the journalists who cover them have an obligation—and an opportunity—to help the public make sense of these dynamics and provide much-needed insight.

Due to a multitude of factors, the politics of race, gender, sexuality, and social identity more generally have been moving more and more to the center of US public debates and struggles, making the symbolic representation of these issues in entertainment as salient as ever. However, the reporters and commentators tasked with unpacking the politics of pop culture have been largely devalued, or simply ignored, by both the journalism industry and the academic journalism studies field. Chapter 1 will explore the complex reasons for this predicament, in addition to providing an alternative historical narrative of entertainment journalism that recontextualizes its longstanding significance in the political communication environment.

1

Why Pop Culture News Matters

Theorizing and Historicizing Entertainment Journalism as Political Communication

When the Golden Globe nominations for film and television were announced in February 2021, news audiences could follow at least five different politically oriented stories related to the awards. Many reports covering the announcement led with the fact that three women had been nominated for Best Director, which was celebrated as a "historic" moment for gender diversity in headlines from outlets such as CNBC, BBC, and the *Guardian*. At the same time, the lack of nominations for black-led films and TV shows sparked a wave of more critical articles, such as the *Los Angeles Times*'s "After a Year Defined by Black Stories, Golden Globe Nominations Fall Short" and PopSugar's "The Golden Globes Didn't Just Snub Black Actors, They Snubbed the Black Experience." Meanwhile, a separate controversy emerged over the Korean American drama *Minari* being relegated to the Best Foreign Language Film category and disqualified from Best Picture, leading to probing "think pieces" such as CNN's "What the Controversy over 'Minari' Says about Being American" and NBC's "What Hollywood's Treatment of 'Minari' Says about the Asian American Dream." Concerns over identity representation also factored into news reports of heterosexual actor James Corden's nomination for a flamboyant gay role in *The Prom* (deemed "offensive" by Buzzfeed and "unfortunate" by the *Advocate*), as well as coverage of the nominations for *Music*, a film that had been excoriated for its depiction of autism and the casting of non-autistic actors in autistic roles. Writing for the *Independent*, pop culture opinion columnist Helen Brown summed up the critical response in a piece titled "Face the *Music*: Why Sia's Dangerous Film Doesn't Deserve a Golden Globe."

As such a headline underscores, the public discourse about entertainment awards—and contemporary pop culture in general—has become about far more than just mere entertainment. Rather, journalists who cover Hollywood news like the Golden Globes frequently highlight their intersection with

Pop Culture, Politics, and the News. Joel Penney, Oxford University Press. © Oxford University Press 2022. DOI: 10.1093/oso/9780197557587.003.0002

hot-button social and political issues, to the point where the pop culture beat now often resembles a form of public affairs journalism. This was illustrated even more dramatically by the *LA Times*'s investigative reporting on the Hollywood Foreign Press Association (HFPA), the controversial group of entertainment reporters who make up the voting body for the Golden Globes. Several weeks after the 2021 nominations were announced, the newspaper published an exposé revealing that the HFPA—whose journalism credentials and professional ethics had long been criticized—had no African Americans among its eighty-seven members. Coming on the heels of the previous year's "racial reckoning" in Hollywood in the aftermath of George Floyd's murder and the resurgence of Black Lives Matter activism, the report sent shock waves through the entertainment industry and received a flood of coverage by news outlets citing the *LA Times* investigation. A few months into the mounting controversy, NBCUniversal announced that it would not air the next edition of the Golden Globes, leaving the future of the awards show in doubt (the following year, the star-studded ceremony was canceled under a full industry boycott, and winners were announced, rather unceremoniously, via tweet). The field of entertainment journalism could thus take credit not only for raising awareness of Hollywood's racism problem but also for pushing the industry toward public accountability and reform in true "fourth estate" fashion.

However, while a great deal of today's pop culture reporting and commentary doubles as public advocacy for progressive social values and political causes, the field is also sharply divided along partisan lines and contains a significant element of conservative backlash. An opinion piece for Fox News, for instance, labeled NBCUniversal "race hypocrites" for dropping the Golden Globes, while commentators on NBCUniversal's news channel MSNBC were simultaneously attacking an African American Republican senator. More pointedly, a Breitbart columnist defended the HFPA as victims of a "Woke Gestapo," complaining that "a major cultural institution that has been around for decades is in genuine jeopardy of being blacklisted into oblivion." In other words, the right-wing news outlet framed the Golden Globes saga as yet another manifestation of an out-of-control left-wing "cancel culture," a theme that has come to define the broader conservative movement in the Trump era and beyond. By following coverage of an ostensibly frivolous entertainment awards show, news audiences thus could find themselves plunged into the center of some of the most contentious political debates of our time.

A marquee episode in the today's "culture wars," the Golden Globes controversy for a brief time became a near-endless resource for journalistic reports and "takes" that examined the political dimensions of Hollywood entertainment and celebrity—that is, until a week or so later, when news outlets moved on to the next wave of pop culture controversy. From a cynical perspective, one could view these coverage cycles as illustrating some of the worst tendencies of for-profit journalism in the digital age: the obsession with click-grabbing entertainment and celebrity topics, the deployment of outrage and anger to gin up audience interest and social media shares, the rapid-fire embrace and subsequent discarding of the polarizing controversy of the day. However, looking at them more charitably, one can identify a rich discourse examining issues of inequality, discrimination, stereotyping, and more, all wrapped inside the glossy packaging of just another day's pop culture news coverage. In some cases, as in the Golden Globes example, politically minded entertainment journalism can even spur institutional change, although the greater public import of reforming cultural symbols like televised awards shows remains open for debate.

The fact that entertainment journalists are so easily able to find these kinds of political angles to cover in the first place reflects the broader intermeshing of the cultural and political spheres, a long-term process that has been documented and theorized by scholars for many decades. In the book *Politics and Popular Culture*, John Street offers a helpful framework for sorting out the various dynamics at play. On the one hand, we can understand "politics *as* pop culture" in the sense that the traditional political sphere—governments, parties, politicians, and the journalistic apparatus that covers them—has taken on more and more aspects of popular media entertainment, reflected in everything from the phenomenon of celebrity candidates to the packaging of politics news in entertainment-style formats like satire and tabloid sensationalism. On the other hand, we can understand "pop culture *as* politics" in the sense that the world of arts and entertainment, including Hollywood film and television as well as popular music, video games, and celebrity culture more broadly, frequently addresses political subject matter in its content and also becomes the basis for politically and ideologically oriented forms of public analysis and critique.[1] This book will focus fairly exclusively on the latter set of dynamics, referred to here as the "pop culture–politics nexus" (as opposed to "politics–to–pop culture nexus," a rich and deserving topic for many other volumes). Yet, as Street emphasizes, these two processes should be recognized as closely interrelated and are in a sense mirror images of each other, illustrating how both spheres of activity are ultimately expressions of the values and identities within the society. We can further add that the growth of modern media technologies has profoundly blurred traditional social boundaries to the point where both entertainment and politics are now experienced and consumed through the same media screens and take on what scholars refer to as "media logics,"[2] making any hard and fast distinctions increasingly untenable.

At its core, journalism trained at the pop culture–politics nexus resembles a mainstream, mass-market version of the kind of critical media studies scholarship that academics have long published for a much smaller and more specialized audience. For more than a century, scholars have devoted serious attention to analyzing mass culture for its political and ideological meanings and effects, from the post-Marxist Frankfurt School to later approaches that incorporate feminist, postcolonial, and queer theory, among others. However, this work has been largely confined to the academic ivory tower, written in often dense prose that can be difficult to access for the lay reader. By contrast, today's entertainment journalism routinely provides ideological discussions and analyses of pop culture to a much broader swath of the public, filling the headlines of mass-market news sites across the polarized digital media landscape. As shown by the example of controversy cycles over a stray awards show nomination or snub, a single morsel of pop culture news can now serve as a springboard for myriad reports and commentaries that explore a host of political issues from varying perspectives.

The broader significance of this journalism is complex and multifaceted, raising important questions about its potential to popularize political ideas in the public sphere and engage audiences who may otherwise be inattentive to political issues through the accessible lens of entertainment and celebrity. The goal in this book is to interrogate these central questions, examining how both news professionals and audiences make sense of the political role played by entertainment journalism as well as how this role may be complicated by its commercial character. However, before beginning to explore how this journalism can be theorized as an impactful form of political communication and chart its substantial historical role in US political discourse, it is first necessary to confront its rather dodgy reputation in journalism circles. As an amalgam of several news formats—including "soft news" celebrity reporting, reviews of newly released Hollywood product, and op-ed-style punditry—that have not traditionally been held in very high regard in the journalism world, it is not at all surprising that it has often been met with hostility and mockery, if it is even acknowledged at all. Furthermore, this negative view is compounded by its close connection to key industry trends in the commercial digital news landscape that have caused much concern and apprehension in the journalism community.

Entertainment Journalism in the For-Profit Digital News Landscape

In the essay "The Crisis in News," journalism scholar Michael Schudson highlights how the use of digital audience metrics has dramatically changed how news organizations are able to assess the appeal of stories, paving the way for editorial judgment based on an "awareness of marketplace success" rather than purely journalistic criteria.[3] In the most extreme cases, Schudson notes, websites now pay writers based on clicks and even peg hiring and firing decisions to the amount of web traffic that their stories bring in. At the same time, these organizations have increased pressure on their staff writers to produce more and more content each day to maximize reach and engagement numbers, a trend that the industry has likened to a "hamster wheel."[4] Making a case for how the commercial motives of internet publishing undermine democracy and the quality of journalism, Robert McChesney points to evidence from digital news companies, such as the owners of the Huffington Post discussing how their editorial judgment has become wholly tied to the "profitability consideration" of attracting clicks and ad revenue.[5] As critics like McChesney and Schudson argue, a digital economy that rewards journalists for the speed, quantity, and crowd-pleasing popularity of their work poses dire risks to professional standards of journalistic quality. Furthermore, the industry's adoption of increasingly sophisticated data metrics to assess its audiences will only continue to exacerbate these risks, as Caitlin Petre argues in *All the News That's Fit to Click*: "Metrics could facilitate a regime of scientific management in which journalists are reduced from expert arbiters of newsworthiness to mere executors tasked with unquestioningly following the dictates of quantified representations of audience popularity."[6]

Among the news formats that industry members understand as attracting valuable audience clicks and attention, entertainment and celebrity news looms large. As scholar Jacob L. Nelson explains, there has been a "consistent observation" within news outlets that "audiences consume more sports, weather, and celebrity news than they do news about politics and foreign affairs" and that "this industry-wide consensus is the reason . . . online news outlets publish so much pop culture content."[7] In their study *The News Gap*, researchers Pablo J. Boczkowski and Eugenia Mitchelstein similarly find that "the stories that garner the most attention from the public tend to be about sports, crime, entertainment, and weather," rather than the kinds of politics and public affairs stories that journalists view as the most important and newsworthy.[8] Their research measures the news content that receives the most online page views and rises to the top of "most emailed" and "most commented" lists, finding that non-public-affairs content (a category that can be defined in different ways, to be discussed later) consistently outperforms traditional political news in the digital information environment, even across varying geographic and ideological contexts. These news consumption patterns—revealed by large-scale quantitative measures that bypass the biases in audience members' stated preferences—raise significant concerns in Boczkowski and Mitchelstein's analysis, as they argue that "trivial" forms of information such as entertainment news that receive the most clicks and shares "aren't enough for the healthy functioning of the body politic."[9]

At the same time, scholarship on the digital news economy also highlights how journalism that forefronts strong opinion and viewpoint—including along the lines of partisan political divides—has become similarly incentivized in the industry's quest for online attention. On the internet, information surplus and intense competition push news organizations to stand out from the crowd and offer something different to attract audiences, and while original reporting is rather expensive, unique opinion and analysis are comparatively cheap and cost-effective.[10] As George Brock puts it, "the quantity of information" on the web "raises the premium on being able to sort it, illuminate its meaning and importance. That also boosts the importance of individual voice."[11] Although this trend began prior to the internet, when talk radio and then cable television demonstrated that opinionated analysis could successfully bring in new audiences for news, Brock points out how "pure-play" online journalism has moved even farther away from the "stiff and solemn" style of traditional journalistic objectivity and neutrality in the pursuit of capturing the attention of target niche audiences.[12] Likewise, Ronald L. Jacobs and Eleanor Townsley find that the "space of opinion" in the news business has greatly expanded over time as news organizations add more and more opinion-based content and innovate a near-endless variety of opinion formats, and this is particularly true for digital-first entities that position themselves as market alternatives to traditional mainstream journalism.[13]

One major consequence of this expansion of opinion, as Michael Serazio highlights in an analysis of contemporary digital sports journalism, is the growth of the "hot-take industrial complex," in which online journalists are pressured to churn out instantaneous reactions to news topics that most reliably get user clicks.[14] Serazio argues that the unique set of demands and constraints of the online news business "forces one into hot takes rather than deep nuanced reporting," which inevitably "radicalizes the tone of digital discourse" in favor of the loudest and most attention-commanding opinions.[15] In the specific domain of sports journalism, such "hot takes" can often be of the nonpolitical variety, and Serazio notes that journalists on the sports beat are frequently ordered by management to avoid sharing explicit political viewpoints so as not to offend segments of the audience.[16] By contrast, online audiences for political coverage are far more segmented along partisan lines, and thus more ideologically driven "takes"—including political commentary on sports as a crossover pop culture phenomenon—appear to make good business sense.

These economic trends are reflected in the rise of partisan news sites that have come to play a significant role in the digital news industry and, according to research, now often lead the news media agenda as a whole.[17] Such "pure play" online news sites with a distinctive, ideologically driven editorial voice have become some of the most reliable sources of today's politically oriented entertainment journalism, including examples such as the Daily Beast on the left and the Daily Wire on the right. As a later chapter will explore, the often intensive focus of outlets like these on political controversies in pop culture is inextricable from considerations of audience interest in entertainment and celebrity topics, as the mere mention in a headline of a blockbuster franchise like *Star Wars* or a marquee celebrity like Kanye West can draw enormous online attention and clicks. Although journalists in the for-profit digital news business are often conscious of avoiding the excesses of audience-chasing "clickbait," as the lowest-regarded industry product is frequently labeled, they are also keenly aware of the emotional pull of pop culture as a driver of audience interest and engagement. When this widely appealing and emotionally resonant subject matter is combined with the most contentious and provocative public issues of the day—such as debates over racism, sexism, homophobia, transphobia, and the morality of "cancel culture" tactics—the results can be truly explosive.

To be clear, entertainment journalism that engages with political issues is hardly a new phenomenon of the digital news economy, a point that will be demonstrated later in this chapter in a section that explores its long and significant history. However, in its contemporary phase, it displays many of the characteristics that scholars and critics associate with major shifts in online journalism more broadly, that is, an emphasis on interpretive voice and partisan viewpoint that can stand out from the competition, coupled with a heightened focus on highly appealing and recognizable topics that can reliably drive online attention and boost audience metrics. Whether such shifts truly represent a "crisis in news," as Schudson puts it,[18] is certainly a matter of debate. However, it is clear that these emergent digital news models conflict with well-established notions of the professional journalistic field as objective, non-ideological, and motivated by the high-minded ideals of "fourth estate" democratic accountability rather than the pull of digital advertising money. The next section will explore how these concerns have helped shape the broader dismissal of entertainment journalism in the academic field of journalism studies, which has tended to view it as a cynical industry cash grab rather than a valued contributor to public discourse.

Partisan Punditry, "Soft News," and the Sins of Commercial Journalism

As noted above, journalism at the intersection of pop culture and politics involves several different common news formats: critics' reviews of movies, TV shows, and other popular entertainment that include ideological as well as aesthetic considerations; opinion-based commentary that addresses the social and political significance of pop culture news topics (colloquially, and often mockingly, labeled a type of "think piece" journalism); and more straightforward reportorial coverage of Hollywood's on- and off-screen controversies that frame such stories as relevant for polarized target audiences. Across the board, these news formats have received relatively scant attention in the journalism studies field which for most of its history has been chiefly concerned with "hard news" public affairs reporting. Regarding the opinion genre, Schudson points out that the "ideologists of professionalism in journalism" have "invariably ignored" the very existence of the editorial page, viewing it as an entirely separate entity despite its routine and widespread inclusion in mass-market news products.[19] The reason for this "shun[ning],"

Schudson suggests, is that the role of explicit political advocacy remains un-comfortable territory for an industry that has come to define its standards of quality and professionalism—indeed, its very identity—through the norma-tive lens of objectivity and neutrality. Although journalism studies has been deeply concerned with how ideology shapes ostensibly objective political reporting, the direct dissemination of ideological positions via the opinion format has been largely marginalized as an object of inquiry, likely because its failure to meet the idealized standards of objectivity is so patently obvious.

As Jacobs and Townsley conclude their analysis of why opinion jour-nalism has been so absent from the scholarly literature, "there is an unstated assumption that the increasing presence of opinion . . . is a threat to serious, objective journalism and, by extension, a threat to civil society as a whole."[20] Furthermore, when editorial opinion has been given sustained attention, the analysis tends to be resoundingly negative. Back in the 1990s, Eric Alterman coined the term "punditocracy" to assail the growth of professionalized com-mentary in print and broadcast news. The pundits, according to Alterman, consist of a small group of political insiders whose highly influential opinion columns and talk shows represent a limited range of viewpoints that serve elite rather than democratic interests. For Alterman, the "punditocracy" represents a threat to both the journalistic profession and democratic dis-course more broadly, not because of the mere fact that the pundits espouse opinions but because their elite opinions are the only ones deemed important enough by the corporate-dominated news business to receive widespread circulation.[21] Here we can recognize how the critique of news punditry folds into broader concerns over the economics of for-profit journalism, as the narrow range of corporate ownership is linked to the narrow range of jour-nalistic opinion that ostensibly parrots the viewpoints of owning interests (notably, this line of argument is key to Edward S. Herman and Noam Chomsky's well-known critique of mainstream US news as an instrument of elite and pro-corporate propaganda).[22]

In recent years, the explosion of new and digital media outlets has greatly expanded the range of publicly available editorial opinion, in terms of both format variations and diversity of voices,[23] yet such concerns remain. For in-stance, David McKnight's work on the conservative editorial commentary of outlets like Fox News emphasizes the danger posed by powerful media enti-ties using their news platforms to spread their preferred political viewpoints and framings.[24] Although Dannagal G. Young offers a more measured anal-ysis of newer partisan opinion formats, arguing that right-wing "outrage" talk programs have a legitimate role to play in public discourse alongside the more ironic and satirical opinion formats favored by liberals, she also raises concerns that the industry of conservative "outrage" spearheaded by pundits such as Fox News host Sean Hannity has become a "vehicle for elite social and cultural propaganda."[25]

Just as the "ideologically influenced journalism of opinion,"[26] as McKnight puts it, tends to be framed as a threat to quality journalism and deliberative democratic discourse, "soft news" formats have also received their fair share of suspicion and critique from academic circles. Framed as the antithesis of "hard news" political reporting, "soft news"—which includes the entirety of news outlets' entertainment, arts, and culture sections—has long suffered from a poor reputation in journalism studies due to its ostensible lack of seriousness and seemingly close relationship to "clickbait" commercialism. Folker Hanusch sums up the normative stance of journalism scholars thus: "Soft news . . . is typically seen by them as an indication of an ongoing tabloidization of the news media, and as such an undesirable development which, in their view, runs counter to idealized notions of what journalism should be and do."[27] As Hanusch argues, such negative assumptions about the category of "lifestyle journalism" (a term that ropes together reporting and commentary on entertainment, music, arts, travel, food, and other non-political topics), have resulted in its neglect and marginalization in the journalism studies field.

As with opinion journalism, when "soft news" does receive scholarly attention, it is often framed as a threat to the ideals of the journalistic profession. This is particularly the case when "soft news values" such as informality, emotion, and sensationalism are seen to transfer to the practice of traditional "hard news" political reporting (i.e., a dynamic of "politics as pop culture," as discussed above). A cross-country study by Fritz Plasser, for instance, finds that professional journalists largely believe that hyper-commercialization and the attending market pressure to cover politics in the style of entertainment spectacle is "responsible for the quality problems of political journalism."[28] If profit motives have devolved political coverage into an audience-pleasing, entertainment-oriented "media circus," as news critic Howard Kurtz once put it,[29] then actual coverage of entertainment and celebrity itself comes to resemble nothing less than an agent of news industry corruption.

However, this negative reputation has recently been called into question as a wave of scholarship in journalism studies and political communication has followed the lead of cultural studies in reassessing the political role of popular culture more broadly. The marginalization and dismissal of formats like "life-style journalism," Hanusch argues, is a problem not only because it is a major component of what the news business commonly produces but also because it may have value for democracy that should not be unfairly discounted.[30] The next section explores these more sympathetic treatments of nontraditional news formats such as entertainment and celebrity coverage, as well as how they can be theorized as a possible bridge between the commercial realities of the news market and the ideals of journalism as promoting an engaged and informed citizenry.

The Public Value of Entertainment Journalism?

In line with Hanusch's call to broaden the scope of journalism studies and reassess the value of "lifestyle journalism," Elfriede Fürsich argues that it can sometimes function as an important locus of public discourse. As evidence, she points to critics' reviews of world music that tackle issues of globalization often lacking in traditional "hard news" coverage of international affairs.[31] Specifically, Fürsich finds that journalists covering the world music genre shifted over time from providing mostly stereotypical representations of non-Western cultures to inviting readers to consider issues such as "unequal access to cultural production, the commercialization of the public sphere, geopolitical transformations, economic inequalities, racism, migration, and diaspora."[32] Fürsich's singling out of the arts criticism format is important to note, as this format stands as perhaps the most esteemed part of news outlets' culture desks. Although entertainment criticism in the popular press has tended to be shrugged off by journalism studies as just another facet of "soft news," some well-known critics—such as Pauline Kael, celebrated for her decades of intellectually provocative film reviews for *New Yorker* magazine[33]—have attained high-status reputations in areas such as literary and film studies, likely due to how their mass-market work parallels more scholarly modes of cultural analysis. Other recent scholarship emerging from the Nordic region—the current global leader in cultural journalism research and theory—has argued for the social and political significance of other, less reputable areas of the newsroom culture desk, including celebrity reporting. Nete Kristensen and Anna Roosvall, for instance, point to coverage of the #MeToo movement against sexual harassment and assault in the entertainment industry to make the case that "issues related to the cultural public sphere should be considered part of the political communication circuit."[34]

This more charitable view of the public relevance of entertainment journalism resonates with a familiar theme in the field of cultural studies, which has long been concerned with uncovering the "serious" meanings of popular culture, popular journalism included. Media theorist John Hartley, for instance, argues that a cultural approach to journalism reveals its integral role in making sense of the varieties of human experience and that entertainment and lifestyle formats are valuable for communicating "what it means to be human . . . and the humanity of those lying outside favored gender, ethnic, national, age or economic profiles" that are typically addressed in the news.[35] Dovetailing with this point regarding identity representation, Marguerite Moritz shows how in the 1970s and '80s, when gay and lesbian issues were largely marginalized in mainstream journalism, celebrity news stories such as tennis star Billie Jean King's public coming out and actor Rock Hudson's revelation that he was suffering from AIDS opened an important new space for the sympathetic media portrayal of sexual minorities.[36]

Cultural studies' interest in the public-serving potential of popular journalism has proven influential in recent decades, paving the way for communication researchers to look for measurable links between the consumption of "soft news" and various forms of democratic engagement. Matthew Baum, for instance, finds that "soft news" TV programs such as *The Oprah Winfrey Show* expose their viewers to political information that they would otherwise be inattentive to and thus serve an important role in expanding political knowledge.[37] However, Baum's position has been challenged by other studies that purport to dispel the theory that "soft news" formats serve as a gateway for accumulating political knowledge.[38] For instance, Nick Couldry and Tim Markham conclude from their research on news audiences that "popular culture is not always the bridge to an effective and expanded democracy that we would like it to be."[39] Specifically, the authors find that news audiences perceive celebrity news to be largely "irrelevant . . . to genuine public issues" and that those who express the most interest in following celebrity stories are also the least likely to be interested in politics and to engage in democratic behaviors such as voting.[40]

However, it is important to note that this body of research considers the genre of "soft news" as a rather monolithic bloc and does not delineate between different types of pop culture journalism when assessing its overall impact on political knowledge and democratic engagement. What happens when journalists who cover the world of entertainment and celebrity do so in a way that explicitly focuses on their political relevance, even at times providing strong ideological viewpoint in the process? For instance, consider a news article lambasting a white celebrity for posting a selfie on Instagram wearing cornrows, a hairstyle deeply associated with African American culture. This would typically qualify as entertainment rather than public affairs content in an academic research study, since it does not reference any specific public policy issue or political process at a governmental level. Yet, seen from another vantage point, it could be considered highly political in the sense that it touches upon racial tensions and power relations that cut to the very core of contemporary US society. This sort of journalism at the pop culture–politics nexus, which deliberately makes the connection between the world of entertainment and issues of public concern that the audiences of Couldry and Markham's earlier study largely failed to see, would seemingly be in far better position to serve as a "bridge to an effective and expanded democracy" than other kinds of "soft news."

Recent research on the news consumption patterns of young people, coming more than a decade after the "soft news" and politics debates of the 2000s, provides evidence that such connections are perhaps becoming more common as the lines between entertainment and politics continue to blur more broadly. Drawing on ethnographic data of young people's experience with news in the social media age, Lynn Schofield Clark and Regina Marchi argue that entertainment news can serve as a gateway to online issue discussion and knowledge gathering, along with other entertainment-oriented media content such as satirical news programs and fictional narratives in TV and film. As an example, they cite how news reports of racist backlash on social media regarding a Miss America beauty pageant winner of Indian descent captured the attention and interest of youth who otherwise did not pay much attention to the news. As the authors put it, "a mundane pop culture event covered by the mainstream news and circulated on social media inspired online debates regarding race in contemporary US society, with youth able to view, critique, and express perspectives in the public sphere from the privacy of their phones."[41]

Following from this point, Clark and Marchi stress how younger audiences are especially attracted to nontraditional news content that provides opinion and perspective on the issues of the day and thus allows for audience identification and viewpoint expression via social media. In contrast to the "objective" news that young people show relatively little interest in, the kinds of stories that these audiences prefer to consume and share online with their peers "offer interpretations and judgments about current events that provide an emotional framework and a moral discourse through which young people can connect with current events."[42] This embrace of opinion in journalism is a clear break from the traditional normative assumptions of the field, which, as noted earlier, tend to privilege objectivity and look askance at punditry as a threat to news professionalism. While young people are certainly not the only target demographic for journalism that voices political ideas through the accessible lens of pop culture (as later chapters will explore in detail), the shifting audience orientations that Clark and Marchi identify suggest how this type of journalism is particularly attuned to emergent patterns of news consumption and political engagement in the digital age.

Entertainment Journalists as Interpretive Communities of Influence

Clark and Marchi's research on entertainment and celebrity coverage as a resource for online youth political engagement suggests that the "soft news" debates of the past need to be revisited in the era of social media. Furthermore, their work highlights how this sort of journalism can function not only as a catalyst for the accumulation of political knowledge and information but also as an agent of political persuasion along partisan lines. In their large-scale study of opinion journalism, Jacobs and Townsley argue that "media opinion and commentaries are important because of the power they have to shape the world of collective representation and opinion formation in real civil societies."[43] As later chapters will show, the potential targets of influence for journalism at the pop culture–politics nexus includes Hollywood executives and creative producers as well as news audiences. In terms of the latter, politically oriented coverage of entertainment and celebrity topics holds the promise of exposing audiences to new and unfamiliar issues and ideological positions in ways that are emotionally accessible and even pleasurable, as well as inspiring identification and peer-to-peer issue advocacy through online sharing, linking, and commenting. In terms of the former, journalistic attention to the politics of Hollywood also has the potential to create an apparatus of public pressure and accountability on entertainment industry decision-makers (as illustrated by the *LA Times*'s takedown of the Golden Globes broadcast discussed above), which to no small degree mirrors the efforts of well-established pressure groups in the media advocacy space such as the NAACP and GLAAD. To an extent, this function recalls the role of the opinion columnist as a policy adviser to elites, which Jacobs and Townsley identify as an important legacy of the oft-derided opinion journalism genre, embodied by foundational figures such as Walter Lippman[44]— here "policy" is in quotation marks, as pop culture commentators in the press often explicitly advocate for change in the way Hollywood operates that aligns with shared ideological agendas.

This notion of entertainment journalists functioning as a kind of political advocacy group through their analyses and framings of pop culture dovetails with the more general theory of journalists as interpretive communities. First introduced by journalism scholar Barbie Zelizer,[45] this theory stems from Stanley Fish's concept of interpretive communities as groups of readers who co-construct the meaning of a text through mutual discourse and shared values.[46] Zelizer argues that journalists similarly create a sense of unity around a "collective interpretation of key public events,"[47] and this theory has since become influential in journalism studies as it has been extended to more areas of news production. Michael Brüggemann and Sven Engesser, for instance, apply the interpretive communities framework to environmental journalists who form a consensus around the science on human-caused climate change as well as a shared stance on how to dispute climate skeptics.[48] Just as these journalists interpret climate change through a mutually agreed-upon understanding of the issue, journalists who cover the intersection of entertainment and politics also hold certain shared values and assumptions—first and foremost, the core belief that pop culture is a powerful tool to advance long-term political change and that its symbolic representations of society and social identity are therefore significant and merit sustained attention, no matter how frivolous they might appear on the surface.

Such a stance is widely familiar in the scholarly fields of media and cultural studies, which, as noted above, have close parallels with certain modes of pop culture analysis in the popular press. Indeed, journalists who address the politics of pop culture from both the right and the left implicitly make the case in their coverage that "media matters," to borrow the title of John Fiske's scholarly book that dissects the political impact of popular media narratives.[49] Increasingly, this argument is made explicitly in entertainment journalism, and not just by left-oriented reporters and commentators who share Fiske's concern with expanding media representation of marginalized groups as a pathway to social progress. In the right-wing news sphere, the "media matters" framework has become increasingly popular over time, in large part due to the influence of the late conservative media mogul Andrew Breitbart and his famous dictum that "politics are downstream from culture." In a characteristic opinion piece for Breitbart's eponymous news site, commentator Lawrence Meyers explains the motto thus:

> Whether you like it or not, or believe it or not, the messaging of popular culture is resonating inside everyone's conscious and subconscious mind. . . . Culture influences politics, and in ways the left has understood for a long time. The right has sat idly by . . . and let an ideological movement take over one of the most important aspects of American society.

Following the lead of Breitbart and other right-wing pundits, Meyers urges his audience to fight back in the "culture wars" by purposively rejecting the "liberal stories" of contemporary Hollywood.

Here, of course, is where the interpretive communities of entertainment journalists on the right and the left sharply diverge. While both generally operate under the shared assumption that "politics are downstream from culture," their coverage of events in the worlds of entertainment and celebrity are shaped by opposing sets of ideological viewpoints and frameworks of meaning-making. Such a partisan divide is indeed a defining feature of both contemporary journalism and contemporary political discourse more broadly, and pop culture discourse in the news is no exception. Just as Brüggemann and Engesser conclude that public discussions of climate change have amounted to "a public debate where an elite interpretive community of scientists and journalists and a competing interpretive community of contrarians seem to drift apart further and further,"[50] we can likewise identify two separate and competing interpretive communities of influence that engage in pop culture reporting and commentary from the left and right banks of the polarized media landscape. Rather than inhabiting wholly separate worlds, however, these two communities are frequently linked through intertextual references, yet often in a reactionary rather than deliberative mode. As a later chapter will detail, right-wing entertainment journalism has positioned itself as a direct rebuttal to the perceived excesses of its left-wing counterpart, as conservative commentators bemoan the "wokeness" of both the mainstream news and the entertainment industry. In recent years, this rhetoric has increasingly centered on the backlash to "cancel culture," in which pop culture figures are castigated in the public sphere (including by journalists as a well as social media commenters and activists) because of statements or actions that are seen as failing to adhere to progressive ideological standards.

How is it that journalism covering the supposedly escapist and "soft" terrain of entertainment and celebrity has become subsumed by the most hardened battles of today's partisan politics? To address this crucial question, it is necessary to consider how the interpretive communities of both left-wing and right-wing journalists who cover the intersection of pop culture and politics have developed over time in a dynamic interrelationship with the broader intermeshing of these two social spheres. The remaining sections of this chapter provide a historical overview that highlights some of the key issues and trends—in particular, the rising prominence of identity politics involving race, gender, and sexuality—that have brought the world of Hollywood symbolism firmly into the purview of political coverage and analysis.

Entertainment Journalism and US Political Discourse: A History

Although it is certainly "on trend" in today's polarized digital news landscape, journalism at the intersection of entertainment and politics has appeared throughout the history of modern mass media, particularly in moments of high-profile public controversy. One of the most notable early examples involves the release of the D. W. Griffith's film *The Birth of a Nation* in 1915, which triggered a wave of public debate in the press regarding the film's portrayal of negative black stereotypes and glorification of the racist Ku Klux Klan.[51] In a front-page editorial demanding that the film be blocked from release, the African American newspaper the *Denver Star* argued that it sent the message to audiences that "all Negro men are low, bestial rapists" and was so incendiary as to endanger the lives and well-being of the city's black citizens. By contrast, many mainstream white newspaper writers vociferously defended the film, such as a columnist for the *Washington Examiner* who dismissed the "avalanche" of angry letters she received for a positive review by insisting on Griffith's historical accuracy in depicting "that portion of the South that was saved from negro rule and supremacy by the Klu Klux Klan riders." One white newspaper in Mississippi even criticized Griffith's film for being too sympathetic to African Americans, accusing it of deliberately pandering to antiracist audiences in the Northern and Eastern United States by including scenes that show the education of black youth. Here, more than a full century prior to current "take" cycles of pop culture controversy, a nascent Hollywood found its way into the crosshairs of political debate on the pages of American newspapers.

Revisiting the editorials that both decry and champion *The Birth of a Nation* for its impact on the public reminds us that concerns about the political influence of Hollywood are far from new and that political journalism by extension has never been wholly separated from matters of pop culture. In cases like *The Birth of a Nation*, the involvement of public advocacy organizations such as the NAACP in mass-mobilized protest and boycott campaigns made certain pop culture phenomena political in no uncertain terms. In retrospect, the commentary in black newspapers such as the *Denver Star* over the cinematic portrayal of African Americans in *The Birth of a Nation* can be viewed as a harbinger of future progressive critiques of "problematic" identity representation in the media that would come to dominate public discourse around the pop culture–politics nexus from the late twentieth century onward.

A similar pattern manifests in the history of the closely related field of sports journalism, which tackled controversies related to the racial segregation of athletes in the early to mid-twentieth century largely along color lines. As Michael Oriard documents, while mainstream white-owned newspapers tended to either avoid commenting on the benching of black players in sports like college football or defended them only on the apolitical grounds of "sporting honor" and fairness, black newspapers such as the *Chicago Defender* and the *Pittsburgh Courier* (along with the Communist paper the *Daily Worker*) "insisted" that the issue of barring black players from the field was "a racial matter, not a football matter."[52] In other words, these journalists used sporting entertainment as a springboard for articulating broader ideological claims about racial justice.

However, apart from the relatively marginalized black and Communist press,[53] political coverage of the entertainment industry for much of the twentieth century tended to involve conservative critiques of perceived liberalism in Hollywood. In the 1920s, a series of high-profile scandals in the press involving film stars such as Roscoe "Fatty" Arbuckle stoked fears that the industry was an out-of-control and corrupting force on the nation, which ultimately led to political pressure from conservative groups such as the Catholic National Legion of Decency to enact industry self-censorship in the form of the Motion Picture Production Code. A key player in this saga was William Randolph Hearst's national chain of newspapers, which sensationalized cases like the Arbuckle murder trial through intensive negative coverage and generally advanced an image of the movie business as morally depraved and in dire need of conservative religious values.[54]

Right-wing political attacks on Hollywood in the press became even more pronounced during the "Red Scare" era of the 1940s and '50s, which saw popular newspaper columnists such as Hedda Hopper and Walter Winchell not only lambasting the industry for its perceived leftist sympathies but also naming names of suspected Hollywood Communists and destroying careers in the process.[55] The formation of the Hollywood "blacklist" under McCarthyism was further fomented by the writings of Billy Wilkerson, owner of the major industry trade magazine the *Hollywood Reporter*. Wilkerson used the "Tradeviews" opinion column in his magazine to rail against the supposed Communist influence on the movie business and call out those such as the infamous "Hollywood Ten."[56] Many years later, in 2012, the *Hollywood Reporter* published a formal apology for its role in the creation of the "blacklist" through its news coverage and opinion columns—a move that underlined the historically powerful influence of entertainment journalism on the politics of the industry and on public discourse more generally (and also marked a definitive sea change in the ideological orientation of the magazine and others like it).

However, the shift away from the staunch conservativism of both entertainment journalism and the industry it covers began in earnest decades earlier, when US culture as a whole started to transform as a result of the upheavals of the 1960s. In the field of sports, this change was vividly reflected in the contrasting attitudes between older and younger sportswriters covering the superstar Muhammad Ali, who by 1964 was a boxing world champion, a pop culture celebrity of the highest order, and a political lightning rod due to his vocal support of the civil rights cause and his affiliation with the controversial Nation of Islam. When Ali aligned himself with the growing anti–Vietnam War movement two years later, seasoned sports journalist Red Smith wrote in his *Washington Post* column that the boxer "makes as sorry a spectacle as those unwashed punks who picket and demonstrate against the war." At the same time, younger sportswriters such as Bob Lipsyte of the *New York Times* and Jerry Izenberg of the *Newark Star-Ledger* were far more sympathetic to Ali's countercultural politics and vocally defended him in their columns, with the latter remarking in a later interview that Ali "gave us a reason to become what we wanted to become . . . the righter of all wrongs."[57]

In *The Revolt of the Black Athlete*, Harry Edwards identifies Lipsyte and Izenberg as examples of an emergent model of the racially conscious sports reporter who "writes not only about developments on the field of play, but also of those influences that might affect athletes off the field."[58] Edwards contrasts this with the more conservative, exclusively white sportswriting establishment of the time, which "remained aloof from the problems of racial justice"[59] and preferred to keep politics out of its reporting. As Serazio notes, such skittishness toward political commentary has become resurgent in recent decades in the sports journalism field.[60] However, the model established by progressive sports columnists during the era of civil rights and black athlete activism proved to be a bellwether for broader shifts in ostensibly nonpolitical "lifestyle journalism," particularly in the coverage of a Hollywood establishment that was being similarly transformed by countercultural currents.

By the end of the 1960s, the US entertainment industry had become increasingly interested in targeting the emergent youth counterculture as a lucrative new audience and addressing the turbulent political environment that had birthed it, which was defined by struggles over issues such as civil rights, the war in Vietnam, and second-wave feminism.[61] In this rapidly changing environment, new kinds of political controversies over pop culture began to arise that pitched conservative reactionaries against mainstream press critics who tended to embrace the more progressive countercultural ethos. One particularly noteworthy saga that rose to the prominence of newspaper editorial pages during this period was the outcry in 1972 over a two-part episode of the TV sitcom *Maude*, in which the title character has an abortion and is not demonized for her choice. Aired on CBS a year prior to the *Roe v. Wade* decision that secured abortion rights in the United States, the episode sparked a campaign led by the United States Catholic Conference to pressure CBS affiliates to pull it from broadcast and sponsors to pull their advertising. However, the pro-choice National Organization for Women (NOW), founded a few years earlier, responded by launching a counter-campaign to pressure affiliates to air the episode and boycott the sponsors who had backed out. All of this activity on the part of organized advocacy groups made the *Maude* controversy into a major political story, so much so that mainstream news organizations weighed in with editorial comment. The *New York Times*, for instance, published two opinion pieces on the subject: an editorial that chastised the Catholic groups for attacking "the American concept of free speech" and a longer piece that praised *Maude* creator Norman Lear's efforts to address hot-button issues such as abortion, birth control, and homosexuality in his programs and thus transform the landscape of television comedy from "a vast playground for witches, Martians, and crazy ladies" into something far more socially relevant and progressive.

The latter piece, written by long-running *Times* entertainment reporter Aljean Harmetz, points to the emergence in this era of an interpretive community of cultural critics in the mainstream press whose views were informed by the left counterculture's challenges to the social, cultural, and political status quo (akin to the generation of sportswriters like Lipsyte and Izenberg noted above). Another *Times* opinion piece written by Harmetz at around the same time, titled "Rape—an Ugly Movie Trend," lambasted numerous male filmmakers for their objectifying treatment of on-screen female characters; it would seem very much at home in the progressive-leaning news outlets of today. Here we can glimpse how the rise of post-counterculture feminist identity politics in the 1970s, typified by the slogan "The personal is political," opened up a space for mainstream journalists to interrogate the political implications of ostensibly routine pop culture representations of female identity. Another key figure in this regard is the critic Molly Haskell, who incorporated feminist analysis into film reviews for news outlets such as the *Village Voice* and in 1974 published the book *From Reverence to Rape: The Treatment of Women in the Movies*. This mass media discourse mirrored the scholarly feminist media criticism that was emerging in academic circles at roughly the same time from theorists such as Laura Mulvey, who famously pioneered the critique of the cinematic "male gaze."[62]

An even more pointed example of this trend could be found in the pages of *Ms.*, the mass-produced feminist magazine founded by activist Gloria Steinem. For the debut issue of *Ms.* in 1972, Steinem and her colleagues chose to feature the DC comic book superhero Wonder Woman on the cover, which was in itself a powerful statement about the relationship between pop culture symbolism and the politics of gender identity. In the accompanying cover story, journalist Joanne Edgar offered a feminist analysis of the character's treatment over the decades and argued that Wonder Woman had been robbed of her radical political potential in later issues of the comic that shifted focus to her relationship with a male love interest.[63] To no small degree, the *Ms.* cover story on Wonder Woman signaled the rise of a new era of progressive-minded pop culture critique that would come to fill the pages of both academic journals and mainstream news outlets in the coming decades.

The example of *Ms.* also highlights how journalistic outlets serving historically marginalized audience groups were particularly attentive to the politics of pop culture representation during a time of growing consciousness around issues of identity. This was especially true of the African American press, which, like *Ms.*, consistently provided alternative perspectives in the news media landscape around politics, culture, and the spaces in between. When another Norman Lear TV comedy, *All in the Family*, became an enormous hit in the early 1970s, numerous African American publications chastised its ostensibly sympathetic depiction of its openly racist white main character, Archie Bunker. Writing in the *Los Angeles Sentinel*, civil rights leader Whitney Young Jr. argued that it was "irresponsible to air a show like this at a time when our nation is polarized and torn by racism," while *Ebony* magazine devoted a lengthy cover article to dissecting the character's potential negative effects on US racial attitudes and asked provocatively in the headline, "Is Archie Bunker the Real White America?"

By the 1980s, publications known for left-wing political commentary more broadly, such as *Mother Jones* magazine, became a steady source for journalism that put the entertainment industry under the microscope of ideological analysis. In its pages, for instance, African American author Cecil Brown published a lengthy 1981 cover story on the portrayal of black characters in Hollywood cinema that made an impassioned case for the political importance of media representation: "If the American audience does not object to the way blacks are treated in the media, then women and other minority groups can only expect similar treatment . . . for we are all ultimately the victims of an electronic plantation mentality which filters the real world and turns its characters into caricatures." Although left-wing political critique of pop culture in outlets such as *Mother Jones* occasionally extended beyond issues of identity politics (such as a cover story published at the close of the 1980s that pilloried the decade's Hollywood films for their mass escapism and alignment with President Ronald Reagan's vision of American values), the representation of social identity proved to be the most natural fit for this mode of journalistic coverage. After all, virtually all pop culture narratives portray characters who are raced and gendered and are thus susceptible to political considerations around issues of stereotyping, marginalization, and the reinforcement of traditional power hierarchies.

This was also true for the growing representation of gays and lesbians in mass entertainment by the 1980s and '90s, as the mere visibility of historically invisible sexual minorities on- and off-screen became imbued with immense political significance.[64] Akin to the African American press, the gay and lesbian press of the post-Stonewall era was likewise a crucial site of progressive-minded criticism around issues of cultural representation. The *Advocate*, a magazine that had transformed from a local LA newspaper into a national glossy title, frequently interrogated Hollywood's relationship to gays and lesbians as a potential pathway for social acceptance and political progress. By the 1990s, when celebrities began to come out of the closet with more regularity and mainstream movies and television began to include more gay and lesbian characters, the *Advocate* led the charge of holding the industry accountable for its representations right alongside nonprofit media advocacy groups such as GLAAD. Cover stories like "Out in Prime Time" from 1996 and "Lesbian Celebrities Are Leading the Way Out of the Show Business Closet . . . So Where are All the Men?" from 1997 took as a given the assumption that pop culture visibility of gays and lesbians mattered politically and that it was thus the responsibility of journalists to push for improved and expanded representation through their coverage. The *Advocate* also gave considerable attention to critiquing gay and lesbian media portrayals for failing to live up to expectations of progress, such as a 1994 cover story on the Fox TV drama *Melrose Place* that chastised the "celibate" treatment of its lone gay character. In a sign of the growing discourse around these sorts of issues in more mainstream journalistic outlets, the article begins with a quote from *USA Today* TV critic Matt Roush, who lamented that "Fox doesn't believe advertisers will support a show in which a gay man has a normal sex life. . . . [W]hen it comes to gay characters, it suddenly turns prudish."

Indeed, by the 1990s, discussing the identity politics of pop culture in mass-market television reviews was becoming rather commonplace, and while minority-serving publications such as the *Advocate* were often at the forefront of such discourse, mainstream outlets were not far behind. Regarding gay and lesbian visibility, high-profile magazine cover stories like *Time*'s "Yep, I'm Gay" profile of comedian Ellen DeGeneres and *Entertainment Weekly*'s "The Gay 90s: Entertainment Comes Out of the Closet" not only documented the increased media visibility of gays and lesbians during this era but also actively participated in the project through their sympathetic and often celebratory coverage. The *Entertainment Weekly* piece, for instance, concludes by arguing that the mainstreaming of gays and lesbians in mass media entertainment will likely create "a more tolerant and compassionate place, at least for one minority. And wouldn't that be absolutely fabulous?"

The fact that mass-market entertainment journalists were now regularly staking out progressive positions on matters of identity politics, often in ways that framed these positions as common sense, helped to solidify the perception among conservatives that the journalism industry in general was an active agent of leftism in the "culture wars"—a perception that remains stronger than ever today. Such complaints became common in the pages of conservative magazines such as the *National Review*, as the presumed "political correctness" of both the entertainment and the journalistic establishments emerged as a favorite bugaboo of the US political right. Take, for example, a *National Review* editorial from 1997 that mocks a Knight-Ridder journalist for using the word "'multicultural' to mean 'good' or 'worthy'" when describing a TV *Cinderella* film that was cast with an African American lead actress. Or consider a 2001 piece from the same magazine by right-wing pundit Jonah Goldberg that attacks what he calls the "anti-stereotype police" of the journalistic establishment for criticizing "monolithically liberal Hollywood . . . for not being liberal enough" and singles out both media watchdog activists and the newspapers that feature them for challenging on-screen portrayals of blacks, women, gays, and Native Americans.

Goldberg's screed against what he calls "celluloid affirmative action," or how "Hollywood has responded to criticism by going overboard with positive stereotypes," highlights a theme that would continue to grow in conservative news commentary in the new millennium. From the viewpoint of the right, the entertainment industry was increasingly bowing to pressure from its left-wing critics—especially those in the journalistic field—to remake popular culture into an engine of progressive identity politics and "political correctness." It was thus conservatives' duty to push back on this trend by loudly rebuking it at every turn, taking a reactionary stance that would continue to accelerate in more recent rhetorical denunciations of "cancel culture," "wokeness," "social justice warriors," and other derogatory characterizations of left-wing discourse. If the politics of pop culture had always bubbled up from time to time over the history of twentieth-century journalism, by the start of the twenty-first century, it had emerged as a key partisan battleground.

The notion that political partisanship has become an increasingly common feature of both pop culture and the journalistic discourse surrounding it makes a lot more sense when considering the broader growth of polarization along cultural lines in Western democracies such as the United States over the past few decades. According to political science research, Americans have become more ideologically polarized than ever before in the past twenty years, and these divisions are deeply rooted in social and cultural identity.[65] As Lilliana Mason finds, the differences between the "red" and "blue" camps of contemporary US politics have less to do with specific policy disagreements than with meaningful differences in social and cultural identification around axes such as race, religion, and ideology. This partisan divide is further strengthened by "social sorting," which describes the tendency of people to congregate with others who share a common culture as well as a common politics.[66] In this environment of what Mason calls "social polarization," where political identity and sociocultural identity have largely become one and the same, it follows that the pop culture symbols and narratives that are commonly used to construct one's sense of self in the consumer society of late modernity[67] have now taken on a heightened political significance. This broader context helps account for how issues of race, gender, and sexuality that animate much of contemporary partisan political discourse in general are the very same that fuel public discourse in the cultural sphere of entertainment and celebrity.

The brief history in this section underscores how political coverage and cultural coverage have intersected at certain moments throughout modern journalism history, particularly when issues of social identity have broken into the broader public conversation and put a spotlight on the politics of representation. However, the overall narrative arc that emerges is one of slow yet steady intensification, culminating in the digital present in which a movie award nomination, a new TV episode release, or even a celebrity tweet can spawn literally dozens of politically minded news and commentary pieces across both left- and right-leaning outlets. The reasons for this, as shown in this chapter, are complex and varied and include economic and technological factors as well as developments in culture, politics, and the spaces in between. As we shift from the theorization and historicization of journalism at the pop culture–politics nexus to firsthand accounts of those who produce and consume it in the present day, we will have the opportunity to further probe its consequences and implications for the future of media production, political discourse, and democratic engagement.

Conclusion

This chapter has outlined the central theories and debates that surround the phenomenon of politically oriented entertainment journalism and that form the groundwork for this book's investigation as a whole. It has considered how journalistic coverage of the latest pop culture controversies relate to key trends in the contemporary digital news ecosystem, in particular the demand for inexpensive, fast-generated content around popular trending topics such as entertainment and celebrity as well as strong editorial viewpoints or "takes" that can evoke emotional responses and spark social media engagement. Furthermore, we have noted how the concerns in the journalism studies field regarding these economic pressures and their impact on the quality of "soft news" relate to broader critiques involving the for-profit nature of the journalism business and its resulting propensity for "hot takes" and "clickbait."

While these lines of critique raise important concerns that will be further explored in later chapters, other areas of theory and scholarship alert us to the potential public value of entertainment journalism. Key here is the notion that the accessible language of pop culture can serve as a bridge to learning about public issues and participating in democratic discourse, particularly through social media engagement with this sort of "soft news" content. For contemporary digital news audiences who often have a broader definition of what constitutes political information beyond the boundaries of traditional "hard news," as well as an interest in opinion and interpretation beyond the strictures of professionalized objectivity,[68] coverage that uses pop culture controversy as a route to political analysis and issue advocacy holds the promise of opening new doors to public engagement and strengthening others that may already exist within the body politic.

The history of entertainment journalism further reveals that it has played an important role in US political discourse at various historical junctures, yet the steady growth of its political consciousness against the backdrop of rising partisanship rooted in culture and identity and battles over race, gender, and sexuality points to its considerable relevance for contemporary political communication. As interpretive communities, entertainment journalists offer ideological framings and critiques of pop culture that underline the perceived significance of media representation and symbolism and, in the process, help make it into a political as well as cultural battleground. However, without hearing the perspectives of the journalists who produce this work, we can only attain a limited understanding of their role in the trenches of today's partisan "culture wars." In the next chapter, we will begin our exploration of the genre's production by examining how entertainment journalists on the left understand the political impact of their work as well as the broader ideological significance of the pop culture subject matter they so assiduously dissect.

2

Progressing Hollywood

Left-Wing Entertainment Journalism and the Push for Diversity and Accountability

Almost immediately after the brutal killing of George Floyd by a white Minneapolis police officer sparked massive Black Lives Matter protests in May 2020, public calls for racial justice came for Hollywood. News reports about racist comments made by cast members of the reality TV series *Vanderpump Rules* led to their swift firing by the Bravo network. In response to excoriating criticism from journalistic commentators and social media activists, the Fox network temporarily canceled the long-running reality show *Cops* which was seen to glorify police brutality. A *Los Angeles Times* op-ed written by African American screenwriter John Ridley convinced WarnerMedia to remove the 1939 film *Gone with the Wind* from its HBO Max streaming service, as he argued that it "perpetuate[s] some of the most painful stereotypes of people of color" (later, it was rereleased with accompanying videos to contextualize the film's depiction of slavery, including a critical panel discussion featuring veteran film critic Molly Haskell). Episodes of TV sitcoms such as *30 Rock* and *The Office* that included blackface gags were similarly pulled by media companies after they resurfaced in news reports and social media, while journalistic exposés about racism on the dating reality series *The Bachelor* led to ABC hiring its first black male star and, months later, firing longtime host Chris Harrison for his handling of racial issues. Again and again, pressure from the popular press, in tandem with advocacy organizations and online activists, compelled entertainment industry decision-makers to take concrete action in an unprecedented "racial reckoning." Responding to the rapidly transformed cultural and political environment, entertainment critics also took the opportunity to champion black voices and stories in Hollywood, from Spike Lee's *Da Five Bloods* to Michaela Coel's *I May Destroy You*. Although it may have been all too fleeting, the post–George Floyd moment was a watershed in entertainment journalism's

Pop Culture, Politics, and the News. Joel Penney, Oxford University Press. © Oxford University Press 2022.
DOI: 10.1093/oso/9780197557587.003.0003

long-gestating coming of age as a socially conscious, politically minded participant in public civic discourse.

This chapter will examine this ongoing shift in entertainment journalism toward an explicit advocacy role in progressive identity politics from a first-hand industry perspective,[1] picking up from chapter 1's historical narrative to chart more recent developments such as the field's key amplification role in hashtag activism campaigns such as #OscarsSoWhite and #MeToo. In addition to entertainment journalism's growing recognition of pop culture as being increasingly intertwined with politics and thus in need of political angles for coverage, particularly regarding matters of social identity, the chapter will also show how the slow but growing inclusion of women and minority journalists in the workforce has contributed to an increasing editorial focus on issues of diversity and representation in Hollywood. From there, it will delve further into the critical approach of left-wing entertainment journalists as an interpretive community, which follows—both directly and indirectly—from a lineage of academic critical theory that understands all cultural expression as inherently embedded with ideological meaning and symbolic of broader power structures. Although this commitment to unpacking the political significance of entertainment has inspired backlash from conservatives who complain about the left's seeming overpoliticization of pop culture, the community of progressive-minded entertainment journalists holds fast to the position that representation matters and is eminently worthy of public scrutiny in the news.

Later, the chapter will investigate how this critical attention to the politics of Hollywood has helped created an apparatus of public pressure, in conjunction with social media activists and organized advocacy groups, to push the entertainment industry toward progressive change. Some of the highest-profile members of the field can point to instances of effecting concrete reforms in areas such as casting decisions, while others stress the cumulative power of the field in collectively shaming Hollywood decision-makers into changing the way they do business with regard to race, gender, and other key areas of concern. However, even as the entertainment journalism of the left has taken on an influential role in the industry it covers as a fourth-estate-style mechanism of public accountability, it remains skeptical about the degree to which Hollywood is committed to meaningful change and how its conspicuous moves to increase pop culture diversity and inclusion may amount to little more than a canny strategy for garnering favorable press for major media corporations.

This skepticism also extends to entertainment journalism's own field of professional practice, as minority journalists stress how there is still much progress left to be made in the news business in terms of centering the cultural and political perspectives of those who had long been marginalized in public discourse. Yet in comparison with other areas of the newsroom that privilege a stance of objectivity that critics see as skewing white, straight, and male, culture departments have for years been on the cutting edge of a more subjective, socially situated approach that is relatively unburdened by the traditional expectations of the journalism profession. This shift toward an unreserved advocacy role in the identity politics of Hollywood—buoyed by the alternative professional expectations of cultural criticism and review formats as well as the historically outsize presence of socially marginalized groups such as gays and African Americans in entertainment—is where the discussion begins.

"Everybody Writes about Questions of Diversity": The Growth of Identity Politics Coverage in Entertainment Journalism

Across the entertainment journalism field, there is a shared understanding that coverage has become more politically conscious over time, particularly in terms of progressive-left advocacy for expanding the representation of historically marginalized groups. While some industry professionals recognize this to be a gradual shift, others highlight specific turning points that have helped push the field into more politically engaged territory and reoriented the sensibilities and priorities of both journalists and editors. Some of these turning points are relatively recent, marking moments of dramatic collision between the worlds of pop culture, news commentary, and social media activism. Yet one entertainment journalist interviewed for this book, with decades of industry experience, highlighted a far earlier phase of the field's transformation into an epicenter of political advocacy around issues of identity and diversity. An openly gay writer and former editor who has covered LGBT issues since the 1980s, he made a case for why coverage of the AIDS epidemic in Hollywood can be considered one of the major milestones in this process:

I really don't think it could be underestimated that the AIDS crisis, I would say especially from around 1988 to 1995 or 1996, had a gigantic impact in how these issues were covered and talked about, and not just in terms of AIDS. We all knew people who got sick and died because we all worked with people who got sick and died . . . a publicist or a producer or a writer you would deal with regularly suddenly wasn't there anymore. If you are a halfway decent human being and you were a journalist who covered this, it was impossible not to cover it in a way as an advocate, as an advocate for visibility, as an advocate for putting government dollars toward finding a cure, as an advocate for not demonizing the sick in pop culture. Obviously, pop culture is only one of the many, many, many places that the AIDS crisis penetrated, but it was one where the earliest sufferers of AIDS were particularly visible, and there were areas within entertainment that were incredibly hard hit. So I think, in some ways, more than sports journalism or business journalism was at the time, entertainment journalism was on the front lines of AIDS coverage, ahead of where many other forms of journalism were. And so from an LGBT perspective, a kind of advocacy began to come into entertainment journalism earlier than it did in other fields.

These comments echo Moritz's finding that news of actor Rock Hudson's death from AIDS in 1985 led entertainment reporters to provide some of the first wide-scale sympathetic coverage of the LGBT community at a time when it was still greatly underrepresented in the mainstream media.[2] However, this journalist also emphasized how the field still had a long way to go in terms of its advocacy of LGBT issues during this period:

In the early '90s, there was a long period of time when if you ran a story about a gay issue or a gay entertainer, you were kind of expected in the subsequent letters-to-the-editor column to run two letters, one of which would always be something like, "Oh, I really like that entertainer and I'm glad you did this story," and the other would always be "I don't approve of that lifestyle and I don't understand why you're giving it attention." So it was a real argument in the early to mid-'90s to stop that, to make the people in charge understand that homosexuality itself was not an issue that it was appropriate to weigh in for or against, to finally get it through people's heads that "I hate gay people" was not a legitimate letter-to-the-editor response to a story about a gay person.

As his account suggests, the editorial shift in entertainment journalism toward a progressive identity politics was not a sudden realization or epiphany across the field but rather the result of intensive battles in newsrooms and editors' meetings over a considerable stretch of time that included a significant role for journalists from marginalized groups.

Several other journalists pointed to the 1990s as a key transitional phase in the field's growing political engagement, when terms such as "culture war" and "political correctness" entered the mainstream public discourse in conjunction with high-profile battles in areas such as education and the fine arts.[3] Yet they also stressed how this period was followed by a retrenchment of sorts, when identity politics largely faded as a central focus of pop culture news discourse, only to be revived again in more recent years. As one veteran entertainment critic surmised:

> I think the reason it feels like there's so much more of it now is because there was this long period, especially in the 2000s, of ""Well, let's just talk about what's cool and what we like." The Gen X critics were very disengaged from this sort of political criticism. . . . And then the millennial generation has been much more politically tuned in, much more interested in political discussions of art.

Similarly, a critic who focuses on the political analysis of pop culture commented that "this stuff is all cyclical. I mean, there were these kinds of blowups in the '90s as well, and so it's hardly the first time that we've had this set of conversations. But I think that we were able to sort of bring the cycle back around some, and that was an exciting thing."

The shift toward progressive identity politics in entertainment journalism thus appears to have been uneven rather than smooth, as different generations of critics and reporters incorporated their varying sensibilities into coverage and reacted to those of their predecessors. Yet with each successive cycle, the field has ostensibly inched closer and closer toward a committed advocacy role around issues of diversity and inclusion, among others. If the '90s represented one important wave in this trajectory—the countercultural era of the late '60s and early '70s can be considered another, as discussed in chapter 1—the period of the 2010s to the present marks the strongest growth yet of a progressive framework in the field. As one critic argued, this renewed journalistic focus on the politics of representation dovetails with larger trends in left-wing politics that have touched all aspects of the entertainment world, from its production to its reception: "This is a subject that it's just mandatory for [Hollywood] executives to be fluent about. It's become a mainstream conversation both for executives and journalists who cover the industry, and for audiences. And I think that's a huge shift from five to ten years ago." While acknowledging that there have "always been queer critics, female critics, critics of color raising these questions," she contended that "that conversation has gone totally mainstream now. It's like everybody writes about questions of diversity."

Beyond tracking broader currents in politics and culture, to what can we attribute this mainstreaming of progressive identity discourse in pop culture news and commentary? As a staffer for a feminist news site underscored, the expansion of outlets on the internet has been a critical factor, providing opportunities for more diverse voices and perspectives to reach an audience without the need for approval from traditional industry gatekeepers:

> Before the blogosphere really existed, you didn't have these sorts of conversations about race and representation and gender in pop culture, because the conversations are so limited to a newspaper or a magazine or just one source with very specific points of view, and very often the specific points of view on the staff. So I think that the conversation has opened up a lot with the advent of the blogging universe.

Along similar lines, a veteran journalist whose career covering the politics of entertainment spans the print and digital eras noted:

> In the old days, I really used to feel that I was writing these sorts of columns really alone. And certainly in recent years, with a much younger group of journalists coming through and all kinds of online publications, it's so nice just to have a lot of other voices joining that debate and adding their voices to those sorts of issues.

Within this context of an expanding digital landscape that targets niche identity groups on both sides of the partisan divide (as chapter 4 will explore in more detail), left-oriented commentary on the politics of race, gender, and sexuality in pop culture has thrived to a seemingly unprecedented degree. However, this development did not happen all at once when digital outlets appeared on the scene. Rather, industry professionals point to a handful of key news cycles during the 2010s that persuaded industry decision-makers to commit more vigorously to coverage that interrogates issues of diversity and representation in all aspects of entertainment.

For instance, just as the AIDS crisis marked a crucial turning point for coverage of homophobia and LGBT rights in the 1990s, the #Gamergate controversy of 2014 became a major rallying cry for journalistic discussions of sexism and misogyny. What ostensibly began as a hashtag campaign critiquing the ethics of video games journalism quickly devolved into a cycle of vicious anti-feminist harassment aimed at outspoken women across the gaming world, from designers such as Brianna Wu to video game critics such as YouTube vlogger Anita Sarkeesian.[4] As one entertainment critic suggested, the #GamerGate controversy—which researchers Alice Marwick and Rebecca Lewis identify as critical to the rise of the online alt-right movement in the 2010s[5]—had a transformational impact on how editors perceive the relationship between pop culture stories and political stories:

> I think arguably the most politically consequential event of the past decade is #GamerGate. . . . It sort of clarified a sense of grievance some people had about diversity and video gaming, but that also provided a playbook by which a lot of really ugly politics on the internet is done now. And so, you know, you can't cover half the story. Increasingly, I see major publications recognizing that the culture half is where a lot of the political work is getting done.

Similarly, another critic remarked that #GamerGate was "a big moment. . . . I think that was one of the first times I was talking especially to the men in the office about how, in that case, gender and video gaming was a huge issue. And it was manifesting in real life."

Several years later, the #MeToo movement targeting workplace sexual harassment and assault became another crucial news cycle in the growing political engagement of the culture desk. On their own, the personal stories shared on social media by survivors of sexual assault and harassment in the entertainment industry were enormously impactful.[6] Yet the journalism covering these stories—coupled with major investigative reports such as the *New York Times*'s exposé on Hollywood studio boss Harvey Weinstein— proved integral in creating momentum for change and made a convincing case for why coverage of pop culture had an important role to play in broader political news discourse.[7] As a freelance critic maintained, #MeToo had a noticeable impact on the editorial priorities of news outlets:

> With all of the #MeToo coverage, that's just become so much wider. . . . It's easier to pitch those kinds of stories now, because I think more places want

to talk about that stuff a little more on a wider basis. It seems like more places want the angle of politics, and specifically sexual harassment or assault. . . . There's definitely a shift now where there's more places that want to delve into that stuff.

With each successive moment of high-profile collision between the spheres of pop culture and identity politics—which also notably includes Hollywood's "racial reckoning" in 2020 following protests of the killing of George Floyd, as discussed above—decision-makers in the entertainment journalism field have become increasingly enthusiastic about pursuing these kinds of political angles in coverage. Again, those with decades of industry experience are especially perceptive of this change in editorial focus, such as a veteran critic who commented:

What I used to find a lot more, say twenty-five years ago, was pushback from people who would say "It's just a TV show, or it's just a movie, then why bring politics into it? That's not a part of the discussion of what this is." And with the rise of representation issues, the rise of diversity issues, there's a whole generation not only of writers but of editors who feel much more comfortable approaching entertainment and pop culture stories as intrinsically political than they used to be.

The field has now reached a point where these angles are actively encouraged by editors in newsrooms, as one entertainment critic for a left-leaning national news site attested:

A piece where I talk about representation or a controversy that has to do with race or sexuality . . . it's actually a lens into pop culture that I sort of am encouraged to look through. [The news site] knows that I'm interested in it, and they like the fact that they have writers who want to weigh into those kinds of social issues.

Likewise, a staff critic for a legacy national outlet who focuses on feminist analysis of entertainment explained that her editors have given her the green light to pursue this angle in coverage "because they have bought into my thesis that pop culture is the way that most people kind of consume social politics and process and think about it." As accounts like these suggest, there is now a significant degree of institutional support for entertainment journalism that centers on the concerns of identity politics, marking an advanced stage of a long-term transformation of the field.

The increasing focus on the politics of identity and representation in entertainment journalism can be attributed to several institutional factors, including the progressive political leanings of editors and managers as well as their economic imperative to serve like-minded target audiences who have an interest these issues (explored in further detail in chapter 4). However, this identity politics "boom" in the news media, as one journalist called it, has been further buttressed by ongoing industry efforts to diversify its workforce and hire more reporters and critics from marginalized identity groups. A Hollywood correspondent for a major national news outlet suggested this relationship directly: "I do think, broadly speaking, that media coverage of all of these issues has significantly been stepped up in the last few years, in part because I think newsrooms are hiring a lot more women and people of color in their culture departments." Here the understanding is that the lived experience and embodied perspective of women and minority journalists make them especially sensitized to issues that face their communities, including representation in pop culture both on- and off-screen. Of course, journalists who are not members of marginalized groups also address these issues in their work, yet there is a clear sense in the field that the social identity of news professionals makes a meaningful difference in terms of how issues of pop culture representation are pursued and covered.

Scholars Maegan Clearwood and Hannah L. Jones advance this exact argument in their discussion of theater critic Diep Tran, whom they identify as an exemplary model for a new type of politically engaged cultural critic writing from an identity-based perspective. Clearwood and Jones emphasize how Tran's subjective first-person perspective as a Vietnamese American woman is central to her ideological critiques of theater productions such as *Miss Saigon*, which contrast with the ostensibly "neutral" and apolitical criticism of many of her white male colleagues in the field. To account for this dynamic, Clearwood and Jones apply a key critical feminist concept known as standpoint theory, which argues that one's knowledge of the world is fundamentally grounded in one's social position.[8] Standpoint theory is thus useful for understanding how diversifying the news workforce is seen as enabling new critical perspectives on culture to emerge that may otherwise be left out.

Indeed, many journalists who cover the politics of pop culture articulate the core logic of standpoint theory when discussing how their own social identity informs their work, even if they don't necessarily invoke the term itself. As one entertainment critic for a national news website put it, "I'm happy to let my political positions and my identity as a trans woman influence the stuff that I write. . . . Criticism is always informed by the person you are and the values you hold." This subjectivity is particularly important, she explained, for covering pop culture that involves members of her community:

> As a trans woman, I've seen enough bad stories about trans people to know that most [journalists] don't put the work in, so I'm automatically going to go into a story about a trans person written by a cis person with a bit of skepticism. They can get it right, they could do it correctly, they probably aren't going to do it as well as a trans person would.

Similarly, an Asian American reporter who covers pop culture and politics explained that her identity matters when covering issues of Asian American media representation: "because we definitely have more familiarity, and it helps with just approaching it in a more sensitive way. We have seen instances where someone who's not part of a certain community really messed up when they write about a community that they're not familiar with or try to exoticize it." Elaborating on this theme, a critic who had worked as a staff columnist for a major national newspaper offered a detailed account of how her black racial identity is crucial to how she has covered African American pop culture differently from her white colleagues. As she explained, she came to this beat directly out of

> frustration with the way that minority artists were covered, particularly by white journalists. . . . Once you get into sort of the bigger prestige news organizations, those newsrooms are often very, very white. But because black people in particular have such an outsized influence on culture, you end up sort of having this white gaze through which we are talking about culture, deciding what's important, why it's important, that can be distorted . . . where you'd have someone who would perhaps make a judgment or a declaration about an artist or about their work that really showed itself to be uninformed when it came to how that person's cultural background influenced their work.

Her own work, she explained, represents a deliberate effort to do away with such distortions, using her standpoint as a black woman journalist to provide a more culturally informed lens on the world of black entertainment.

Such concerns over problematic and insensitive coverage underscore the need for news organizations to hire more journalists who are members of the communities they report on to "get the story right." As a Latina journalist suggested, the blowback from past mistakes in coverage of marginalized groups has persuaded at least some publications to take these matters more seriously: "There are absolutely missteps. When a publication gets hit with that kind of negative press or negative sentiment, then they become aware of that issue, and then it becomes extra sensitive for them, and they're more cautious around that." A key aspect of this increased sensitivity, she said, manifests in how editors choose to assign stories with the social identity of the journalist in mind. Speaking about coverage of a Netflix series on the late Mexican pop singer Selena, she commented:

> We are now at a point where it would be a mistake for an editor to approve a story that doesn't come from someone who is of Mexican or Mexican American descent. And that's not to say that race is always a factor, because if you're a great writer, if you have a good idea, I think that still holds weight. But now there's more consciousness around the decision.

Beyond the matter of deciding "who gets to tell those stories" when they arrive at culture desks, she also contended that the entertainment journalism field has become more proactive in seeking out diverse voices who bring their unique standpoints and concerns to the table: "Right now, the landscape is changing, where editors are looking to diversify what they publish, and they're looking for not just people of color, but we're talking about trans, immigrant stories, LGBTQ." While she stressed that this shift in editorial practice is tied above all else to news outlets' considerations of their changing target audience (a point to which chapter 4 will return in a discussion of industry economics), her remarks also suggest how entertainment journalism's focus on cultural matters has placed it at the forefront of the broader industry's current push for cultural diversification, in an echo of the historical progression noted at the beginning of this chapter.

Later we will see how these efforts to expand diversity in cultural reporting and commentary still have a long way to go, leaving minority journalists to contend with problems such as tokenism and pigeonholing even as professional opportunities grow. In many ways, the ongoing push for increased inclusion within newsrooms mirrors the push for progress in Hollywood representation on- and off-screen, a project that has become a chief focal point of entertainment journalism of the left. Yet before approaching the question of how this journalism may help effect these kinds of changes in Hollywood by acting as a watchdog-like pressure group, it is first necessary to examine how it functions as an interpretive community. Drawing both directly and indirectly from long-standing traditions of academic critical theory and cultural studies, this journalism has worked to popularize a way of understanding pop culture as a lens through which to observe broader discrepancies in power as well as a symbolic model for intergroup relations throughout the society.

"All Art Is Political": The Interpretive Approach of Left-Wing Entertainment Journalism

Increasingly, Hollywood itself has made identity politics and issues of diversity and inclusion a major focus of both on-screen production and off-screen industry discussions, to a degree that has fueled an intensive right-wing backlash that now dominates the pop culture coverage of conservative news outlets (discussed in detail in chapter 3). Regarding the choice to forefront political interpretation and analysis in their work, many left-wing entertainment journalists see it as unavoidable and even obligatory, given the way in which Hollywood now openly and explicitly embraces progressive social politics across so much of its output. For instance, as one critic remarked regarding his politically minded pieces, "people look at it, and they say, 'Why do you bring politics into it?' sometimes. But, you know, [the 2019 TV series] *Watchmen* is very much engaged with race and racism. [The 2019 film] *Charlie's Angels* is conscious feminist statement.... They are talking about these issues." As another critic put it, "issue-related pop culture isn't just on the fringes of entertainment. It's right in the center of it. So if you cover entertainment, if that's what you do, there's absolutely no avoiding it." Along these lines, a senior journalist for a left-leaning news site explained:

I'm always looking as an editor and as a writer for those moments where either the two worlds [of pop culture and politics] intersect or echo each other. And I think, obviously, that happens more and more. The two are not only interconnected, they're sort of inescapable at the moment. . . . If you look at our site on any given day, you will see us looking for those moments where pop culture isn't just a comedy show, but it's a comedy show telling us something. . . . We are always looking for kind of extension moments.

As he suggested, finding these moments when the world of entertainment extends into issues such as racism and sexism has become so frequent and so consistent that it is now a near-daily occurrence in coverage.

However, as much as contemporary Hollywood's conscious engagement with progressive identity politics makes these kinds of angles obvious and at times mandatory, the critical framework that left-oriented entertainment journalists adopt does not necessarily rely on pop culture being explicitly political in its content. Rather, as a journalistic interpretive community, they work from a shared set of assumptions about the ideological function of entertainment and the arts that, as will be explored more below, stems from academic critical theory and cultural studies. At its core, this framework boils down to the position that "all art is political," in the words of one critic, or, as another put it, "everything is politics, everything is political." Elaborating on this theme, one left-wing film critic stressed that "movies exist in a social context, they are produced by forces, by bodies with social power. And therefore there's always a politics to them. . . . I think because movies have politics, a political perspective is a legitimate way to approach them." Similarly, another critic said:

> I think it's really important to look at movies as more than just "this is entertainment," you watch for two hours, and it doesn't mean anything, and then it doesn't impact you in any way. I mean, movies do something, they say something, they represent something, they put forth certain points of view, they put forth certain politics, they either reinforce or subvert the status quo.

In particular, the fact that all cultural narratives, whether fictional or nonfictional, involve individuals who are marked by race, gender, and other dimensions of identity means that they are understood to be relevant symbols for discussions of power and representation in the broader society. As one critic explained, "I think pretty much any movie has 'Is this cast diverse? Are various point of views represented? Are people of differently able bodies and different sexualities?' All that stuff is in there." A journalist who specializes in coverage of diversity in the entertainment industry likewise asserted, "I think that anything starts to become political when people realize that [Hollywood] is a system that has historically favored white men," while another noted that "most of the people making those projects are still straight white men, and they make them from a straight white male point of view. And so it is not hard to look critically at what they're making and say, 'Hey, how maybe would this have been different if a woman of color had made this?'"

This commitment to examining pop culture through the prism of ideology and power differentials between social groups marks an important distinction from entertainment journalism of the right, which, as chapter 3 will show, tends to reject the "all art is political" framework and often advocates for a depoliticized pop culture sphere. Entertainment journalists of the left are well aware of this line of counterargument and see it as a further manifestation of ideology and power at play. For instance, a left-oriented film critic explained:

> Because I think everything is political, I think to say "keep politics out of movies" is taking a very privileged look and not realizing that it's probably your politics that are in the movie and that's why you're not noticing them. . . . If a movie is reinforcing the status quo, then you probably won't be mad about it because it's your status quo. So I think it's often a very privileged take to hear something like "keep politics out of *Star Wars*" or "keep politics out of Marvel." . . . The reality is these movies are made by people who also have their own set of political values and considerations.

Another critic echoed this view by contending that "when people say 'we don't need to talk about politics,' it just means that they don't want their particular politics questioned," while another still succinctly remarked that when it comes to writing film reviews, "not being political is a political choice."

In addition to affirming the core concept that "everything humans make has a political dimension"—one of the fundamental tenets of post-Marxist cultural analysis going back to Antonio Gramsci[9]—entertainment journalism of the left is informed by a range of scholarly research and theory that stresses the importance of media representation of marginalized identity groups. Within academia, class-based critiques of hegemony and counter-hegemony in the "culture industry" (as Frankfurt School pillars Theodor W. Adorno and Max Horkheimer famously termed it in the 1940s)[10] have been expanded on over many decades by incorporating the insights of feminist, queer, postcolonial, and critical race theory, among others. The academic field of cultural studies, pioneered by theorists such as Stuart Hall who incorporated the dimension of race as well as class into ideological critiques of mass media representation,[11] has been particularly influential in shaping left-progressive criticism of pop culture both inside and outside the academy. As Isabel Molina-Guzmán puts it, "Stuart Hall's work on culture, representation, ideology and hegemony positions Hollywood as a cultural institution informed by and informative of U.S. social values and norms. Thus contemporary debates over Hollywood's diversity are indicative of broader social conflicts."[12] In recent years, scholars such as Molina-Guzmán have increasingly drawn attention to the issue of diversity behind the camera, which has been shown to lag behind progress in on-screen representation due to a range of structural and institutional barriers.[13] Although journalists who address the politics of representation in their work have varying degrees of familiarity with this body of academic research and theory, it appears that they have absorbed many of its key ideas as they have filtered into the broader public discourse.

In fact, quite a few of these journalists have engaged directly with this kind of scholarship as part of their educational background. One writer for a feminist news and culture blog who completed a Ph.D. in literature noted that "all of the research skills that I have and the critical thinking skills I have are the ones that I learned in academia," while a freelance film critic who received a Ph.D. in cinema studies recounted that "as I went through undergrad and took a lot of humanities courses and cultural studies courses, I just came to reflect more on the politics of representation. . . . It got me thinking a lot about how power is manifest and reflected in popular cultural texts." A columnist who writes about the politics of pop culture for a major national legacy news outlet similarly described how her approach is deeply informed by her experience in academia:

> I majored in the humanities in college and actually ended up writing a thesis on the intersection of art and politics. And I think what I do is broadly informed by a couple of big ideas that have their place in the academy . . . the insight that artistic work is created under political conditions that inevitably affect the work in question.

Even those who did not encounter much in the way of critical theory and cultural studies in their formal education are sometimes familiar with scholarly media research on the politics of representation through citing it in their coverage. It is common practice at many news outlets—particularly those aimed at a more sophisticated target audience—to incorporate academic studies and commentary into pieces as a means of bolstering arguments and providing added insight. For instance, a staff reporter at a major national news site explained that "especially in the diversity and representation coverage, there's a lot of academic research out there. Every year, they release these reports looking back at the year, and oftentimes they're finding that there's not a whole lot of diversity in representation. And so that's often a good place to start in terms of covering these issues." Similarly, another journalist who covers issues of Hollywood diversity noted how the annual reports of the USC Annenberg Inclusion Initiative[14] have become a particularly prominent reference in mass-market coverage: "That study is very frequently cited when it comes to discussing these types of topics."

Accounts such as these underscore how the critical approach of left-oriented entertainment journalists has been meaningfully shaped by academic studies of media and culture that have broadly proliferated in higher education in recent decades. It could even be argued—as conservative firebrand Andrew Breitbart once did in his screed against the influence of the Frankfurt School and "cultural Marxism" on both mainstream journalism and the American political left more generally[15]—that this critical theory has trickled down over time from colleges and universities into a range of professional institutions, including journalism, where graduates are now employed.

Moreover, the commitment of entertainment journalists to critically analyzing the politics of media representation can be understood not only as a consequence of critical theory's influence but also as part of the process of advancing its spread in the public sphere. One reporter who cited scholarly research in her coverage of Hollywood diversity explained that "I always felt like part of why I gravitated more toward journalism was just because it felt like we could write to a much wider audience, and we could incorporate academic research in our reporting but bring that to a wider audience." A freelance entertainment journalist who is also currently working on a graduate degree likewise expressed how she uses popular journalism as a conduit for advancing the insights of critical theory:

I did my undergrad in equity studies, so a lot of race, gender, disability theory. . . . Going to school and learning about these things in an academic setting and getting to put language to these things that I was experiencing and thinking and feeling for years and years is really gratifying. And one of the biggest reasons that I do what I do is to give that language to other people. . . . That's incentive to work with really big ideas and do it through this more accessible lens of talking through pop culture.

To be clear, many members of the field do not share this academic background and may be largely unaware of specific scholarly reference points—a point to which chapter 7 will return in a discussion of how entertainment journalism can forge closer connections with the academic disciplines that can greatly aid in the sophistication of its discourse. Yet, generally speaking, entertainment reporters and commentators of the left tend to understand the public impact of their work in terms of advancing the critical education of a largely receptive audience.

Although later chapters will explore the intensive blowback from more hostile audiences, it is important to stress that these left-oriented journalists typically view themselves as addressing a like-minded public that shares their core concerns regarding topics such as race and gender yet is seeking to better understand them as they manifest in specific cultural contexts. In other words, if these journalists take on a role of translating the critical insights of academic media and cultural studies for popular mass consumption, then the imagined audience can be thought of, metaphorically speaking, as fully signed up for the class. One left-wing entertainment critic elaborated on this dynamic by way of another common metaphor:

Often it's more about preaching to the choir, but . . . the choir needs to be preached to, they're the ones who show up there at the service, they're the ones who came and wanted to listen to the preaching, the ones who kind of want to take away something . . . so I don't think it's so bad to give them a sense that they're on the right track.

A later chapter will explore the question of the real-world impact this journalism has on members of the public (as well as that of its right-wing counterpart) by examining the experiences and perspectives of engaged audience members who actively share it on social media. For now, we shift our attention to another major target of potential influence for progressive pop culture news and commentary: Hollywood itself. As the discussion will show, politically engaged entertainment journalists of the left are deeply mindful of their role as watchdogs for the entertainment industry and proactive instigators of institutional change. Moreover, the broad ideological alignment between these journalists and their pop culture subjects means that this coverage can be greatly impactful in the push for diverse representation in entertainment, even as the news business continues to grapple with its own parallel issues of inclusivity.

"Shame Is a Powerful Tool": Influencing Hollywood as a Pressure Group

When reporters and critics publicly call out Hollywood for its treatment of issues regarding race, gender, and sexuality, is anyone in Hollywood listening? In other words, does this journalism play an active role in pushing the entertainment industry toward more progressive on-screen representations and off-screen actions? Although the answer may not be so clear-cut, there is compelling evidence to suggest that entertainment journalism functions as a watchdog-like pressure group for the industry it covers. When considering the impact of their work on Hollywood, journalists are often quick to downplay their own relative power over an entertainment industry that is, by any estimation, immensely powerful in comparison. Yet, at the same time, their stories of concrete and tangible influence on the Hollywood creative class, sometimes as individual critics and more often as collective agents of agenda-setting, suggest a relationship that is growing in significance.

To be certain, the notion that entertainment journalists can simply force the industry to change by publicly reprimanding its conduct is far from the more complex reality. Many journalists who produce these kinds of critiques point to the fact that for-profit entertainment companies are chiefly accountable to the audiences who provide their bottom-line revenue. Since journalists have less of a direct role in the profit-making process, their voices, by extension, are less of an immediate concern. As one staff film critic remarked about the question of influencing Hollywood:

> I think critics are a very, very, very small part of the ecosystem for them.
> They don't really care all that much about reviews. They care about what

people will look for on-screen. And they also care about their perception because it can cause harm to them, but I think they might be a little more worried about fan communities sometimes than they are about critics. They're still driven primarily by what they think will put people in seats.

Another critic similarly stressed a disconnect between journalistic critics and fans, explaining that "the cultural conversation can often be very siloed off from who's actually spending money and how."

However, one entertainment journalist questioned the idea that audience behavior is largely removed from critical discourse in the news media, suggesting a path of influence that flows first from critics to audiences and then from audiences to the industry: "I wouldn't necessarily go so far as to say that I think our method of reviewing is what's impacting studios, but I do think that we have an impact on the audience, and how the audience spends their money is then what determines what gets made or not made." Although this indirect form of influence is partial at best—after all, the well-known phenomenon of the "critic-proof" box-office hit belies the notion that journalists can simply dictate audience behavior—it is nevertheless important to consider when assessing the impact of this journalism on Hollywood decision-makers. By helping to cultivate a politically engaged mode of consumption and interpretation that foregrounds left-progressive concerns regarding representation and diversity (as discussed above), this journalism can potentially help shape what audiences look for in entertainment and, in turn, what the industry chooses to provide as a means of securing their money.

However, the influence of this journalism on Hollywood is not always conceived of in such indirect and abstract terms. Some reporters and critics are quite optimistic about the capacity of their field to spark industry change, often in concert with activist groups and vocal supporters on social media. For instance, a staff reporter who covers issues of racial diversity in Hollywood for a national news site highlighted the example of the #OscarsSoWhite campaign as an amalgam of social media activism and advocacy journalism that made a major collective impact on the Academy Awards:

I think #OscarsSoWhite is a really good example . . . that was completely just public pressure on the Academy. And that came from a lot of activists speaking out, reporting on that activism, reporting on the larger problem of diversity in representation. That, I think, is a very clear example of where that really seemed to make an impact. . . . [The Oscars] do seem to be conscious of their public image. And they do seem to think that if you don't nominate a diverse slate of nominees, people will protest, and people will draw attention to that very publicly, whether it's through reporting or through activism or through social media.... Public pressure seems to be a pretty big component in holding people accountable or at least making them aware that next time, you have to do better, because people will respond if you don't.

The #OscarsSoWhite campaign—launched in 2015 by activist April Reign and covered extensively by red-carpet reporters and commentators—led directly to the Academy of Motion Picture Arts and Sciences diversifying its voting membership to include more members of color.[16] Of course, Reign and the thousands of social media users who amplified her hashtagged call for change deserve much of the credit for this victory, yet it is also clear that the public pressure forged by activist networks on platforms such as Twitter does not exist in a vacuum. Rather, campaigns such as #OscarsSoWhite can be understood as phenomena of the hybrid media system, which scholar Andrew Chadwick describes as the dynamic interaction between newer media logics such as crowdsourced online civic expression and older logics such as media gatekeeping and professionalism.[17] In their book *#HashtagActivism: Networks of Race and Gender Justice*, scholars Sarah J. Jackson, Moya Bailey, and Brooke Foucault Welles identify this precise dynamic as a broader pattern of "how Twitter activism, within this interconnected environment of media and platforms, influences journalistic and political narratives in the United States."[18]

Framed in this context, the relative success of #OscarsSoWhite can be understood as a product of social media activists and ideologically aligned journalists working together to bring awareness to the cause. When giving widespread coverage to viral activism campaigns, journalists help to amplify them and propel them forward, further grabbing the attention of industry power brokers in the process. Along these lines, a staff writer for a feminist news and culture blog emphasized the role of her website in elevating social media activists' calls for changes in on-screen representation: "I think that it is important for these movie studios to listen to this backlash. And I think that a site like ours can act as an amplifier for people's voices that maybe wouldn't be heard otherwise."

This key relationship between activists and journalists in creating public pressure on Hollywood is also notable in the #MeToo movement, which many news professionals cite as another important case study in how reporting on the entertainment industry can actively change the way it does business. Moreover, as one journalist who writes on feminism in pop culture suggested, the outpouring of online #MeToo and #TimesUp activism that began in 2017 was itself fueled in part by the long-building critical feminist discourse in the journalistic field:

> I do think that things like #TimesUp are very much sparked and supported by a conversation that was also happening in entertainment journalism for years leading up to that about the representation of women in media. . . . I hear from people I interview and reps of studios all the time about that stuff, and I do think that it is shifting the conversation.

Again, the community of entertainment journalists can be seen in this context as one crucial component of a hybrid media network of advocates and activists, both amateur and professional. It may be difficult to disentangle exactly where this journalism's influence begins and ends within these hybrid networks, but there is a strong sense within the field that its contributions are consequential in mounting public pressure on the industry.

Although such efforts to bring progressive reform to Hollywood do not always achieve their intended effect, one veteran entertainment editor stressed the importance of reporters and activists working in tandem to advance shared goals: "Any power that journalists like me who do this have is collective and cumulative. . . . And so when a ton of writers and journalists and advocates all sort of write pretty much the same thing, I know that that gets noticed." Likewise, many journalists referenced a sense of their communal power as a group when considering the capacity of their work to push for change in Hollywood. As one staff pop culture writer put it, "I don't think it can ever necessarily be down to one specific person alone, but the kinds of conversations that pop culture journalism has over time can shift the narrative in really interesting ways." A columnist for a major national news outlet similarly stressed how she and her colleagues form a collective apparatus of accountability when their critiques of Hollywood become a chorus:

> Maybe not my piece individually but I think as part of a larger thing, when there are other pieces on it or people have taken notice . . . I do think it sort of changes things and has [industry members] look at themselves in a different way, knowing their world isn't insular, knowing that there are people from the outside looking at this.

Despite the many reservations and caveats outlined above, this notion of entertainment journalists serving as watchdogs over Hollywood—a direct manifestation of modern Western journalism's foundational identity as a "fourth estate" holding elite institutions to account[19]—can be highly important for their sense of professional mission. One film critic for a national news site commented:

> I think it's part of my job to hold people in positions of power responsible for their behavior, and people who cast movies and make decisions around those movies are certainly people in positions of enormous power. . . . I'm pretty much a small fish when it comes down to that, but hopefully the larger conversation is helping to push against the industry in progressive ways.

Again, while they may be skeptical of their individual impact, these journalists find value in their role as contributing to broader watchdog efforts that they see as having a cumulative impact.

Another critic who writes on issues of race in pop culture was quite forthright in drawing the parallel between her identity as an entertainment industry watchdog and the public service role of her colleagues in more traditional "hard news" political reporting:

> Part of the job of being a journalist is holding officials accountable. And so if you're covering city hall or Congress or the president, that's going to work one way. If you're covering culture and entertainment, that's going to look a little different. The power dynamics are going to be different in those situations. . . . You're looking at who gets opportunities and who doesn't and why that is. You're looking at the difference in budgets. . . . I would say I'm kind of bringing that watchdog ethos to what I do now.

Her account powerfully underlines how members of the entertainment journalism field have come to take on a serious public mission of advocacy and institutional reform—a far cry from the long-standing stereotypes of the culture desk as fun but inconsequential "soft news."

In her specific case, the watchdog role has paid some tangible dividends when it comes to spurring concrete change in Hollywood. She is a columnist who has written for some of the most high-profile major news outlets in the United States, so her audience—and, by extension, her influence—is likely larger than those of other members of her cohort. Although her experience may be relatively unique, it does suggest how entertainment journalism can in certain contexts lead directly to concrete steps toward reform in Hollywood:

> While I was at [one news outlet], one of the things that I wrote about quite a bit was *Saturday Night Live* and the fact that there was a stretch of time where they just did not have a single black woman in the cast. . . . And the thing is, once you can call attention to this rather embarrassing fact, and the fact that NBC and [producer] Lorne Michaels didn't appear to be doing anything about it or care about it very much, that was the nudge that resulted in *SNL* basically holding showcases where they invited a slew of black women to audition for the show. And the result of that was Leslie Jones being hired and another black woman being hired as a writer.

This victory may represent incremental progress, but for a critic who has long championed the cause of making Hollywood more diverse, it is clearly a point of pride. Furthermore, she related another story in which she could directly trace the influence of her journalism on industry decision-makers:

> There's a minority actor I wrote about when I was at [one news outlet] who had created this web series . . . and when I interviewed him, he was telling me about the difficulties that he was facing as a queer person of color going on auditions and being told, "Well, you're too specific" or "You're not right for this role." . . . But that article that I did on him, he came back later and said, "You're the reason I have an agent now. Somebody saw that feature and called me." So it is gratifying when things can have an impact.

Cases such as these, where an individual work of journalism can be credited with triggering a specific outcome, may be relatively rare, but this is not to say that reporters and critics are unaware of the concrete effects of their work. A television critic who focuses on representation and diversity noted that "it's hard to know" if one of his pieces made a specific impact in Hollywood, "because often when they change stuff, they won't admit that you're the reason they did it." However, he related a telling anecdote about a time when he publicly confronted a group of broadcast TV executives at an industry event announcing a new lineup of programs:

My first question was, "You don't have any women starring in any shows here, what is the deal?" And they had a real hard time answering it, and so that gets in everybody's story. It wasn't just my story that had that in there . . . it was in the Associated Press and the *Hollywood Reporter* and *Entertainment Weekly*. And then, when something like that happens, . . . they get embarrassed . . . and then you start to see that open up and they have shows starring women. Often that's how I find it works. I might ask a tough question at a press conference, and then their inability to answer it doesn't just show up in the work I do, it shows up across the board, and it becomes this sort of wave of negative stories where everybody is saying, "Look, why don't you have any gender diversity in your shows?" And then that makes an impression.

This story is particularly helpful in illustrating how the entertainment journalism field functions collectively as a pressure group for Hollywood—on key issues such as diversity and representation, news reports and critiques form a mutual discourse in which individual journalists pick up on one another's cues and create shared conversations across platforms and outlets (the story from the beginning of chapter 1, recounting how an *LA Times* exposé on the diversity problems of the Golden Globes kicked off a barrage of negative coverage across many news outlets and led to the awards show's cancellation, is another typical example). As this critic emphasized, the cumulative effect of such discourse is often what convinces industry executives that change is necessary, as the chorus of criticism creates a reputational liability that is simply too much to ignore.

Furthermore, he stressed that as a pressure group, journalists must be aggressive in their rhetoric for their critiques of Hollywood to result in actual change. While he lamented the necessity of using heated tactics that have become controversial in "cancel culture" debates, he contended that his decades of experience working in the field have proved their effectiveness:

I really think that you should be able to just create a story where you kind of describe what's going on and [industry executives] get the message and they just do it. But that's not how it works. . . . To get them to understand that, you have to shame them publicly. You have to constantly put before them the evidence of what they're doing that is so negative and destructive and hurtful. You have to constantly show them that these are the people they're victimizing. . . . It's harder to get them to change when you make that case to them privately, because they can ignore it and feel like they won't have any consequences. So it has to be a public thing, where the network gets called out, and the corporation that owns the network gets called out. . . . These stories come out, and they create a huge public backlash, and they embarrass the crap out of the people who run the network. And then those people eventually go to the producers of the show and say, "Look, this has got to change," and then they force them to change. And that's the progression of it.

Such tactics of public shaming have created a substantial backlash of their own, and chapter 3 will explore how complaints about "cancel culture" have become a central preoccupation of right-wing pop culture commentary that is often framed in direct reaction to its left-wing counterpart. However, it is apparent that the chorus of shame from Hollywood's progressive press critics has become a driver of industry change, at least in certain moments. This is particularly observable in the wave of cancellations and firings that gripped the entertainment industry in 2020 following George Floyd's murder by police and subsequent Black Lives Matter protests, discussed at the beginning of this chapter. In moments like the "racial reckoning" in the aftermath of Floyd's killing, the pressure that journalists mount on Hollywood to make progressive reforms can be especially forceful, creating a climate in which industry executives may consider making dramatic and unprecedented changes to avoid public embarrassment.

More broadly, the recent growth of this critical news discourse seems to have had a lasting impact in terms of how Hollywood decision-makers handle matters of racial and gender diversity. For instance, a reporter for a major national outlet who covers representation in film stressed that there is now an expectation within the industry that intensive press criticism will follow major missteps around these issues:

These executives know that when they do interviews, they're going to be asked about it, and they're going to be made to look backward if they say, "Oh, I don't have anything in the next two years that's being directed by a woman," or "My slate is all white." And shame is a powerful tool. I don't think they want to be publicly shamed. . . . I think it's had a significant impact on how Hollywood casts, the pride they take now in diverse casting or giving certain properties to women to direct.

As his account suggests, entertainment journalists as a pressure group have helped to create a forceful—and possibly lasting—set of new industry norms around considerations of race and gender politics, essentially training industry decision-makers to anticipate negative backlash and to take preemptive steps to avoid it. Sometimes, though, these changes are only made begrudgingly after criticism has been piled on, as one journalist surmised:

> I don't know how much of Hollywood wants to listen to the bad criticism or critiques, or that it just becomes so overpowering that they sort of have to. It still causes them to change, which I guess is still a good thing, but I'm not sure how much of it is just the overwhelming sense of people criticizing something that they feel, "OK, I guess we've got to do something about this."

As an example, she pointed to alterations made by producers of the Netflix series *13 Reasons Why* after she and many other journalists sharply criticized the show's handling of teen suicide and self-harm:

> They did seem to make a conscious effort to say, "OK, we are listening to this kind of critique and we're going to try to change it." I don't think that they completely listened, because I don't think they really did a good job of changing it, but I think the outcry was so much that they sort of had to.

The relationship between Hollywood and its progressive-minded press critics, however, is not always as contentious or fraught as such a framework might suggest. While some industry figures can be reluctant or even hostile to the kinds of reforms that left-leaning commentators are pushing for, it seems many are quite receptive and willing to listen. This may be attributable to both groups tending to have a shared set of political viewpoints and ideological orientations—a notion that conservative critics would readily assert. Indeed, one of the most striking differences between entertainment journalists of the left and of the right is the degree to which they sense that their targets of criticism in Hollywood are paying attention to them at all. As chapter 3 will show, conservative journalists almost universally maintain that the entertainment industry does not listen to or care about what they have to say. By contrast, many left-leaning journalists can point to examples where they have received supportive responses from their subjects of commentary. For instance, a staff entertainment critic for a major national news outlet said:

I wrote a story where I kind of snuck in a line needling a very large studio for not making as progressive choices as another company even though they kind of portrayed themselves to be the standard-bearers of inclusiveness and progressiveness. And a week later, I heard from the rep from that studio saying, "Hey, we're actually working on rolling out some LGBT narratives in the next year. Let's talk."

Of course, such a response may contain an element of face-saving damage control, but it also says a lot that this studio representative would be responsive to a journalist's critique about LGBT representation in the first place and, moreover, could point to plans to redress such concerns. Another staff journalist who often focuses on Hollywood diversity provided a similarly revealing account of how this kind of work has sympathetic ears in the industry: "I do a lot of interviews and reporting that puts me into circles with TV executives and publicists and TV showrunners and people who work in the film industry, and they will say all the time that they appreciate when someone like me is championing the way they're approaching LGBT representation and racial representation on their shows."

As these accounts suggest, a rough consensus has more or less emerged between entertainment industry figures and their progressive-minded journalistic interlocutors on the cause of diversity and inclusion. This is not to say that there are not important exceptions to this alignment or that commentators on the left feel that they have nothing more to fight for in terms of pushing the industry toward further change. Indeed, a great amount of left-oriented commentary aimed at Hollywood typically involves calling out the industry for not going far enough in making progressive choices on- and off-screen. However, it is a conversation that is ultimately taking place within a cooperative framework—a conversation that includes journalists, industry professionals, amateur activists on social media, and long-standing media advocacy organizations such as GLAAD and the Hollywood Bureau of the NAACP. Although these various stakeholders often disagree sharply over what specific steps are needed to create progressive change in the symbolic field of pop culture, they appear to be committed to a mutually reinforcing project to advance a shared set of ideological goals.

Chapter 3 will explore how the concerted nature of this project fuels an intensive reactionary backlash in conservative journalism that targets "Big Hollywood" and the mainstream media in tandem as co-conspirators of social and cultural re-engineering. Before shifting attention to the world of right-wing pop culture news discourse, however, it is important to address how its practitioners' cynicism regarding the project of "woke-ing" the entertainment industry, as it were, is shared to a degree by some of their left-leaning counterparts who fear that such dynamics are now becoming exploitable as a means of serving corporate bottom lines.

"Just Another Way to Sell a Product": The Corporate Exploitation of Diversity Discourse

One of the consequences of the push for progress in both Hollywood and the journalism that covers it is that taking steps to expand diversity and inclusion has become a reliable way to obtain favorable news coverage. This represents the flip side of journalists calling out the entertainment industry for its perceived failures and missteps—when Hollywood figures and decision-makers act in ways that are seen to align with progressive values, they are likely to be applauded by the very same journalistic community that serves as an adversarial pressure group in other contexts. For right-wing commentators who are broadly critical of the push for progress in the first place, such a pattern is grounds for skepticism regarding the entertainment industry's true motives when making appeals to progressive ideology. As one conservative film critic argued, for instance, "Marvel doesn't really care about woke issues, it's just branding superheroes as feminine or queer or whatever because it's good corporate branding." In other words, he accused entertainment companies of being solely concerned with upholding their public reputations to remain viable profit-making entities, with the strategy of expanding diverse representation being merely a cynical way to secure positive publicity at a time when "woke issues" have become popular in the public sphere.

This sort of cynicism about the corporate exploitation of identity politics is also voiced by some entertainment journalists on the left who actively participate in the push for progress in Hollywood. However, while their right-wing colleagues seem to invoke such critiques as a way of denouncing the project of pop culture diversification altogether, they are more concerned with how the economic interests of Hollywood can incentivize superficial and cosmetic changes that sell this project short. For example, one left-wing entertainment critic lamented:

[Hollywood] has gotten better at progressive virtue signaling without necessarily making big changes. You keep seeing headlines like Marvel just put their first-ever gay character in a movie, and then it turns out to be an unnamed man who is on the screen for thirty seconds. . . . Perhaps it's a sign that people have noticed the pressure against them . . . but it's unclear to me that that will actually shift in meaningful ways very quickly.

Along these lines, another critic noted:

You can see Disney doing a few things in particular to try to garner good coverage, like touting the inclusion of openly gay characters in *Avengers: Endgame* and the last *Star Wars* movie, but the inclusion is so brief and so vague that it's almost insulting. And they've created it that way so they can lift it out for international markets, so it's really kind of pitiful, and I think it's really revealing of what the end goal here is, which is maximum profits.

Here the fact that studios are so willing to reverse their own moves toward diversity when it is economically expedient, such as when releasing a film in more socially conservative countries, draws the motives for these moves into question. Although some critics like herself may call out this self-interested behavior on the part of Hollywood, others, she suggested, simply take the bait and provide the celebratory headlines that such efforts are ostensibly designed to generate.

Some pop culture news commentators on the left take this line of critique a step further, arguing that the trend of media corporations championing their newly diverse representations is ultimately about appealing to new target markets and advancing the cause of capitalism, not progressive social change. As one such pop culture critic put it:

It's really easy for people to put a trans woman in a movie and then say, "Wow, look at her, she's in the movie. Isn't that great?" . . . but that's a super easy thing for capitalism to do, expand the number of markets it's selling to, and if that includes other identities, great. A harder thing for capitalism to do is to critique itself and to see its own blind spots and to see the ways in which it is actively making the world worse. . . . We are not in a place where the industry has changed the capitalistic way in which it does business.

A left-wing film critic similarly expressed "skepticism about corporations that trumpet their wokeness," suggesting that they simply

> sell liberation as another product. So when a mega corporation like Disney says "we have female superheroes," just so they can sell more products and continue perpetuating this really excessive consumerist lifestyle and grow their monopolistic empire, I get kind of suspicious. . . . It feels like a legitimate critique of the culture industry has been turned into just another way to sell a product.

When it comes to the journalism that examines these trends, there certainly seems to be room for critique that questions the underlying motives of the entertainment industry in making appeals to progressive identity politics. After all, the journalists quoted above make these very sorts of arguments in their published work. However, it is also true that Hollywood routinely receives favorable news coverage from mainstream and left-leaning outlets for its diversity and inclusion efforts, to the point of being predictable enough to arouse suspicions of cynical manipulation in the first place. Chapter 7 will explore how the parallel profit motives of commercial news outlets risk exacerbating this potential for the exploitation of identity politics, as the imperative to target segmented audience groups with identity-affirming news content can lead to simplistic and flattened coverage of media diversity that trades depth for surface-level appeal. For now, we can consider how the model of entertainment journalism as a pressure group pushing Hollywood for meaningful change may be compromised as the entertainment industry learns how to work the relationship to its own advantage. Now that progressive critiques of media representation have become so well established in the news media landscape that they can be foreseen and anticipated in advance, the threat of cynical gamesmanship on the part of savvy Hollywood decision-makers grows more pertinent.

The Struggle to Diversify the Entertainment Journalism Field

Just as Hollywood has come under scrutiny for making slight and superficial changes to placate calls for diversity and inclusion, so, too, has the journalism industry that covers it. Earlier in this chapter, we saw how news organizations have been taking some steps to hire more journalists from marginalized groups, helping to provide their target audiences with an expanded set of perspectives on culture and politics. Although these hiring practices have moved the field closer toward an engaged public advocacy role around matters of social identity, minority journalists nonetheless raise important concerns about how the news business has been handling these efforts. As journalism scholar Nikki Usher contends, the overall picture for the journalism industry remains quite grim, as "racial, economic, and geographic diversity are worsening given the financial pressures on the news" to cater to affluent, largely white audiences.[20] For obvious reasons, this issue is especially pertinent for entertainment journalists who advocate for increased cultural diversity in their professional work, as they seek to ensure that their own field is living up to the same standards that they rigorously apply to their Hollywood subjects.

The push for expanded representation within culture and entertainment departments follows broader diversity initiatives in the journalism business that have been implemented over several decades. However, the notion that newsroom diversity alone leads to improved coverage of minority-group issues has been challenged by numerous scholars who find that entrenched journalistic norms of objectivity and neutrality continue to privilege a white male lens on the news despite the shift to a more diverse workforce.[21] Notably, the area of cultural criticism and commentary seems to be somewhat of an exception to this pattern due to the very nature of the format, as critics are expected to provide subjective opinion rather than objective fact and are thus in better position to cast off the baggage of neutrality norms and embrace their socially situated standpoint. Like political opinion columnists, who are also given institutional license to speak subjectively on public issues, cultural critics may be relatively free of the journalistic constraints of objectivity that have traditionally privileged the "default" white male lens. Because of this, the field of pop culture commentary has held the promise of empowering marginalized voices and perspectives in ways that can far surpass other parts of the newsroom.

Judging from firsthand accounts of minority entertainment journalists who address issues of identity politics in their work, this promise is being fulfilled to a degree, yet there is still a long way to go in terms of diversifying staffs to the point where marginalized standpoints move meaningfully toward the center. One obstacle that minority journalists still face is workplace tokenism, a dynamic whereby their marginalized status becomes a rationale for limiting the expansion of diversity hiring since it is perceived by managers as "enough." As an Asian American freelance entertainment critic noted regarding opportunities to publish pieces that address identity politics from a minority perspective:

> I feel that even though editors are interested in sourcing these stories, there aren't that many publications that recognize the sheer amount of viewpoints around a certain topic. And they might feel as though, "well, we've got, like, our piece on race for the next two weeks, you know, box checked." . . . There is this feeling of you get to write your story and be the singularity with which these topics are looked at. It can be frustrating. There are so many viewpoints and so many experiences in one realm of identity that need to be talked about, explored, published.

Furthermore, she pointed out that "there just isn't that much diversity in the people who run the publications," and therefore these decision-makers may have a narrower sense of what constitutes the full scope of diversity when it comes to the intersectionality of multiple identities and the unique perspectives that they embody.

This sense that editors treat hiring minority journalists as checking compulsory boxes, rather than making a more sustained commitment to diversity, was also highlighted by a freelance Latina journalist who was surprised to find that her minor contribution to a news outlet was being exaggerated by management for strategic PR purposes: "I only wrote for them once, and they're pretty big. And they included me in their diversity report as like 'hey, we're doing really great stuff, we've got [journalist's name] writing.' . . . I thought that was interesting because I had literally only written for them once, and the things I wrote about were being touted as this groundbreaking thing." In this context, she was being used as a token to bolster the reputation of the outlet as being minority-friendly, and the disconnect between her actual role and the souped-up image in the diversity report suggested the insincerity and shortcut-taking with which these initiatives can often be handled by industry decision-makers. Like her above-noted colleague, she attributed the problem to the fact that despite progress in inclusive hiring practices for lower-level roles, the industry is "still predominantly filled with gatekeepers who don't look like me."

An African American entertainment critic whose decades of experience have led to him serving in consulting roles for various newsroom diversity initiatives expressed a more acute sense of frustration with the industry's struggles to move beyond minimal-effort tokenism:

> Somebody like an editor will come to us and say, "What can we do about diversity in our newsroom?" And somebody like me will sit down with them and just say, "Just take ten minutes and think about the issue. You know your news organization, think about it. What do you think the problem is?" And nine times out of ten, they can name that problem, it's just do you have the will to deal with it? . . . I feel that answer is not satisfying to a lot of people. What they want is a checklist—do this, do this, do this, do this. And they want it to be stuff that they can kind of do and it doesn't take much.

As his comments underline, change that centers the perspectives of marginalized voices in cultural journalism and beyond requires far more effort than mere quick fixes.

In addition to the problem of tokenism, minority journalists who cover pop culture also point to how their dedication to discuss matters of identity politics from their own embodied standpoint can result in compartmentalizing that limits the scope of their assignments and even their career development. An entertainment reporter who covers Asian American and LGBT representation as a member of both groups stressed how this kind of in-group specialization can be both a blessing and a curse. While he agreed that "you want someone who actually comes from the place of being gay and then writing about gay stuff," he also noted:

> It kind of sucks if you're one of those people and you just feel, "Well, I would like to write something that's not about like my community every single day of my life." I think that there's a tendency to do that. I mean, the entire industry was a bunch of straight white guys for the longest time writing about everything, so I guess that's a small win for minorities and people of color and women. But it also kind of pigeonholes them into those pieces.

Likewise, an Asian American staff reporter remarked that "sometimes you feel this burden that you have to cover something that concerns your community," while a Latina journalist expressed how she didn't want her freelance career to be limited to "writing about brown issues for brown people. . . . I think it takes a certain kind of editor to appreciate that and give me opportunities." This burden of representation is especially heightened when members of marginalized groups make up only a small portion of newsroom staffs and freelancer pools, which places more pressure on any given individual to speak for their entire community. At the same time, minority journalists largely agree that covering issues from an in-group standpoint is enormously valuable for the quality of coverage. The seeming solution to the pigeonholing problem, therefore, would be to expand workforce diversity to such a degree that these assignments do not dominate the workload of minority journalists who also wish to branch out into more areas.

This push for broad meaningful changes to newsroom diversity will continue to be a major issue moving forward for the journalism industry as a whole. Notably, the specific area of entertainment reporting and commentary appears to be at the forefront of such efforts due to its sensitivity to cultural experience and emphasis on point-of-view subjectivity in place of performed neutrality. Yet it is also still grappling with the ongoing problems of tokenism and pigeonholing in a very profound way. Ultimately, we can understand entertainment journalism's push for progressive reform in Hollywood and within its own professional ranks as two prongs of an ongoing common project, stemming from an ideological commitment to intersectional social justice as an organizing principle of all social life.

Conclusion

This chapter has shown how entertainment journalism in mainstream and left-leaning news outlets has increasingly taken on an active advocacy role to help advance progressive values around race, gender, sexuality, and more within the public sphere. Although this shift has been long in the making—a point also addressed in chapter 1—the emergence of many high-profile pop culture and politics news cycles in recent years has led entertainment editors and other industry decision-makers to focus increasingly on pursuing political and social justice angles in pop culture coverage. Sagas such as the #MeToo movement in Hollywood and the response to the #GamerGate controversy, both watermarks in the resurgence of feminist activism in the 2010s, have demonstrated to the industry in no uncertain terms that the world of entertainment is rich with political significance and worthy of journalistic political analysis. Moreover, not only do reporters and commentators keep close tabs on today's progressive social media activism aimed at reforming the symbolic cultural field of Hollywood, but they also often help to amplify and extend it by affording it increased visibility in the hybrid media environment. We can thus understand the community of left-wing entertainment journalists as a key contributor to this broader project of social, cultural, and political transformation, seeking to increase diversity and inclusion in pop culture while holding public figures such as Hollywood celebrities accountable for racism, sexism, homophobia, transphobia, and other forms of bigotry.

These efforts, inspired by traditions of academic critical theory that view pop culture as an inherently political and influential symbol of broader social relations and power inequities, have begun to make a concrete impact on the way Hollywood does business. Although entertainment journalists are often skeptical of their power over an entertainment industry that is primarily concerned with extracting profit from audiences, they nonetheless form a collective voice as a pressure group that is sometimes too loud for Hollywood decision-makers to ignore. These industry figures can now anticipate waves of negative press attention if they fall on the wrong side of the concerns of progressive identity politics, leading to preemptive maneuvers that can sometimes amount to meaningful progress and other times merely "virtue signal" to shore up corporate public reputations. Even so, the emergence of entertainment journalism as an apparatus of public accountability and instigator of change in Hollywood underscores the significant role that it has come to play in contemporary circuits of political communication and social advocacy.

This role has sharpened as the entertainment journalism field has taken steps to become more inclusive of voices that are able speak to the politics of social identity from the standpoint of lived, embodied experience. A later chapter will discuss how members of the news audience can find great value in hearing and learning from the perspectives of journalists from marginalized groups who use the symbolism of pop culture to interrogate matters of social inequality, discrimination, stereotyping, and myriad other struggles close to home. However, the expectation that these journalists serve as representatives for their respective identity groups can also lead to the problem of pigeonholing, which, along with workplace tokenism, continues to hinder meaningful change within the news business. Like the push for accountability and progress in the world of Hollywood entertainment and celebrity, the push to transform the journalistic apparatus that covers it remains on-going and incomplete. Chapter 3 will explore how the ostensible progressive consensus between the mainstream entertainment and journalism industries forms the backdrop for a caustic right-wing backlash, with the conservative media apparatus framing itself as a rebellious and irreverent alternative to "woke" cultural dogmatism.

3

Pop Culture Warriors

Right-Wing Entertainment Journalism and the Fight against "Big Hollywood"

When actress Gina Carano was fired from the hit Disney Plus *Star Wars* spinoff series *The Mandalorian*, the conservative news media was ready for a counterattack. For months, Carano had been igniting controversy with her social media posts that supported Donald Trump's false 2020 election claims and mocked Democrats, Black Lives Matter activists, coronavirus masking policies, and gender pronouns, among other targets. Conservative news outlets were following each step of her story closely, linking the social media backlash against her various tweets to broader grievances over "cancel culture" that have become central to contemporary right-wing rhetoric. After Carano shared a post that compared the plight of conservatives to that of Jews in the Holocaust, Disney moved swiftly to terminate her employment on *The Mandalorian*, leading to outraged headlines on the right such as the Federalist's "Lucasfilm Bows to Leftist Internet Mob." Yet beyond receiving a flood of sympathetic coverage from outlets such as Fox News, Breitbart, and Newsmax, along with a sit-down interview on *The Ben Shapiro Show* to air her side of the story, something rather unprecedented happened next. Shapiro, cofounder of the conservative news outlet the Daily Wire, announced that the company would be co-producing a new film starring the embattled actress as a direct rejoinder to her treatment by Hollywood: "We could not be more excited to be working with Gina Carano, an incredible talent dumped by Disney and Lucasfilm for offending the authoritarian Hollywood Left. This is what Daily Wire exists to do: provide an alternative not just for consumers, but for creators who refuse to bow to the mob."

The Daily Wire's creative partnership with Carano marked a notable new chapter in the conservative news media's ongoing war against an entertainment industry establishment that it views as irredeemably "woke" and hostile toward its own. By expanding the Daily Wire's brand to integrate entertainment content production with "culture war" news coverage, Shapiro

Pop Culture, Politics, and the News. Joel Penney, Oxford University Press. © Oxford University Press 2022.
DOI: 10.1093/oso/9780197557587.003.0004

provided a revealing example of how right-wing institutions have become increasingly united in their oppositional stance toward Hollywood and in their collective identity as "the cultural resistance" (a *Star Wars*–inspired term used by Shapiro in a tweet promoting a Carano-themed discount offer for Daily Wire memberships). As this chapter will explore, this "cultural resistance" is aimed at countering not only Hollywood itself but also much of entertainment journalism in the mainstream news media, which is similarly perceived to be unfairly biased in favor of progressive social values and political causes.

Framing themselves as a freethinking alternative to an oppressive media and cultural regime that dictates the lines of social acceptability in ever-narrower ways, the conservative media has increasingly taken on the mantle of freedom of expression and unencumbered aesthetic pleasure that has long been associated with the counterculture of the left—even as it still sometimes reverts to a stance of censorious moral guardianship that it had typically taken in decades past, such as when fulminating outrage over the inclusion of LGBT characters in children's cartoons. While many of their ideological opponents may dismiss their constant—and at times logically inconsistent—grievances about an out-of-control "cancel culture" in both Hollywood and the progressive media discourse around it, conservative news professionals maintain that these themes strike a deep chord with their audiences and drive mobilization within the broader conservative movement. To understand today's right-wing politics, there is perhaps no more appropriate place to start than with the entertainment section of right-wing news outlets.

However, the shift in conservative journalism toward the terrain of Hollywood as a major front in its "culture war" battles with the left is still ongoing and incomplete, as the very topic was long perceived as being so foreign and alienating to conservative audiences that it was to be avoided at all costs. This chapter begins the examination of the political role played by entertainment journalism of the right by charting this shift in editorial focus, spotlighting the firsthand accounts of conservative journalists and editors who have been leading this charge. Later it will explore the tension in right-wing entertainment journalism between a more extreme hyper-partisan approach that fully embraces a "culture war" mentality and a more moderated approach that makes conscious appeals to traditional journalistic values and standards. While the latter suggests the potential for a productive cross-cutting public discourse on the politics of entertainment, the former highlights the worrisome role of pop-culture-based rhetoric in fomenting far-right anger and hatred toward socially marginalized groups. In both cases, the political significance of the conservative news media's engagement with pop culture is substantial and unmistakable, as many of its own professionals acutely recognize.

"People Have Started to Catch On": The Conservative Market for Pop Culture Coverage

In stark contrast to its left-wing counterpart, coverage of entertainment and celebrity topics in the conservative news media is inherently controversial. Even when journalists on the right strongly criticize Hollywood on political grounds, these discussions are typically met with some resistance from segments of the conservative news audience who perceive anything Hollywood-related to be unworthy of their attention. These sorts of reactions stem from the long-standing view in the conservative movement that the entertainment industry—seen as an epicenter of left-wing activist causes—constitutes one of its chief political enemies. As such, even unfavorable coverage can raise the ire of audience members who would prefer to block out the world of contemporary pop culture entirely from their everyday news consumption.

As several journalists noted, these right-wing pop culture avoiders tend to make themselves heard anytime conservative news outlets venture into Hollywood-related territory. For instance, an opinion columnist who writes critically about pop culture lamented:

> Sadly, when I do write those columns, I get emails and comments from people and they proudly say, "I don't even own a TV" or "I don't have cable," "I would never watch the Oscars," things like that. . . . They're disgusted by Hollywood, and they say, "I would never go see any of these movies, I won't give these people any of my money." They're very proud of saying "I don't participate in it," when what they're really saying is "I pretend it doesn't exist."

An entertainment editor for a conservative news site similarly explained that a certain percentage of its target audience "hates culture coverage," noting that "there are people who actually really believe, for very good reasons, that there's no excuse for writing about these things or elevating them because they are so corrupt that they should not be touched."

However, the conservative world is currently undergoing a long-term shift in its attitudes toward pop culture as a legitimate subject of political discussion and concern. Many believe that part of this shift is generational in nature, as younger conservative audiences are imagined by the industry to be more fluent in pop culture than their elders. One conservative columnist who often focuses on pop culture recounted:

> At first, when I started, I got a lot of kind of cranky older people saying, "Well, I just don't go to movies anymore. I don't watch TV, that's all trash." . . . However, a new generation is coming up. And weirdly for an older guy, I have got a very young audience, and they are not the same. They agree with me, and they are saying, "Yes, you know, this has got to change, we can't just sit around." . . . When I started, they weren't talking about this, and now they are, and now they pay attention. And the younger they are, the more they pay attention.

Yet, beyond this generational change in the audience, there has been a more fundamental evolution in the right-wing political imagination that is closely tied to the influence and legacy of one conservative leader in particular: the media entrepreneur and pundit Andrew Breitbart. One journalist recounted:

> The line that gets repeated constantly in conservative media, in conservative circles more broadly, is Andrew Breitbart's adage that "politics are downstream of culture." People really believe that in conservative circles, now more than ever, and so that's definitely influenced the conservative media's approach to culture coverage. . . . It is absolutely true that the conservative movement more broadly, and conservative media as a consequence of that, has discovered that pop culture is an arena it needs to be present in. That is absolutely based on this gradual realization that the culture is an essential arena for political conversations, or at least for conservatives to understand. Because you can't fight a culture war when you don't understand the culture.

Breitbart, a former entertainment industry professional who died in 2012 after having launched the popular right-wing news site that bears his name, looms large in virtually any discussion of the right's relationship to pop culture. He is typically credited in the conservative movement with making pop culture a central focus of news coverage and political commentary, which he did with both the Breitbart site and its predecessor, the pointedly titled Big Hollywood. As he described his philosophy in his book *Righteous Indignation*, "Hollywood is more important than Washington. . . . What happens in front of the cameras on a soundstage at the Warner Bros lot often makes more difference to the fate of America than what happens in the back rooms . . . on Capitol Hill."[1] Many right-wing journalists who cover entertainment readily quote his famous "downstream from politics" line as a sort of decree for the conservative movement to take pop culture more seriously and move beyond the reactionary stance of outright avoidance. For instance, one veteran columnist cited Breitbart as a personal influence on his approach to tackling pop culture in the face of conservative antipathy:

> I was friends with Andrew Breitbart, and he was out there [in Hollywood] and knew these people, and he always said that politics is downstream from culture, so to ignore the popular culture is to eventually lose in politics, I believe. Whether you participate, whether you like it or not, is one thing, but to try to pretend that it doesn't exist is a sort of ostrich head-in-the-sand kind of mentality that I think is counterproductive to anybody who cares about politics. Because eventually, what you see in popular culture will end up in politics. So that's why I write about it.

Although journalists who cover entertainment topics for right-wing outlets report that their audience still includes a sizable contingent of pop culture avoiders, they are optimistic about what they see as a vastly growing interest in their work. One columnist explained:

> I started talking about [pop culture] more than fifteen years ago, and when I started out, it was like me talking about it and maybe Andrew Breitbart, and the conservatives would just stare at us. . . . They liked us, they thought we were nice, but they had no idea what we were talking about. Now people have started to catch on. There's more movement in the culture than there was before . . . they understand what I'm talking about. And a lot of those older voices that just were saying, "Why are you even talking about this?" those voices are fading away.

Similarly, a writer and editor who specializes in conservative entertainment coverage described a recent surge in audience interest that he attributed to "a perfect storm" of factors:

> I think Hollywood content has gotten more progressive, I think Hollywood reporting has gotten more progressive, I think the culture has gotten more divided, and I think that more people are realizing what Andrew Breitbart once said—politics are downstream of culture. So I think you put all those things together, there's more of an appetite for what's going on right now, the coverage that I write.

Again, the constant refrain of Breitbart's mantra signals the way in which it has become a powerful organizing logic of contemporary conservative thought. At the same time, however, journalists who are committed to Breitbart's culture-centric approach must make the argument over and over to their audiences to persuade them to get on board. One commented, for instance, that "as a conservative culture writer, I am always aware that my job is probably to persuade, because there is that section of the audience that's going to be inherently skeptical of the project. So just everything that I write, I'm aware that it needs to be persuasive to that kind of reader." In this context, persuasion refers to reaching out not to audiences with different political beliefs but rather to those conservatives who remain suspicious about the Breitbart project, as it were, of engaging with the world of entertainment and celebrity as a route to "downstream" political advantage. In other words, it is a matter of tactics, not ideology. In this way, conservative pop culture news and commentary are rather distinct from their left-wing counterpart, which, as discussed in chapter 2, addresses an audience that is imagined to be widely in agreement about the need for progressive political change in entertainment narratives and representations.

By contrast, the push to adopt Breitbart's tactic of targeting "Big Hollywood" to advance the goals of the political right remains an ongoing concern and an incomplete project. One entertainment writer and editor pointed to the rise of Donald Trump as a TV-celebrity-turned-president as a milestone in the right's shifting approach but noted that even this has not completely phased out an ingrained aversion to pop culture discussions among conservative news audiences: "Especially the 2016 election helped conservatives understand that they need to be following pop culture closely. And it helped, I think, some beltway Republican types understand that

culture drives politics, so I think there's an increased awareness of these issues and their importance. But it can still elicit strong reactions in either
direction."

The sense that there are obstacles left to overcome in realizing Breitbart's
vision of a concerted right-wing battle over pop culture is underscored by
the fact that entertainment journalism is still relatively marginal in the conservative news sphere. This is especially true for review-based cultural criticism, a genre that has been traditionally positioned as service journalism
of a "consumer guide" variety. Given the long-standing tendency in right-
wing circles to deliberately avoid all things Hollywood, it is not surprising
that conservative news outlets have not been quick to prioritize it. One
freelance conservative film critic expressed a notable frustration with the
lack of opportunities to publish his long-form movie reviews, lamenting
that "pop cultural criticism is not welcome in general in the right-wing
publications . . . they don't do much of it besides internet clickbait. Most
publications now will publish something brief about whatever it is, but they
do not cover culture in general. They do not have film critics, music critics
even less so."

Those who do work in this specific capacity are often quick to point out
how rare it is. A right-wing film critic who has the uncommon distinction
of publishing in a national news outlet more known for left-leaning commentary noted that "I think it is fair to say that I'm one of maybe ten conservative film critics working in the country on a regular basis for money,
you know, certified by Rotten Tomatoes and in a critics group and all that
sort of thing. There are not many of us." Another journalist who writes
film reviews from a right-wing perspective similarly remarked that "one
of my canned jokes is that you can fit all the conservative movie critics
in a clown car and have plenty of elbow room left over. There aren't that
many people who are looking at culture and in Hollywood from a right-
of-center point of view."

Precisely why this is the case may not be entirely clear at first glance, especially when considering that journalists who cover Hollywood from
the right frequently point to a growing interest in their work. One likely
reason is that there are still lingering assumptions about the conservative news audience as being pop culture avoiders on ideological grounds,
even in the face of generational change and the widespread influence of
Breitbart's "downstream" maxim. In addition, one critic surmised that part
of the explanation may be that the arts in general are fundamentally more

compatible with left-progressive dispositions and worldviews, which can account for a lack of interest from both right-wing journalists and their audiences: "I am very sympathetic to the idea that there frankly aren't that many conservatives who would have any interest in this sort of career path, that this sort of creative or creative-adjacent endeavor is the sort of thing that more likely is of interest to folks on the left." Such a theory is supported by research conducted by Dannagal G. Young, who finds that key psychological differences between partisans of the right and those of the left can explain their diverging media preferences. According to Young, left-wingers are more comfortable with artistically minded genres such as satire that operate with a playful ambiguity, while right-wingers prefer the more didactic, no-nonsense style of talk radio.[2]

However, while acknowledging that conservatives may be inherently less likely to develop an interest in Hollywood entertainment to the point where they want to discuss it for a living, the above-noted critic also highlighted the sense of exclusion that they may end up encountering in the field if they do pursue this line of work. To this point, he recounted a story of meeting another conservative member of the film critic community and posing the question directly:

> I said, "Why do you think this is, why do you think there's so few of us?" And he said, "Look, the professional rewards simply are not there. If you're a conservative and you're writing about movies, you look around and you see a landscape that is ninety-nine percent liberal. Why would you go into a business like that? Why would you go into a business where you don't see anyone like you?" I don't think it's necessarily a function of outright discrimination. I think there's a lot of self-selection. Why would you go into this business if you have no chance of succeeding? And that's kind of the message that we send to conservatives who are interested in writing about movies. Conservatives look at this world, and they see that there's no place for them, so they see no reason to pursue it.

Whether the "ninety-nine percent liberal" claim is accurate or not, it speaks powerfully to conservatives' broader perception of a journalistic establishment that is deeply biased against them and actively hostile to their views, mirroring their criticism of Hollywood as similarly unwelcoming territory dominated by the left.

"A Site Like Mine Will Be a Corrective": Framing Coverage as a Counterbalance to Left-Wing Dominance

This sense of a profound ideological imbalance, both in pop culture and in the news apparatus that covers it, is key for understanding how right-wing entertainment journalists frame their collective identity as a small band of rebellious outsiders taking on a powerful status quo. Still marginal within conservative circles but quickly gaining ground, and largely cast out by a left-leaning media mainstream (at least as they see it), these journalists envision themselves as being at the very cutting edge of pop culture discourse. Although the perception of imbalance that animates this outsider identity may be exaggerated—after all, there is no shortage of media outlets that cater to right-wing viewpoints—it has clear consequences for how conservative journalists approach entertainment topics in their coverage.

Specifically, much of this journalism is framed as a direct response—a rebuttal, even—to left-oriented pop culture news and commentary that is viewed as unfairly dominant in the media landscape. As one editor for a right-wing news website described her approach to story selection, "the process for me is basically identifying things that are either under-covered by the media or I think could benefit from having conservative coverage in the media." To illustrate this point, she noted:

> I wrote about a Christian TV series that really has been ignored by the mainstream media despite being the largest crowdfunded entertainment project in history. That's a good example of a time where I identified something as not being part of the conversation and wanting to kind of elevate it or amplify it. . . . I decide to jump on those stories when I know that there's a conservative perspective that needs to be included in the larger conversation.

An editor for another conservative site similarly stressed the theme of righting the perceived wrongs of the mainstream news media's approach to pop culture coverage, explaining, "I think that a site like mine will be a corrective in a way." To clarify, he gave the example of a left-wing activist celebrity:

> Like an Alyssa Milano, who's got a huge Twitter following. [She] may share erroneous information to her millions of followers. Now, the *Hollywood*

Reporter and *Variety* and Deadline, they will not report on that, they will ignore that. But I think it's valuable that a site like mine, for example, would say, "Hey, no, she's got this wrong. She just shared this information that is inaccurate with millions of fans."

By pointing to major entertainment industry trade publications as in need of correction due to their ostensible left-wing bias, he underlined the sense that he and journalists like him are on the outside of the establishment looking in, "pointing out the hypocrisy," as he put it, of the perceived liberal media powers that be.

As he elaborated, this emphasis on "correcting" the pop culture journalism of the left suffuses every aspect of corresponding coverage of the right, from celebrity news to reviews of film and television. Regarding the latter, he described how he often crafts pieces in direct reaction to left-leaning movie reviews, which he follows intently and uses as a springboard for his own criticism: "I read a ton of it. I get a steady stream of entertainment stories, and I'm keenly aware . . . if they're going to review a movie and say, "Well, there weren't enough people of color in it," and maybe it's set in World War II where that just wasn't the reality, then I will poke fun at that for sure." Indeed, the very subject of this sort of conservative entertainment criticism is often the mainstream journalistic discourse around pop culture—perceived as overly slanted toward the left—even more so than the pop culture content itself.

In a telling example, he said:

When the [2016] *Ghostbusters* movie came out . . . the media seemed to rally around it, like it needed to be successful and the media was going to make sure it was successful. . . . There are certain movies and themes where the media serves as not just reporters but cheerleaders. The *Washington Post* basically called men misogynist if they had an issue with the lady *Ghostbusters* remake. My issue was the trailer sucked and the movie itself was mediocre, and I don't want to be lectured to by the media about not being skeptical of a project.

Here his negative assessment of the film, which featured an all-female lead cast and a message of feminist empowerment that incited right-wing backlash more generally, was secondary to his frustration with the film's positive reviews in major left-leaning news outlets. In keeping with broader conservative rhetoric that lambastes "the media" as a whole on the grounds of pervasive ideological bias, his comments highlight how right-wing enter-tainment coverage often boils down to a kind of media criticism that seeks to poke holes in a seeming journalistic consensus around pop culture. Just as conservative commentators bemoan political reporting in mainstream outlets such as the *Washington Post* and the *New York Times* as unfair and even "fake," they likewise focus their ire on the Hollywood-themed com-mentary in these same outlets as further evidence of worrisome imbalance.

Another conservative columnist offered a similarly revealing account of how this journalism is produced on a day-to-day basis in direct response to its left-wing counterpart. As he explained, when he looks for a topic for his next column, the work of other, more progressive-minded film critics serves as the raw material for fashioning his own reactive commentary:

> When I see some of these movies get really just hammered on Rotten Tomatoes, a movie like *Peppermint*, it's not as good as *John Wick*, but it's a totally serviceable revenge action movie, and the only reason it is stuck in the low teens on Rotten Tomatoes is because of the choice of villain. . . . There has been kind of a constant refrain that it is unacceptably racist to cast the Mexican [drug] cartels as villains in pulp exploitation movies, which strikes me as totally, totally bonkers, because the cartels themselves are just objectively terrible. . . . And so, as a conservative, I look at that, and I think, "You people are nuts." I cannot fathom looking at the world and thinking the cartels aren't the real problem here, it's portraying the cartels as bad that's the real problem. I look at that, and it flummoxes me in a certain way that I think does not flummox ninety-eight percent of critics.

As accounts like these illustrate, conservative coverage of pop culture is very often reactionary in a quite literal sense, as journalists use the ever-expanding corpus of left-leaning entertainment news and commentary as a starting ground to bounce off of and provide ideological counterweight. Furthermore, their stated drive to speak back to "ninety-eight percent of critics," or simply "the media," evinces how these journalists conceive of their work not only as oppositional to the news media mainstream but also as a kind of righteous cause—no pun intended—to perforate its seeming lock-step ideological conformity. The next section explores this dynamic fur-ther by examining the key arguments and rhetorical tactics of right-wing journalism's attack on "Big Hollywood" that have flowed downstream from Breitbart and his ilk.

"There's Not Allowed to Be a Brad Pitt on the Right": The Grievance-Based Interpretive Approach of Right-Wing Entertainment Journalism

At its core, right-wing entertainment journalism is animated by a deep sense of grievance toward Hollywood for its perceived unjust treatment of conservatives. This reactionary framework, in which conservativism is positioned as the victim of an entertainment industry committed to its wholesale destruction through the spread of left-wing ideology both on- and off-screen, cuts across nearly all pop culture news and commentary that appears in right-wing news outlets. Although such a framework could certainly be accused of exaggeration, it is nevertheless crucial for understanding how conservative journalists approach the terrain of entertainment and celebrity and use it as a rallying ground to mobilize anger and outrage toward the left.

One of the key tenets underlying this reactionary framework is the belief that left-wing messaging dominates pop culture to an overwhelming and totalizing degree, creating an imbalance so extreme and lopsided that it violates the principle of free and open democratic discourse and must therefore be vigorously resisted. Indeed, conservative commentators readily point to what they see as concrete evidence of this complete cultural domination as a means of justifying their resentment. One asserted, for instance, that "if you take a look at every single late-night comedy show on television, every single one, with no exceptions, every single one is an anti-Trump, anti-conservative show. . . . It's only legitimate to express one side of the political question. That is a very widely held opinion in Hollywood." As he went on to suggest, conservatives feel so aggrieved by this progressive media environment not just because they disagree with its viewpoints but because they see it as inescapable and fundamentally invasive:

> You're surrounded by left-wing ideas. You cannot be a right-winger in this country and not know what the left is thinking. You would have to live in your basement, you know, because it's ABC, it's CBS, it's NBC, it's every TV show, it's every movie that you go to see . . . you will hear the opinions of the left.

In addition to the perceived dominance of left-wing ideology in film and television entertainment, conservative anger is further animated by the ostensibly uniform leftism of Hollywood celebrities who use their fame and public prominence to champion progressive causes and lambaste the right. Speaking about the conservative audiences he targets with his opinion columns, one journalist explained:

> [They have] little appreciation for Hollywood being the moral voice of society or for the celebrities having the right to be a moral voice. Everyone has the right to speak out, no one disputes that. But I find among my constituents there is not a lot of sympathy for these actors, actresses, directors, producers, making moral pronouncements and kind of judging others. They tend to react to that in a similar way to Hillary Clinton's comments about "the deplorables" that Trump followers then took as a badge of honor. I see it often in a similar way with Hollywood's critique of things that may be important to us.

Here we can glimpse how the broader populist grievances of contemporary conservatism align closely with the specific resentment toward the pop culture sphere. It is not just that progressives in high-status institutions such as Hollywood voice opposing political viewpoints, but it is the fact that they are seen to look down on right-wing folks with disrespect and scorn that feeds into feelings of victimization at the hands of contemptuous elites.

Regarding celebrities making public political statements, there is, again, a perception of gross ideological imbalance that fuels conservative commentators' sense of indignation. As one put it regarding celebrity activism:

> None of it would be important if there were two sides. I mean, you used to have a Hollywood where there was Gregory Peck on the liberal side and Charlton Heston on the conservative side. They were friends, they liked each other. And now you are just canceled, you lose your job, you lose your livelihood if you don't toe the line. That's what I think is wrong. It's not that Brad Pitt has an opinion . . . that's not the important thing. The important thing is that there's not allowed to be a Brad Pitt on the right. The problem is not that somebody gets up and says something at the Oscars. The problem is that everybody gets up and says one thing at the Oscars.

Although there are certainly outspoken conservatives in Hollywood, anyone who has sat through the Oscars telecast in recent years can recognize a degree of truth to this perception of ideological consensus. In fact, many commentators on the left, such as the journalists discussed in chapter 2, tend to look quite favorably on the entertainment industry's concerted efforts to champion progressive causes in recent years. For conservatives, however, this is taken as an insult—a sign that they are entirely unwelcome in the pop culture sphere.

As the above account further highlights, the sense of victimization in right-wing cultural commentary is buoyed by episodes in which conservative members of the entertainment industry are seen to be actively excluded and shunned—"canceled"—because of their political beliefs, such as in the Gina Carano saga that opened this chapter. One conservative entertainment critic, for instance, explained why he devoted a large amount of coverage to an incident in which the stars of the TV sitcom *Will & Grace* tweeted that they wanted to know the names of industry members attending a Trump fundraiser event in Los Angeles so that they could avoid working with them in the future. As he explained:

> Demanding uniformity of thought annoys the hell out of me. So that's why I wrote about that. To be so blatant about it, to openly advocate, because somebody thinks differently, because your opinion they think is wrong, they should be denied the ability to make a living, is such bullshit. The producers of *Will & Grace* are following [series stars] Eric McCormack and Debra Messing on Twitter, and they saw that. They think, "Well, we're not going to hire [conservative actor] James Woods to be a guest star." Or if a grip or a gaffer or second assistant director or whatever happens to be moderate or center-right, he's following them on Twitter, suddenly that guy thinks, "Fuck, I've got to make sure that nobody suspects anything if I go into work, I could be replaced tomorrow." So it just creates a horrible situation. It pisses me off.

In certain cases, this feeling of ideological persecution on the part of Hollywood is born of personal experience. Some conservative journalists (including, quite notably, the late Andrew Breitbart) worked in the entertainment industry at various parts of their careers, and their ostensible experience of mistreatment helped inspire them to become professional critics of Hollywood. For instance, an entertainment reporter for a right-wing site described how things were early in his career:

I was pursuing a job in the entertainment industry . . . and it was a difficult time. I was a conservative Christian, and that was a difficult thing for me to square with. Because I know that in a place like Hollywood, to get by, you have to network with people, and you network with people by getting very close to them. And if people you get close to you have very strong different opinions from yours, you very much fear that could harm your professional chances. So that was a hard difficulty for me to deal with.

Shortly after this negative experience, he was recruited by the founder of the right-wing news site for which he now works and discovered what he believed to be a far more welcoming professional environment. Another conservative columnist who had a successful career as a movie screenwriter described being "blacklisted by Hollywood" when he began to publish right-wing commentary:

I think what I have done has cost me literally millions of dollars. I made a very, very good living in Hollywood. When I went public with some of this stuff, my phone stopped ringing in Hollywood. I was selling two and three scripts a year, which is a lot of dough. And my phone stopped ringing almost instantaneously and almost completely.

As these stories underline, there is a palpable sense of alienation from the entertainment industry that conservative commentators draw upon in their antagonistic approach to the subject matter. In addition to personal experiences of exclusion when working in Hollywood, a further source of this alienation involves how they perceive the industry to ignore or even actively shun them in their professional capacity as entertainment journalists. For example, an entertainment editor for a right-wing news site decried how studios treat her outlet as a kind of pariah on the Hollywood beat: "I do think they deliberately, in many cases, will shut off access from someone like me. . . . Not granting interviews, not granting behind-the-scenes access that other people would probably get." At the same time, however, she noted that these same studios will occasionally reach out in a friendlier manner: "when they have something that's like Christian entertainment that they want to promote, they'll bring us in. But it's kind of like they just want you in that case. . . . They ignore us until they have something they want to pitch to our audience." As she suggested, such uneven treatment further feeds into the perception that Hollywood is fundamentally unfair toward conservatives, cynically exploiting them when it is economically desirable to do so while coldly eschewing them when it is not.

In stark contrast to entertainment journalists of the left, who, as chapter 2 showed, often point to concrete instances in which their politically oriented exposés and critiques have been listened to and even acted upon by industry figures, their counterparts on the right describe a far chillier relationship with Hollywood professionals. As one conservative entertainment critic put it, "I don't think what I write impacts Hollywood at all, honestly.... People on the right joke about the bubble that liberals are in, and I think it's true. I don't think they get the messaging from my site and like-minded sites." Along similar lines, a columnist remarked that when it comes to right-wing commentary on pop culture, "I don't believe that Hollywood listens.... I'm not sure that the people who are in decision-making positions read it or are open to it. I think they'd be better off to do so, because why you would alienate or immediately write off forty percent of a potential audience is bizarre to me." As he suggested here, conservative entertainment journalists view Hollywood as disdainfully ignoring both them and the audiences they see themselves as representing, reinforcing the alienation that underwrites their oppositional stance.

It is precisely this notion of Hollywood's intolerance toward conservatives—seemingly manifested in everything from its press relationships to its hiring practices to its narrative messaging—that provides the central rhetorical framework of contemporary right-wing pop culture criticism as a battle against leftist cultural oppression. The irony of co-opting the left's own anti-oppression rhetoric around such issues as race, gender, and sexuality may strike some as galling, but it is nonetheless crucial for understanding how the pop culture sphere, as a relative bastion of progressive politics, is mobilized for conservative anger and grievance.

"The Bigger Issue Is Free Speech": Adopting Liberal Rhetoric in Attacks on "Cancel Culture"

Within this framework, commentators position themselves not as enforcers of traditional social hierarchies but rather as champions of freedom of expression and the rights of all individuals to participate fully and openly in social and cultural life, no matter what their political views are. The fact that such rhetoric readily makes appeals to traditional liberal values of freedom, tolerance, diversity, and equality is not lost on right-wing critics of "Big Hollywood." Take, for instance, one conservative columnist's rationale for why "Hollywood is such a good target at this point" for political criticism:

> The left is no longer liberal. I mean, I consider myself a liberal. I'm a conservative because I'm a liberal, by which I mean I want people to be free, to say the things that they think, to act in accordance with their own beliefs, to worship as they please, to write as they please. The left is no longer the liberal side. The left is now the side that tells you what you should think, what you should say, what you can't think, what you get fired for saying. . . . So what makes Hollywood so attackable at this point is not that they're liberal. It's that they're leftist, and that's a totally, totally different thing.

The distinction that he draws here between liberalism and leftism is now a familiar refrain in broader political criticism of the progressive left, in which the term "illiberalism" is often invoked to describe its perceived intolerance of views other than its own around issues of identity politics. Through this rhetorical framing, critics of identity politics position themselves as the true inheritors of the liberal tradition that values freedom of expression and the questioning of elite authority in open democratic debate. In addition to attacking college campuses for this perceived "illiberalism" (which has emerged in recent years as another favorite target of right-wing ire),[3] conservative commentators use the entertainment industry as a key mobilizing symbol of the left's perceived dogmatism and quashing of free expression.

Indeed, freedom of expression and the fight against ideological tyranny have emerged as the preferred rhetorical framework of right-wing criticism of the pop culture world, far more so than any direct engagement with the issues of race, gender, and sexuality that constitute the core concerns of the industry's progressive politics. While debating the merits of expanding media representation of women and people of color, for instance, can make conservative commentators vulnerable to accusations of bigotry, reframing the debate in terms of freedom of expression puts them in more comfortable territory and provides a firm sense of having the moral high ground. One right-wing entertainment critic and editor, for example, explained that of all the issues that he covers, "I think what I care about the most is expression right now, where we can't say certain things and we can't tell certain jokes and we can't have certain opinions. And I think that's extremely dangerous . . . people are aghast when someone defends free speech in our culture. And I will fight with my website on that." Within this framework, the actual content of the controversial jokes or opinions is beside the point; what matters only is the principle of having the right to voice them publicly without the threat of material retaliation. In this way, conservative critics appeal to centrist liberal ideals, rather than blatant far-right prejudices, in their attacks on Hollywood's "political correctness" and "cancel culture"— although it could certainly be argued that those prejudices often remain as subtext if not explicit text.

To bolster the case that they are concerned with freedom rather than big-otry or hateful extremism, conservative news commentators often emphasize solidarity with entertainment industry figures associated with the left who have become targets of "cancel culture." One such journalist commented:

> When it comes to free speech and creativity, I consider [comedian] Ricky Gervais a significant ally. And Ricky Gervais, I'm pretty sure, hates Trump, would never vote the way I vote. But I aligned with him because I think the bigger issue is free speech, creative expression. . . . I think those are values that we need to hold dear as a culture. [Comedian] Dave Chappelle is the same way. I don't think he votes the way I do, but I consider them key allies in what I think is one of the biggest issues of our time . . . there's a collective pressure to silence some people and to not have their views heard.

This notion of freedom-of-expression values being more salient than any right–left political divide was likewise invoked by a conservative film critic:

> I don't look at it as a partisan issue, in large part because a lot of times what you see in these "cancel culture" debates, a lot of it is intramural. A lot of it is leftists going after leftists and attacking fellow travelers. And I have found in almost all of these fights that I am defending people who are Democrats just as often as I am defending people who are Republicans. . . . I don't even know that it's ideological except in the sense that I believe that it is bad to try to destroy people's lives over something they say on Twitter or something they say in DMs that gets leaked four years later.

This particular line of argument, which shifts focus from the substance of speech controversies to the tactics with which they are pursued (i.e., calls for "canceling" both media content and Hollywood careers), appears to be highly persuasive for certain segments of the news audience. Chapter 6 will look at how the backlash against "cancel culture" has emerged as a key catalyst of audience engagement with entertainment journalism, in some cases even cutting across partisan lines. Tapping into this distaste for hard-line tactics of moral censure—such as demanding someone be fired from their job over an offending social media post—conservative commentators reframe the debate in a way that effectively sidesteps the weighty matters of identity and representation that fuel the rhetoric of their colleagues on the left. In essence, pop culture commentators on the right are engaging in a different debate altogether—one in which they are ostensibly in a more favorable position to "win" by taking on the mantle of freedom of expression that resonates so powerfully with deeply ingrained individualist American values.[4]

"I Want My Entertainment to Be Entertaining": Appeals to Depoliticize Pop Culture

In addition to targeting the tactics of "cancel culture," another important and closely related rhetorical strategy of conservative pop culture criticism is to tap into audience's potential exhaustion with the mixing of entertainment with political messaging and to position the right as the defenders of pure fun and amusement. As discussed in chapter 2, pop culture journalism of the left tends to operate with the core understanding that all cultural symbolism is imbued with political meaning and performs an ideological function in society—the post-Marxist Gramscian turn that has inspired generations of media criticism in academia and beyond.[5] We have also seen how much of the entertainment industry has come to broadly align with this philosophy as well, propelling its sense of political consciousness and inspiring more explicit social advocacy throughout the sphere of cultural production. Since conservative critics perceive the political engagement of both contemporary Hollywood and its mainstream news media interlocutors as being uniformly leftist and oppositional to their values, the notion of freeing entertainment from politics altogether becomes an attractive proposition. Here commentators on the right repudiate the notion of pop culture having an innately ideological character that is so fundamental for their colleagues on the left, championing instead a vision of entertainment as a welcome sanctuary from political—and "politically correct"—concerns.

As one conservative film critic put it:

[This is] another issue where the right and the left just kind of disagree. I don't believe that the personal is the political. I do not believe that all art is inherently political, or that all art is propaganda.... I think that it is possible to enjoy something that has, quote, bad politics to it, which may put me outside of the mainstream of film criticism, or at least it certainly would separate me from the far-left critics who kind of explicitly look through this stuff with that lens.

This sense of fighting for a depoliticized space of pop culture, free from concerns over whether symbolic representations are either progressive or problematic for the broader society, is an important recurring theme in conservative commentary. Akin to the backlash against "cancel culture," it frames political activism as a fundamentally unwelcome and invasive force in entertainment, threatening to upend its ability to bring aesthetic joy and pleasure to its audiences, in addition to muzzling the free expression of its creators.

In articulating this stance, another right-wing columnist pointedly commented:

I want my entertainment to be entertaining. Nobody goes to the movies thinking, "What I really want to do it be bitched at for ninety minutes about how racist the society is." They go to the movies to get away from that shit for an hour and a half. And too often, especially in award-winning movies, because Hollywood is so liberal, that is what gets awarded. That's what gets attention. But, you know, the best movie for my money last year was *Avengers: Endgame*. It was awesome, and it got nothing, no love at all from the Academy. The storytelling was great. The acting was good. There were emotions. It was everything. But because it wasn't about some social injustice, or some overarching theme that fits a certain narrative, it was ignored.

Here the Oscars—along with the journalistic film criticism that frequently influences them—are evoked to symbolize a perceived left-wing dominance over the adjudication of cultural value, or what is held up by elite institutions as "good" (i.e., progressive political messaging) versus what is dismissed as "bad" (i.e., everything else).

Of course, ostensibly escapist and apolitical entertainment such as *Avengers: Endgame* continues to thrive in the pop culture marketplace and command a huge audience—in fact, this particular "popcorn" movie became the high-grossing film of all time upon its 2019 release.[6] Yet, as the above comments suggest, conservative news commentators are frustrated less with the economics of the entertainment industry than with how hierarchies of status are accorded within it by elite institutions. In their book *Cultural Backlash*, political scientists Pippa Norris and Ronald Inglehart identify the threat of declining social status as a key driver of right-wing populist politics more generally, particularly as older white men seek to protect the hegemonic status that they have traditionally been afforded and that they see as imperiled by recent shifts in social and cultural values.[7] Within this framework, we can recognize how the conferring of status in the pop culture field, including awards shows and movie critics' reviews, feeds into to this broader dynamic of backlash. Specifically, many appear to be resentful because they feel that their "traditional" cultural tastes—and the social identities that they symbolize—are being actively devalued in status while cultural content that reflects newer, more politically progressive sensibilities is held up in institutional high esteem.

At its core, the conservative response to this shift toward a more politically conscious status hierarchy in pop culture revolves around a call to "leave politics out of it." In other words, allow audiences to enjoy escapist Hollywood entertainment without being confronted with critiques about its politics of representation that knock it down a peg, or allow celebrities to say what they want in public without being met with politicized judgment and condemnation that threaten their social standing as well as that of their fans and sympathizers. As one columnist put it regarding this framework, "the left is demanding purity . . . [the right] just wants to be left the fuck alone. Now it's 'if you don't celebrate me, then you're the problem,' and they'll poke around and try and find something that you're not sufficiently woke on so that they could be mad at you." Again, we can observe how conservative rhetoric frames pop culture as a space of innocent pleasures that is being spoiled by the contentious concerns of politics in general and progressive identity politics in particular. By exclaiming "leave politics out of it," right-wing commentators position themselves as defenders not just of freedom of expression but also of the right to unencumbered fun.

As chapter 2 has shown, left-wing critics have a ready response for such calls to depoliticize pop culture, which, as they note, also represent a frequent audience response to their own politically oriented entertainment journalism. Maintaining that cultural symbolism can never be truly separated from issues of ideology and power, they argue that the desire to take politics out of pop culture is in reality a desire to preserve an ideological status quo that runs deep in seemingly mindless entertainment and harmless fun. The conservative cry to "leave politics out of it" is thus interpreted as an attempt to preserve a cultural space that centers the white, male, heterosexual, cisgender experience, along with traditional conservative values more broadly.

Although there may be considerable merit to this line of counterargument, it is nevertheless important to consider how the rhetoric of "leave politics out of it" puts the right-wing backlash against pop culture progressivism in a seemingly more favorable position than it would be in if it were to mount an explicit and full-throated defense of an ideological status quo. After all, the impulse to use pop culture to escape the troubles of the world and revel in uncomplicated pleasures of pure spectacle is greatly widespread, if not universal, and therefore making appeals to such desires has clear tactical benefits. Like their appeal to freedom-of-expression values, their call to depoliticize pop culture in the name of good, simple fun helps conservative commentators shift the terms of debate to their ostensible advantage and avoid directly confronting the sensitive matters of identity politics that preoccupy their left-wing counterparts. Defending a racial and gender hierarchy may be viewed as a losing proposition in the contemporary social and political climate. But defending the right to be entertained without being put down for it is an argument that right-wing news commentators believe they can win.

"It's Really Important to Engage with Culture and Not Rage at It": From "Red Meat" to "Nuance" in Conservative Pop Culture Coverage

As outlined in the previous section, conservative entertainment journalism tends to follow a common set of patterns and present a consistent set of ideological viewpoints. However, those who work in the field are quick to draw a distinction between the more aggressively hyper-partisan style popularized by sites such as Breitbart and a more moderate style that tends to be invoked with the singular descriptive "nuance." The former is defined as being entirely couched within the framework of "culture war," with journalists and editors taking every available opportunity to score attacks on leftist Hollywood and "own the libs," to use a phrase common in right-wing circles. The latter, by contrast, ostensibly seeks to generate a right-of-center conversation around pop culture that resembles its left-wing counterpart in terms of its studious approach to cultural discourse and appeals to traditional journalistic values.

In some ways, this distinction maps neatly onto the familiar highbow–lowbrow dichotomy that is perceptible across the media landscape. In the world of conservative news, more intellectually minded publications such as the *National Review* or the libertarian *Reason* are known for featuring lengthy essays and reviews, while sites that follow the Breitbart model of partisan media warfare are far more tabloid-like in terms of "quick hit" coverage that emphasizes sensational appeal. This distinction within conservative pop culture journalism appears to have an ideological component as well, as those who adhere to the "nuance" model tend to self-consciously back away from what they see as the extremism of the far right, particularly regarding sensitive topics such as racism and homophobia.

Within the conservative news media landscape, journalists who cover pop culture often speak of the hyper-partisan tabloid style in derisive terms, even when affirming its utility and market value. For instance, one remarked that "there's a lot of stuff that is very bad" in the field, and while he upheld that "there's obviously a place for that, and some people have been very successful with it," he also joked, "I don't think anybody is going to be collecting volumes of takedowns of the libs in Hollywood like people read the collected works of critics we have known and loved throughout the years." A veteran conservative columnist similarly knocked the hyper-partisan style for its negligible quality while also admitting its appeal and profitability: "There's always a market for bitching about Hollywood, just like there's always a market for bitching about the media. Pointing out the obvious . . . it's the preaching to the choir, throwing red meat to the base. . . . It's comfort food. I guess it's nothing more than that. I don't think it's any deeper." "Red meat" is indeed a frequent shorthand for this type of coverage within the field, suggesting both the vociferous passion with which it is consumed by its riled-up target audience and its "common man," anti-elitist appeal.

It is unclear how many conservative journalists would positively embrace the "red meat" label for themselves. Rather, it tends to be invoked when pointing out the perceived weaknesses of others in the field (although it should be noted that the news company that is most commonly associated with the "red meat" style, Breitbart, declined to participate in the research for this book). For right-of-center journalists who identify more with the "nuance" approach, "red meat" serves as a useful point of comparison to distinguish their own pop culture coverage which aspires to be more thoughtful and in-depth. Along these lines, a conservative entertainment critic commented:

> A lot of people in my niche will write a "Jim Carrey put out a crazy tweet" [article]. And that's fine. It's news to an extent. But I try to give more context to the stories I write, to kind of connect more dots to make it more interesting. . . . I would rather write a story that looks at a larger theme for an emerging trend as opposed to these sorts of quick hits.

In similar fashion, an entertainment reporter for another right-wing news outlet explained:

> I try to move away from writing pieces that are like "Oh, this celebrity said this," unless they said something really, really outlandish and crazy. You know, Breitbart almost on a daily basis has an article that "this celebrity said this on Twitter about Trump," you know, and I tend to not write about that because we already know what a lot of these people think and what they believe. There's just no point in writing a whole article about what Cher said on Twitter for the hundredth time about Trump. So I try to focus on something that has a little bit more to it, a little bit more impactful.

In addition to noting the relative depth of their pop culture discussions, these journalists also tend to stress how the tone of their Hollywood-targeted criticism differentiates their approach from the more pugnacious "red meat" style. One remarked, for instance:

> I think there are people on the right side of the aisle who are pretty "red meat"-driven, who are really aggressive. And that's their brand, that's who they are, you know, it is what it is. But I don't try to go there. Just to give you an example, [left-wing filmmaker] Michael Moore is heavyset, but when I critique Michael Moore, I don't say "the fat Michael Moore." I critique his movies or his commentary or what he's doing or what he's saying. I try not to get nasty. And I think at the end of the day, I am a journalist, and I try to keep holding on to that even though the world of journalism is sort of shifting and changing and growing less disciplined.

As these remarks suggest, those who identify with the "nuance" approach tend to understand it as a matter of maintaining professional journalistic standards in the face of a heightened hyper-partisanship that prioritizes attacking the opposition by any means necessary.

An entertainment editor for a conservative news site even went so far as to say that such as a distinction in tone shapes her entire professional approach:

> I don't think that sort of rage clickbait that plucks everything from Hollywood and frames it as evil is productive. . . . I sort of preach this in conservative circles, [that] it's really important to engage with culture and not rage at it. So some of that really angry clickbait stuff that you will occasionally see in conservative media about the Oscars or whatever it is, I don't think it's particularly helpful. Sometimes it's completely warranted, and you have to do it, but I think also just being able to engage with Hollywood and the entertainment industry is really important.

As she further explained, this notion of fashioning a more measured discourse with the world of Hollywood and celebrity comes down to the guiding editorial principle of "nuance":

> For my job as a culture editor, I only want to publish something that's appropriately nuanced on pop culture. I don't like publishing things that are just like screeds against the latest pop star. . . . A lot of times it's better to sort of say with empathy, "Why is this popular?" because it is connecting with people for some reason. What is it in our culture that's making this resonate? So I prefer to come at things from that perspective. I think it's much more productive, much healthier.

This desire to take a less combative and more inquisitive tone in pop culture news commentary is shared by some conservative journalists who have professional aspirations to transcend the "red meat" function of hyper-partisan media, although their opportunities to do so may be uneven. One freelance conservative critic, for instance, complained that in contrast to the professed "nuance" ethos of some members of the field, his intellectually minded essays on film were sometimes molded by his editors into "red meat" by the affixing of provocative headlines:

You need a hook, and the hook still tends to be culture war. So that is reflected more in the headlines than in the contents. And often [articles] with
incendiary or striking headlines make thoughtful arguments that do not
lend themselves to "own the libs" rhetoric. . . . Almost no writer chooses
his headlines; those are editorial decisions made by the publisher. I'm not
sure if one percent of the things I write come under a headline of my own
choosing.

He noted that some of his pieces published on a right-wing site were given
headlines that made it sound as though he was directly attacking feminism
(with the trigger word "feminist" featured prominently), which he claimed
was a deliberate mischaracterization to make the articles fit better with the
site's hyper-partisan house style. While he seemed to begrudgingly accept
this arrangement as a reality of working in today's right-wing news sphere,
another conservative journalist described how he left a staff position at a "red
meat"-style news outlet in part because "they wanted to cover stories that
I found very tabloid-y, and that just wasn't what interests me."

Despite the protestations of some journalists in the field, the "red meat"
approach to right-wing pop culture coverage is clearly not going anywhere,
as long as its target audiences keep clicking on the incendiary headlines.
However, it is also clear that there is a palpable tension within this journalistic community between industry demands to serve hyper-partisan "red
meat" and personal sensibilities and professional ambitions that may run
counter to that impulse. This tension is well illustrated in the account of an
entertainment reporter for a right-wing news site who found himself making
a transition from one end of this spectrum to the other. As he explained, a
few years back, his reporting was squarely in the "red meat" camp, yet his
stance against the "cancel culture" of the left led him to reconsider his participation in attack-style journalism on the right:

During the #MeToo movement, myself and others included, I think we
were so giddy over our anger at Hollywood. . . . We were very quick to want
to just smear every single person, every single celebrity in Hollywood at the
time. So yeah, cancel culture is a really bad thing, and I've moved away from
it. I've changed. . . . I try to focus on positive things, or just maybe do more
sarcastic tongue-in-cheek kind of stuff, but I've moved away completely
from rage or anger toward people.

Although his desire to distance himself from belligerent "culture war" attacks on Hollywood would presumably put him in conflict with the demands of the conservative news business, in this case, his employers appeared to support his shift to a less aggressively partisan mode of entertainment reporting:

> As time has gone on, I've been more encouraged to just kind of write more straightforward pieces. . . . Especially when it comes to very sensitive matters like LGBT issues, sexual matters, I try to keep the reporting very straightforward, like "who said what," "this is what's happening," that kind of thing. When it comes to issues like that, there is so much nuance to the equation that those kinds of things I'd prefer are left up to serious conversations and dialogue in the public square. . . . I don't think that should be handled on online forums or duking it out on Facebook or on Twitter. That's mainly why I've shifted away from that. There's just a lot of nuance to them, and I think that people should be able to talk more freely and have an open dialogue about it rather than these hit pieces online.

Again, we see how the term "nuance" is used to signify an alternative model for doing conservative cultural criticism that avoids the excesses of hyper-partisanship and "red meat" outrage. Moreover, his comments suggest the discomfort that some conservative news professionals appear to have with the more extremist side of right-wing rhetoric that exploits prejudice and fear toward vulnerable identity groups such as the LGBT community (a trend that has notably skyrocketed in the era of Trump's domination over the conservative movement).[8] Although he noted that he still sometimes writes pieces that poke fun at "political correctness going off the rails" in pop culture, he also evinced a degree of disillusionment with the more hard-edged, identity-based right-wing attacks on Hollywood:

> After being in this for several years, I've learned to see that the culture war that we talk about, there's a lot of gray and fog in it. And it's not quite the war that I was taught to see several years ago where there are clear dividing lines, and those people are over there and those people are over here. It's a very, very murky, messy thing . . . there's a lot of nuance, and I try my best to address those nuances.

His account thus shed lights on a more moderate wing of sorts within conservative entertainment journalism that backs away from full-throated "culture war" in favor of a more traditional journalistic stance of neutrality and objectivity, at least when covering some of the most hot-button issues around identity politics.

In addition to pulling back from hyper-partisan attacks on Hollywood and adopting a more straightforward tone for reporting on it, another way in which "nuance" journalists distinguish themselves is with how they handle coverage of conservative-oriented pop culture. Right-wing entertainment productions—often themed around Christianity—exist as a relatively small part of the pop culture landscape, and there appears to be some pressure within conservative news media to provide positive coverage as a means of advancing the "culture war" into more favorable territory. However, journalists who lean toward the "nuance" approach take pride in resisting such pressure for partisan cheerleading. One right-wing critic explained: "As a movie reviewer, I review movies. If I spot political material in there, I will note that for the reader, especially given that my audience is primarily right-of-center readers. What I will not do, though, is give points if the content is right of center and weak. I'm not going to say, 'Oh, it's great,' even though it's not." In other words, he stressed that his professional identity as a film critic supersedes his role as a partisan operative, to the point where he would not allow the latter to interfere with the integrity of the former.

Similarly, an editor for another right-wing site claimed that she consciously avoids the kind of partisan-driven cheerleading that she views as a shortcoming of her left-wing counterparts:

> My big critique of a lot of entertainment media coverage, which certainly skews left of center, is that some of it is sort of like clickbait that's reflexively favorable to its celebrity subjects. And so I try not to do that, either. Whether it's a conservative, you know, Clint Eastwood doing something or a liberal, I try not to just hand out applause for a celebrity doing something, or anyone in pop culture doing something valuable. We'll try to apply the same standards of rigorous analysis that we would apply to a politician to a celebrity.

Again, we can see how "nuance" journalists in the conservative news sphere appeal to notions of journalistic professionalism and objectivity as a way of distancing themselves from "red meat" hyper-partisanship. In this case, treating a well-known Hollywood right-winger like Eastwood with an even hand, as opposed to an automatic thumbs up, becomes a mark of distinction for those who seek to fashion a more measured form of conservative pop culture coverage that aspires to be more than just "culture war" ammunition.

To a degree, this "nuance" approach can be understood as an economically motivated strategy, targeting a news audience that is right of center but may also shy away from far-right "red meat" that revels in extremism around issues such as race, gender, and sexuality. One conservative journalist who runs a pop culture news site suggested as much when explaining how he tries to differentiate his coverage from that of outlets like Breitbart:

> I am building a brand. And you know, the Breitbarts of the world are bare-knuckled, that's their MO. But I'm not quite that, it's not me, and it's not what I'm trying to do. . . . I want to show more positive things. . . . [*Captain America* actor] Chris Evans was hanging out with [Republican senator] Ted Cruz. And I'm thinking, I kind of want that in the conversation as well.

As he indicated, this less "bare-knuckled" style serves as a strategy for courting audiences who lean conservative but who can also be fond of Hollywood entertainment and do not view it solely as a partisan enemy to be vanquished.

"I Really Agree with Their Concerns on Representation": Finding Common Ground for Dialogue?

Although there may be a pragmatic element to taking this more moderate stance in pop culture coverage, it appears to be more than simply an exercise in niche-market positioning. Rather, these "nuance" journalists seem to be rather sincere in their rejection of a far-right cultural politics that willfully demonizes marginalized identity groups and their desire to carve out a less extremist space for right-of-center pop culture commentary. To this point, they tend to be outwardly sympathetic toward left-wing criticism about the need for more diversity and inclusion in the entertainment industry. Rather than rail against these arguments as undue "political correctness," as is common in "red meat"-style coverage on the right, they appear to accept them as fundamentally valid but seek to expand on them in ways that resonate with the conservative movement's preoccupation with its own perceived cultural marginalization.

One journalist of this type explained:

I really agree with their concerns on representation in general, and how the media lacks representation from minorities, from people who have different socioeconomic backgrounds, and certainly from people with different cultural and regional backgrounds. And so I definitely believe that it's an important goal to make the media more representative of the country as a whole. . . . You have all these people around the country whose voices are not represented in the mainstream media.

As a conservative commentator, however, her discussions of pop culture diversity tend to be a bit different, focusing on groups such as those who live in rural areas and who share a distinctive "heartland" culture, whom she sees as underrepresented by Hollywood:

I to try to be in tune with how my tastes might reflect the tastes of other people who are outside of the sort of coastal areas, and then I try to write from that perspective. I'm from Wisconsin, I didn't grow up in a city, and I didn't grow up on the East Coast, so to me, it's really important to represent that the best I can.

Here her comfort with diversity rhetoric seems to position her to the left of the most hyper-partisan forms of conservative discourse, even if she is susceptible to accusations of appropriating such rhetoric in equivocal fashion to simply bolster a right-wing agenda.

In addition to extending calls for pop culture diversity to include regional as well as racial, gender, and sexual identity, one "nuance"-leaning conservative film critic emphasized the need for ideological diversity in political discussions of entertainment:

People see the world in different ways, and I'm totally open to the argument that, for instance, film criticism is lacking in African American voices and that lack of African American voices actually has a serious negative impact on how films are judged and perceived. Or that there are too few major female film critics, that having that voice and that perspective in the discussion is good and useful and worthwhile, because being a woman changes how you look at the world and changes how you experience certain things. And I think the same thing is actually true of being a conservative, because ninety-nine percent of film critics kind of come at all of these issues from the same basic lens. There is a useful dynamic to having a different point of view on these things.

Again, we see how these more moderate "nuance" journalists express affinity with the core concerns of their left-wing counterparts while also making the case that diversity and inclusion rhetoric serves their ideological purposes as well. Here the fact that most entertainment criticism in the news is left-wing in orientation—which, as discussed earlier, is a major preoccupation of and rallying point for conservative pop culture coverage as a whole—provides the basis to argue that adding more right-wing perspectives would help diversify the field and make it live up to its own calls for increased inclusivity.

This rhetorical move to uphold "diversity of thought" as equivalent to diversity along the lines of race, gender, and sexuality has become quite familiar in conservative discourse, particularly in debates over the politics of college campuses which have become a favorite topic of the right in recent years.[9] Just as college campuses have been accused of hypocrisy for championing the cause of diversity while ostensibly narrowing the range of representation by disinviting conservatives from speaking appearances, both Hollywood and mainstream entertainment journalism have been similarly criticized for selectively applying the principle of inclusivity in a way that leaves out groups who lean conservative. Of course, this argument is vulnerable to counter-critiques of false equivalency and cynical exploitation, but even so, it suggests that there is a serious intellectual debate to be had in the public arena regarding the full scope of the politics of representation.

More generally, the phenomenon of "nuance" entertainment journalism within the right-wing news sphere signals how at least some conservatives contribute to the critical public discourse around pop culture on terms that are recognizable to their progressive-left counterparts. In fact, many of the core arguments that are advanced by conservative commentators, such as the moral dangers of "cancel culture" and the potential overpoliticization of arts and entertainment, find sympathy with some progressive-minded members of the entertainment journalism field. For instance, regarding the issue of "cancel culture," a reporter who covers LGBT representation for a left-leaning news site noted concern over "the fact that any small thing that can be taken out of context is used as fodder for clickbait that incites a pitchfork mob of outrage, and everything gets blown out of proportion, and things aren't considered with nuance. There's a lot of validity to those criticisms." Tellingly, his appeal to journalistic "nuance" in this context indicates a common set of values that he shares with certain conservative colleagues in the field. Here the rejection of hard-line "cancel culture" tactics of moral censure represents an appeal to moderation that is attractive for news professionals on both the left and the right who wish to distance their work from the most extreme, ends-justify-the-means forms of partisanship.

Regarding the call to carve out a depoliticized space for the pleasures of Hollywood entertainment, chapter 2 has already shown how some left-wing commentators counter that such a notion is simply a form of hegemony in disguise. Yet others are more charitable to this line of argument. For instance, a film critic for a left-oriented news site lamented that focusing exclusively on whether a movie has "good" progressive politics can be problematic in her line of work:

> I think it is very hard to judge a film if you're always holding everybody in-volved up to your own personal purity test. And I think it takes a little bit of the joy out of watching a movie. The reality is that I started writing about movies because I love movies, you know. So I think if you are holding eve-rything up to a very exacting set of standards all the time, it can become really difficult and, honestly, very disheartening.

Along similar lines, another left-leaning critic explained:

> In the broader critical community, this is a huge tension right now. I think there are a lot of people, maybe particularly younger critics, who kind of go in ideology first. And I understand why and don't think that's necessarily bad . . . but I do get a little worried that we will miss talking about the aes-thetics of a film. I think it's really important for film critics to pay atten-tion to, like, what's on the screen? Is it any good? Should these people keep making this art? And not just thinking about "Do I agree with the ideas of this thing?" That's a pretty vapid way to approach criticism.

As these remarks suggest, the criticisms that conservative news commentators often raise about the work of their left-progressive colleagues in the field are not theirs alone but rather dovetail with difficult discussions and debates that are taking place inside those very circles. Moreover, the concerns that some left-leaning journalists express about the potential excesses within their own ranks suggest that there is room for productive conversation on these issues across the left–right divide. One such reporter for several left-leaning news outlets contended:

I think the best cultural critics I've read provide such extraordinary nuance and thought to these arguments about these pieces of art that we consume. And I do feel there have been heightened [political] tensions around pretty much anything, and I think that's unfortunate. I personally have never felt like I've had to pick a side. I am on the side of nuance and a lot of interesting thought and debate on what we consume with our media.

Once again, these repeated appeals to "nuance" coming from both ideological directions indicate a shared set of precepts about the practice of journalism, pointing to the promise of fashioning a deliberative space for pop culture discourse in the news media that springs from this common foundation.

A Platform for Far-Right Extremism?

However, the true breadth of this space for respectful cross-cutting debate on the politics of pop culture may not be as wide as such a formulation might suggest. Rather, the "nuance" approach to cultural coverage represents only one part of a conservative news ecosystem that has increasingly moved farther to the right, along with much of the Republican Party, in the era of the Trump presidency and its aftermath. It is important to stress that the ample attention given in this chapter to the voices of "nuance" conservative entertainment journalists is partially due to the fact that they were some of the only ones on the right who were willing to participate in this academic research in the first place. Given that academia is frequently targeted by the conservative movement as a political enemy in roughly equal measure to Hollywood and the mainstream news media, it is not surprising that the more hyper-partisan, "red meat" contingent within the field would decline to be involved. Indeed, many journalists who work for these types of news outlets (including Breitbart, as noted above) turned down the invitation to be interviewed for this book. Some were openly hostile; for instance, one high-profile right-wing commentator replied to an email asking for an interview by exclaiming that the request "sickens me."

From journalists' interviews alone, it is thus difficult to capture the true tenor of "red meat" right-wing coverage of Hollywood and the threats it can pose to civil discourse on issues of cultural power and representation. Yet it is nonetheless important to take stock of the severity of the hyper-partisan rhetoric that circulates within the more extreme side of this landscape. At a time when the QAnon conspiracy theory—which alleges that Hollywood celebrities join Democratic politicians in worshiping the devil and abusing children—is believed by nearly a quarter of Republicans and forty percent of those who follow far-right news sources,[10] the extent of the problem is difficult to overestimate.

As an anecdotal illustration, consider one audience member's response to a Breitbart article that accused Hollywood of engaging in "reverse racism" and argued that "there is just no question that Hollywood's two-decade blacklisting of conservatives and conservative ideas is about to extend to white people, most especially white men." A participant in the audience research study presented later here in chapter 6, this white male in his seventies had shared the Breitbart link on Twitter and made the following comment when responding to interview questions: "There is no doubt in my mind that lesbian Nazi-like women are extortionists if high-profile young stars don't convert to their political thinking." He further remarked, "Blacks like [sports journalist] Jemele Hill have only two cards in their wallet, victim card and race card, and MSM [mainstream media] are currently biased toward blacks because they're afraid to be branded racist . . . trash the whites, give whites 'slander' tags, and there's little downside from their workplace environment."

Obviously, this individual speaks only for himself and not for Breitbart or any other news organization, nor does he speak for the conservative news audience writ large. Yet the disturbingly bigoted tone of these comments provides a glimpse into the far-right extremism that traffics within the broader right-wing discourse around pop culture and identity politics. Chapter 5 will show how this sort of hateful rhetoric is routinely directed at minority and female journalists on social media because of their progressive-minded coverage of the politics of representation. Here we can consider how the more extremist "red meat" style of hyper-partisan news on the right provides spaces for this rhetoric to germinate and flourish, as audiences are ginned up with heated claims that they are being culturally oppressed and victimized by the very forces that call for an end to historical oppression.

Conclusion

This chapter has shown how pop culture reporting and commentary have emerged as a key focal point of contemporary conservative news media as backlash against the progressive politics of cultural and social identity has grown more central to the broader conservative movement. Framing "Big Hollywood" as one of its chief political enemies due its embrace of progressive social values regarding race, gender, and sexuality and its perceived exclusion of and hostility toward conservatives, right-wing news outlets have begun to make pop-culture-themed cultural grievance into one of their major selling points. Furthermore, by rhetorically aligning with freedom-of-expression and aestheticist values as a strategically convenient—if rarely consistent—ploy to gain a moral high ground for the right in today's "culture wars," conservative entertainment journalism has fashioned a forceful set of arguments that have far-reaching public appeal.

Later, chapter 6 describes how engaged news audiences on the right, as well as some on the left, take up the crusade against "cancel culture" in the world of entertainment and celebrity as a major facet of today's citizen-level political expression and discourse. By shifting the framing of the debate from concerns over the oppression and symbolic erasure of historically marginalized social groups to concerns over a restrictive and ideologically rigid environment around artistic and cultural expression, conservative news commentators provide a road map for broader rhetorical struggles against the left's push for progressive social, cultural, and political transformation. It is important to note that this rhetoric sidesteps the seemingly uncomfortable position of defending age-old prejudices while positioning the right more favorably as home to a freewheeling antiestablishment counterculture that is unrestrained by "political correctness" and "wokeness."

However, not all right-wing news is so careful to avoid voicing these prejudices when vociferously attacking Hollywood's moves to expand diversity and inclusion and hold industry members accountable for offending words and actions. Although conservative entertainment journalism contains multiple facets, including a "nuance" contingent that ostensibly seeks to engage in good-faith debate with its left-progressive counterpart, it can also serve as a platform for promoting animosity toward marginalized groups that lie at the center of its discussions of identity politics. Yet racism, sexism, homophobia, and other forms of bigotry are not the only forces that contribute to the phenomenon of "red meat" pop culture discourse in the news. Chapter 4 will examine the economic pressures of the news business that prioritize the fulmination of outrage on both sides of the partisan divide in the quest for online attention and clicks.

4

Hot Takes and Clickbait

The Impact of Commercialism on the Pop Culture–Politics Beat

Perhaps the most telling sign of the success and ubiquity of today's politically oriented entertainment journalism is the fact that it has become the subject of withering satire within the industry itself. Writing in *Vice*, humorist David Schilling offers "How to Write a Think Piece," a mock instructional guide that defines the titular subject as "an article so infuriating and controversial that you would have to share it with all of your friends on various social media platforms." Schilling uses the hypothetical example of a piece that angrily objects to anti-gay comments made by a reality TV show star, joking that "I really didn't want to write an article about Phil Robertson from *Duck Dynasty*, but the internet cycle of outrage meant that I had to. . . . Sure, I could have tried to ignore all the chatter . . . but I wanted to be connected to a hot SEO [search engine optimization] topic."[1] Schilling then proceeds to offer tongue-in-cheek advice suggesting that authors of such articles skimp on their research, offer deliberately extreme and controversial opinions to rile up readers and inspire social media shares, and slap on a "crazy headline" to ensure that the piece receives the online attention that it was deliberately designed for. Through satire, Schilling thus lays out a litany of complaints surrounding the contemporary production of journalism at the pop culture–politics nexus: that it is facile, rushed, uninformed, potentially insincere, and, above all, a cynical ploy for digital ad dollars.

The questionable economic motives of this journalism are likewise satirized in John Herrman's "Take Time" from the Awl, which pokes fun at what he derisively terms the "content industry" for hastily mining every pop culture tidbit as the source of reactionary "take" articles that exploit audience interest and leave "no attention on the table." Herrman offers the example of a story about celebrity nude photos leaked on the internet, remarking that "there were takes on privacy and gender and consent and free speech issued with and without conviction," all because of the "pull of a guaranteed

Pop Culture, Politics, and the News. Joel Penney, Oxford University Press. © Oxford University Press 2022.
DOI: 10.1093/oso/9780197557587.003.0005

audience." He then jokingly accuses "virtually every outlet that publishes news" of becoming a "take generator" as a result of the boundless industry appetite for this kind of coverage.[2] Like Schilling's *Vice* piece, Herrman's "Take Time" humorously makes the argument that this type of journalism is the result of the perverse incentives of the online attention economy, which rewards sensationalized content about trending pop culture and celebrity topics, regardless of its quality or sincerity.

Although the poor image that emerges in satire pieces like these is clearly exaggerated for effect, there are shades of truth, as discussed in chapter 1, to this sort of characterization of the contemporary online news business. Yet to complicate the idea that pop culture serves as a trusted formula for guaranteeing lucrative audiences for digital journalism outlets, consider a 2018 report from Vox that raises red flags about the downsizing of culture desks across the industry and the weakening of the job market for entertainment critics and other key staff roles: "From major newspapers to tiny websites, anyone with enough money to hire new journalists usually wasn't putting it toward an expanded culture section."[3] How is it possible that entertainment and celebrity coverage is viewed by the industry as the ultimate form of crass commercialism, while at the same time professional roles for this journalism are dwindling at alarming rates?

This chapter interrogates this seeming contradiction by examining the candid insider perspectives of news professionals who work at the intersection of pop culture and politics. As the discussion will show, the profound financial stresses of the news business writ large have put pressure on entertainment journalism to adopt narrow formulas that serve specific industry needs, often emphasizing sheer quantity over quality and professional expertise, blockbuster subject matter over coverage of niche and artistic fare, and "quick hit" speed over long-term gestation and development. These same economic pressures have also contributed to entertainment journalism's growing engagement with hot-button political issues that spark valued audience identification and affect, yet in ways that risk exploiting issues such as identity politics for short-term monetary gain and flattening the complexity of public discourse in the process. Through an exploration of entertainment journalism's precarious position in the broader for-profit digital news economy, this chapter makes the case that the industry's widespread devaluing of cultural expertise and failure to recognize its vital role in journalism's broader public service mission have contributed to the field's often bemoaned weaknesses and "clickbait" excesses.

"It's Hard to Make a Living at This": The Culture Desk in a Financially Strained Industry

As the journalism industry suffers financial setbacks and painful cuts to staff positions, the model for entertainment reporting and cultural criticism has been significantly destabilized. On the one hand, industry demand for coverage of pop culture and celebrities remains high, as these topics are seen to be effective in capturing the attention of online audiences and satisfying bottom-line needs for clicks and shares. On the other hand, discussions of cultural affairs in general are often perceived by many news companies to be a nonessential, even expendable, add-on to the more bread-and-butter product of breaking news and politics coverage. This contradictory status of pop culture within the news business—at once seemingly both a bread-winner and a superfluous extravagance—has led to a complex and uneven professional landscape in which roles are often blurred and day-to-day operations are marked by tension and uncertainty.

In decades past, news companies that were flush with profits from a healthy and sustainable advertising market expanded their coverage into more and more areas. In the case of entertainment that meant establishing the model of the full-time staff critic who regularly reviews new Hollywood releases, a phenomenon that stems from as far back as the 1910s.[4] These staff critic positions were eventually filled by high-profile, senior-level talents who served as public faces for their respective organizations—think Roger Ebert for the *Chicago Sun-Times* and Gene Siskel for the *Chicago Tribune*, icons of newspaper film criticism's glory days—and commanded considerable salaries and high organizational status. However, multiple factors have since complicated this model and put it on a path toward possible extinction, even as some of the more well-known entertainment critics in the field continue to thrive on a case-by-case basis.

For one, the "straight review" of new entertainment releases, as it is typically referred to in the industry, has lost some of its luster due to several interrelated factors. These include the flooding of the market with seemingly interchangeable product from myriad online critics of various stripes, the rise of aggregator sites such as Rotten Tomatoes and Metacritic that flatten these reviews into mere data points for calculating numerical scores, and the growth of social media as a platform for amateur opinion-sharing on a mass scale. This crowding of the field of pop culture opinion has prodded professional entertainment criticism to reinvent itself and find new angles such as political commentary to stand out from the competition—a phenomenon explored in detail in this chapter—yet it has also imperiled the careers of many journalists who have staked their professional viability on their critical expertise.

One journalist who had formerly worked as an entertainment editor for a major digital news outlet shared a revealing account of how these changes have affected the careers of her colleagues:

> I saw the impact of this personally as the entertainment news team kind of broke apart.... I had people on my staff, one of whom had worked in entertainment and written about television for a decade, another one about film for a decade, ... Seeing my colleagues and what they've done and seeing how culture and entertainment desks around the industry have shrunk, I definitely think that there is a devaluing of its importance.

As she suggested, this devaluing of pop culture expertise in the industry stems from the fact that key decision-makers—and perhaps news audiences as well—are unable to distinguish it from the sea of opinion that is now available online:

> It has to do with this idea that everybody's opinion on pop culture is equal. And I personally, as elitist as it sounds, disagree with that. Opinions are not formed equally.... When they've been doing it for a decade, they might have more insight.... They understand not only what makes a film, if it's good or bad, but they understand the industry and they understand why things work and why things don't work. And I think what people don't respect about pop culture writers is that these people do this for a living ... there's a little bit of a lack of understanding that that is literally their expertise.

As she went on to argue, this confusion over the unique contribution of the professional entertainment expert is further compounded by industry practices that flatten the role of "writer" to include anyone who publishes under a byline, which is an increasingly expanding list due to budgetary pressures for employees to multitask and serve more and more professional functions at news outlets:

> My view of the last twenty years is that writing in the media is the only field where everybody gets to be categorized as doing it regardless of their

capacity to do it and whether they actually do it as a job. And I mean that in the sense that putting a Band-Aid on someone does not make me a doctor, but somehow in this field, everybody gets to kind of feel like they have access to being a writer. And I don't think that's actually good for the industry; it devalues a lot of people who are actually experts in their field and are good at what they do.

Indeed, there is a shared concern within the community of professional entertainment critics that the financial pressures of the industry to maximize content output from all directions have made their traditional distinguished status more precarious. As a film critic for a major digital news site underscored, these professional roles are shrinking as cash-strapped news outlets pressure their reduced staffs to become jacks-of-all-trades and work on more than just criticism:

> It's very, very difficult to get a staff job, and when we do, it's so much different from staff jobs that people ten years older than you were getting . . . you know, you review three movies a week, and that's your job. Now it's like you need to know how to report, write profiles, write about television, do interviews, cover festivals, you have to do everything. So there are very few publications left that are willing to support criticism.

Although this expansion of professional duties may be partially a simple cost-saving maneuver, she argued that it is also a consequence of how management gives entertainment coverage a lower organizational priority: "The people who run these publications just don't really see the value of it. They don't really care, I don't think, about our culture or see the value of it. And so that makes it very difficult."

Of course, the for-profit journalism industry *does* value pop culture content for its ability to gain clicks and audience attention, so it is not as though decision-makers are cutting back on this area of coverage entirely. Rather, as the above accounts highlight, their relative lack of interest in cultural affairs makes them less willing to invest in senior-level staff positions that ensure quality output in this area and more willing to find other, cheaper ways of churning out pop culture content regardless of its distinction. Another critic for a digital news outlet emphasized this idea when noting the industry's shift from hiring full-time entertainment critics to relying on less expensive freelance labor as a substitute:

I think culture writing is very valued. I think culture writers are undervalued. . . . I can see the traffic for the site, and culture writing is consistently at the top, we bring in a lot of readers. However, there are a lot of recently graduated English majors who want to talk about how *Breaking Bad* is drawing on [Michel] Foucault and are happy to write essays about that. So the market is kind of flooded, and I think culture writers in general are not paid particularly well, and their labor is not particularly valued.

Although it is certainly possible that younger freelancers can produce quality criticism on pop culture topics, it seems as though many industry managers are willing to take whatever they can get as long as it fills the hole for content at a low cost. Within this model, experienced critics who come with high price tags along with esteemed reputations are often perceived as unnecessary and antiquated—relics of an earlier era in which news outlets could afford to pay a premium for gold-standard work. In many cases, these kinds of positions are being methodically eliminated, as one critic explained: "Lots and lots of publications will either lay off or just let their staff retire, and then they won't be replaced, or they'll be replaced by freelancers who are paid absurdly small amounts of money to review films."

This industry trend appears to be particularly pronounced at newer, digital-native news outlets that are struggling to establish a sustainable financial model in the face of steep competition and a challenging online advertising market (along with downmarket legacy outlets that have experienced steady declines in audience and revenue).[5] The aforementioned Vox report on the decline of cultural criticism staff positions includes a long list of digital outlets that have seen these kinds of cuts, including the AV Club, the Fader, Complex, Inverse, Fusion, and MTV News, among others.[6] The Covid-19 pandemic also exacerbated many of these dynamics in the early 2020s, with major rounds of staff layoffs and furloughs at companies such as Buzzfeed that are known for pop culture coverage.[7]

However, for a handful of elite news outlets with strong national reputations, the picture does not appear to be nearly as grim. A columnist who covers pop culture and politics for one such outlet gave a far more optimistic impression of the field:

At the level of the *LA Times* or *Washington Post* or *New York Times*, generally they're bringing in people with more experience. . . . We need actual original thought out there, and there's a hunger for it. So we're seeing our subscriptions go up. You know, many of the major papers that were dying, or established publications that were dying before, are actually now making money or at least breaking even. So that means something . . . we're actually kind of moving toward a direction where I think journalism is becoming pretty vital again.

As her comments underline, the journalism industry's financial struggles and pressures are distributed very unevenly, and those who work for outlets at the top of the hierarchy may not be feeling the same pinch that colleagues are experiencing elsewhere.[8]

While full-time staff for entertainment criticism and other Hollywood-related output may be thriving within an elite circle of the most prestigious and established outlets, those who are outside of this circle tend to be quite anxious about what the future holds for the profession. For instance, one pop culture critic who works for a digital-native outlet commented, "I have a full-time staff job, but I wake up every morning and assume that this isn't going to be my forever. And everyone has kind of a half exit plan in hopes that we won't have to use it." Similarly, a critic for another digital outlet explained:

When I first started delving into cultural criticism, there was always this sort of wheel turning that was, like, you have to find a way to basically justify your own existence. Because as journalism as an industry has shrunk, the number of critics who are employed to write full-time has shrunk precipitously. And so the fact that I was doing this in a time when the journalism industry is still basically trying to stabilize after years and years and years of shrinking . . . even if that pressure wasn't put on me by my bosses or just externally, it definitely existed for me in my own head.

As noted above, when the number of these tenuous staff critic positions becomes smaller and smaller, freelance critics have more opportunities to fill the vacuum that is left behind. However, freelance journalists are similarly unnerved by a system that they see as undervaluing their labor as well. Far from being the winners in the shifting economic landscape of digital journalism, they are among the most vulnerable. As one freelancer candidly remarked: "It's hard to make a living at this. I wouldn't recommend it to anybody. And I don't know what the future is going to look like, so I can't tell people that it will get better or that some model for paying for writing is going to work out." Another freelancer stressed that although editors seek out their labor in general, the freelance market for entertainment criticism is extremely competitive, and individuals often struggle to find opportunities. Referring to one of her published pieces on the topic of cultural appropriation in superhero films, she noted:

> That's a story idea I had been pitching for a year . . . that took more than a year for it to get published. And I easily pitched over thirty-five publications for that, everything from the *New York Times* to *Atlantic* to Vox to the Ringer, that either got a rejection or silence. But these are things that are very meaningful to me and topics I want to explore and that I think are really necessary to be added to the lexicon of pop culture. . . . You really have to do it for your own personal interest, because you'll get a lot of rejections on these stories.

Her account of pop culture news commentary as a kind of personal passion project, as opposed to a reliable professional gig (in her case, she also works as a corporate communications professional, which serves as her primary source of income), further suggests how the industry treats this form of journalism as less than worthy of sustained investment.

Yet, in addition to an increasing reliance on lower-paid freelance labor, this shift away from dedicated staff roles for entertainment journalism is also happening internally within newsrooms that are stretching existing staff into more and more areas. In some cases, editors will assign pop culture stories to reporters from other departments, such as breaking news, to ensure a steady flow of content on the latest trending topics. As one of these breaking-news reporters explained, such pieces tend to be "really short, quick hits that are around three hundred, four hundred words at most," although the headlines affixed to them by editors can sometimes make them indistinguishable (at least at first glance) from more in-depth commentaries produced by full-time critics. On news sites and on social media, all journalistic content is essentially compressed into the format of the clickable headline, which can have the effect of blurring the boundaries between different types of journalistic labor and the varying status levels of those who perform it.

The fact that pop culture stories intersect so regularly with political issues also means that designated political journalists tend to cover them frequently as well, partly out of their interest in the subject matter and partly out of organizational necessity. At one major digital news site, for instance, a staff journalist described how pieces that examine the politics of pop culture are "spread out among a lot of different people," including members of both the politics and the culture desks, because "there's only so much that we as a publication can do" without the resources for dedicated staff to cover this specific beat. A journalist who specializes in entertainment coverage for another news site expressed some frustration with these sorts of arrangements, arguing that the involvement of political commentators in entertainment criticism can detract from its quality: "A lot of what happens is non-culture people, non-culture writers, end up writing hot takes . . . people who are very knowledgeable in real-life politics write about the politics of fiction, which is just kind of a little bit strange." Here he suggested that political journalists' lack of training in cultural criticism results in work that is naive in its analysis and contributes to the poor reputation of the field.

The next section details the effects of the industry's challenging economic realities on the content of entertainment news, which includes potential positives as well as the sorts of threats to journalistic quality indicated here. As we shift to this discussion, it is important to consider how the strained financial picture outlined above forms the backdrop for all day-to-day decision-making at the levels of management, editorial, and journalistic production. To summarize, pop culture coverage—particularly that which mobilizes cultural expertise and critical acumen—is a deeply imperiled part of the journalism landscape even as it is positioned as innately commercial and appealing to audiences. Due to its long-ingrained lower status in industry circles, it is especially susceptible to cost-cutting pressures regardless of its capacity to garner clicks, resulting in a workforce that often feels destabilized, undervalued, and uncertain of its future. However, both staff and freelance journalists in the field have adopted numerous strategies to navigate such pressures and secure their own industry viability. This includes the growing political engagement of entertainment journalism, which has become a means of boosting its overall reputation and status within the broader field, as well as a way of meeting the financial demands of a news business in crisis.

"Everything 'Politics of *Game of Thrones*' Works": How Economics Shape Pop Culture–Politics Coverage

As many journalists working at for-profit digital news companies will readily admit, the economic need to maximize audience clicks is an unavoidable and undeniable force in shaping coverage decisions. Although some outlets—particularly legacy organizations with strong national and global reputations—may be relatively more insulated from these pressures on a day-to-day basis, the traditional "wall" between business and editorial only extends so far in an industry that faces existential risk around every corner. One entertainment critic for a national news site was quite candid in remarking that "that's all anybody's trying to do, we're all trying to harvest clicks, everything we write is trying to harvest clicks because of the way the digital media landscape is set up." Interestingly, the outlet for which this journalist works has a reputation for in-depth reporting and a more intellectual tone than many of its competitors—a reminder that not all click-chasing is reducible to the cliché of quick, dumbed-down "clickbait." Rather, the economic demand for clicks manifests in many ways depending on the identity of the outlet and its specific target audience.

Although there is no universal formula for harvesting clicks in the digital media landscape, there are clear and identifiable patterns. For entertainment journalism, which has traditionally been positioned in the industry as audience-grabbing "soft news" that helps prop up news organizations that cannot survive on traditional public affairs alone,[9] one of the most common of these patterns is to focus coverage on the most widely popular, event-level pop culture topics. Notably, this editorial focus extends to pieces that examine blockbuster entertainment franchises and A-list celebrities through the lens of hot-button political issues that similarly promise to maximize audience interest.

An entertainment reporter for a major left-leaning news site broke down this dynamic in no uncertain terms:

> Once you have a big hit piece of pop culture, you want as many pieces out there as you can, because it's good for traffic and it's good to get eyes on it. . . . It is in a publication's best interest to churn out as much content and as many pieces on *Game of Thrones*, because everyone will click on it. Everyone who clicks on it looks good for advertisers.

As he elaborated, stories on his employer's site that look at the political aspects of "big hit" pop culture constitute one key variation of this coverage strategy: "It's not like an end-all be-all, but if you have something that's like mass consumption like *Game of Thrones*, yes, of course, everything 'politics of *Game of Thrones*' works." An entertainment reporter for a right-leaning news site described a nearly identical dynamic; while the tenor of their political commentary may be quite different, their coverage focuses on the same sorts of event-level entertainment properties as a means of drawing the largest audience: "Overall, pop culture pieces generally do well. . . . And I think the reason for that is because it's all about brand recognition. It's very easy—you see Marvel, you see the celebrity, people know who that is. And if it's correlated with something that's a political hot topic, that will generate clicks."

One of the consequences of prioritizing the biggest pop culture and celebrity topics in coverage is that it leaves less room for analysis of smaller-scale and niche entertainment that does not have the advantage of such "brand recognition." One commentator for a national news site told a revealing story about how she had to put off writing about the feminist politics of the 2019 film adaptation of *Little Women* due to organizational pressures to shift her focus elsewhere:

> One of my editors came to me and said that she thought it was time to write a piece on Adam Driver, because *Star Wars* [*The Rise of Skywalker*] had come out, and he was a lead and very, very buzzy and hot. And I said, "Oh, that's so boring, I just want to write about *Little Women*," and then she said, "OK, but you have to write about Adam Driver first because that's going to be the traffic getter here." So that was sort of a case where I had to rearrange my personal ideal priorities for the health of the site.

Another critic for a major national news outlet, who noted the "insane traffic" she got for a piece on the gender politics of *Game of Thrones* as well as similar results for pieces about the blockbuster comic book hit *Joker*, surmised that "those are things that people are already inherently interested in . . . more people watch *Game of Thrones* and *Star Wars* and superheroes and therefore are more willing to engage in political arguments about that than in political arguments around the moving, forward-thinking female movie that not as many people are seeing." The sense of weariness in her remarks was echoed by a freelance writer and former entertainment editor who lamented this dynamic more acutely:

> When something is really, really important, people will latch onto it, and there are pop culture products that for whatever reason touch a whole bunch of people, and then it's very easy to see the value in them. But I think the economics doesn't always work out for things that may be what I would call experimentation, "let me write about this thing that I don't know is

super popular yet, but it might be, or this thing that is kind of obscure, but it still makes for a good story." I think I see less of that. So there's less risk being taken about things that are not so obviously popular.

Similarly, a freelance journalist who writes about literature as well as high-profile film and television described the difficulty that he faced in publishing an analysis of relatively obscure literary novels: "Nobody wants a two-thousand-word piece on two books that nobody's really read. That's not profitable. . . . That had been a piece that I'd been thinking about for probably ten years, because nobody wanted it, they weren't going to publish it."

Concerns over the propensity for news outlets to play it safe in coverage decisions by prioritizing reliably mega-popular pop culture also surfaced in a different way in comments from a reporter who had written extensively about the #MeToo movement in Hollywood. When accounting for the impact of this journalism on the broader public conversation around sexual harassment and assault, she remarked:

I think the fact that with #MeToo, it was a lot of very famous actresses speaking out . . . unfortunately, I think that did make a difference. You know, I wish more sort of less famous, more marginalized voices would make a difference, but sometimes it does seem to be like if it's someone very notable or very famous, people take note of that.

In this case, the bias in coverage that she noted toward maximum familiarity to ensure audience clicks means more than just sidelining more obscure entertainment and cultural content. When it comes to stories that filter political issues and activism through the attention-grabbing appeal of celebrity, there is a potential to marginalize voices that are not as well represented on the Hollywood A-list—in the case of #MeToo, this includes women of color and others who do not fit the mold of a marquee name like Gwyneth Paltrow or Ashley Judd.

Bearing these risks in mind, one of the ways journalists navigate the pressure to prioritize the most popular subject matter within pop culture is to be strategic in tying what they most wish to address in their journalism to the A-list topics that they are frequently compelled to cover to satisfy the bottom-line needs of employers. Specifically, several journalists noted how they would plan out a work of political analysis or commentary in advance and then wait for an opportune moment to hitch it to a relevant popular trending topic in the entertainment world. For instance, one free-lance journalist who has written extensively about racial representation in pop culture recounted:

> I have various things that I'm interested in writing about that are sort of on the back burner, and if you see something that can tie into that, you say, "Oh, I'm going to write about that." . . . People very much want to read stuff about the biggest thing that's happening right now . . . that's the job. So you try to write about the biggest thing that's happening right now and bring in things that you've been thinking about for longer.

Another freelance journalist detailed a similar process for publishing her critical commentary on media representation of women's weight and body image in major news outlets: "That was something I was thinking about and wanted to write about. . . . Whenever I see a media story or something else that's coming out, like a TV show or a movie that I can use to kind of talk about these things as an entry point into a bigger political discussion, I will pitch that piece." To illustrate, she described how she strategically used the high-profile release of the controversial Netflix series *Insatiable* as an oppor-tunity to get her work out on a major international news site: "I pitched an article about fatphobia, but really just using *Insatiable* as something through which to talk about that topic. So that's kind of how it works."

This notion of using the biggest pop culture of the moment as a "news peg" to successfully publish long-germinating works of political commentary was also highlighted by a staff columnist for a major national news outlet who recalled preparing for a story on the 2017 film *Wonder Woman* a full year in advance of its theatrical release: "Those things can be very long-term in the making. I'm trying to think ahead to, OK, what is going to be an impor-tant cultural touchstone I can use as a prism through which to talk about gender?" At the same time, she rejected the idea of being forced by editors to write about big-ticket Hollywood properties that she would otherwise not want to cover, emphasizing that she loves watching, thinking about, and writing about blockbuster superhero movies like *Wonder Woman* regardless of their newsroom prioritization.

Following from this point, most entertainment journalists—with the ex-ception of breaking-news reporters who are typically assigned "quick hits" by editors—assert that they have a large degree of control over what they cover in the world of pop culture, at least until their work is either accepted or rejected by editors. Thus, the model of writing about "the biggest thing that's happening right now" can be understood as an internalized strategy for journalists to navigate the economic pressures of the industry rather than a clear-cut dictate from above. Furthermore, these journalists also tend to push back on the notion that they are somehow forcing a fit between the issue discussions that they want to have and the pop culture topics that they must prioritize in coverage. Rather than "digging" for something in a film or TV show that's just not there, as one columnist put it, the key is to find the right moments of opportunity where high-profile and audience-grabbing pop culture auspiciously aligns with the social and political content that journalists seek to advance in the public discourse.

A Boom Market for "Strong, Spicy, Passionately Argued Things"

One of the most recognizable pressures in the digital news industry, well documented by journalism scholars (as discussed in chapter 1), is the push to stand out from the crowd with unique angles and perspectives. Since so many news outlets are competing to be heard over one another in the ever-expanding attention economy, news organizations have come to emphasize opinion as an economic strategy to differentiate themselves[10] and provide audiences with a "unique selling proposition," to borrow a term familiar in marketing circles. In an online information landscape overflowing with digital-native and legacy outlets, news itself becomes something of an interchangeable commodity, a process further exacerbated by the rise of online news aggregators, blogs, and social media. Thus, unique opinion and viewpoint are increasingly valued by news organizations as a solution to the problem of getting lost in the digital crowd, giving rise to what journalism scholar Michael Serazio jokingly terms the "hot take industrial complex."[11]

As many reporters and critics attest, this dynamic has been just as transformative for entertainment journalism as it has been for traditional political coverage and can at least partially account for the growing trend of integrating political opinion into pop culture reporting. Those who have worked in entertainment journalism for many years are especially attuned to such a shift in the field. For instance, a former editor with decades of industry experience commented:

I think there's much more of a market, even in the oldest publications, for stories that bring a perspective to something or come at something from a certain point of view, than for straight-up "who, what, when, where, why" reporting. I think "What's our take on this?" is something that you hear even editors at legacy publications say, much, much more often than you did twenty-five years ago.

He went on to suggest that this long-term change in editorial emphasis has resulted in "an entire generation of journalists sort of defining themselves publicly by their takes on things," which he also related to the emergence of social media as a training ground for aspiring journalists to develop their unique voice and perspective and get noticed by potential employers.

The pattern of culture and entertainment editors strategically prioritizing opinion-driven "takes" over the commodity of basic "who, what, when, where, why" reporting appears to be especially pronounced for digital-only outlets that, in contrast to many legacy organizations, tend to position their brand identities more firmly in terms of their partisan political leanings. One reporter for a left-oriented news site described how this strategy is explicitly communicated by editorial staff as a means of courting a loyal audience:

People come to us because they know that we kind of have a sharp angle in a lot of our stories. And I think my editors are always encouraging of that, because it just kind of makes us stand out a little bit more. . . . People come to us not necessarily for the daily news but for some more analysis on a news story.

A senior entertainment reporter for another left-leaning news and culture site offered a similarly revealing account of this dynamic:

One of the core tenets of [our site] is the content that it produces is really strongly worded columns. And so anytime I have an idea for one of those, they're happy to have them. . . . It can be good for the bottom line, especially when the stories sort of take off if they're particularly passionate or incendiary. . . . Because we're a digital outlet, [my editors] appreciate the fact that a passionately argued piece does well with our readers and makes more of an impact than just a summary of the news.

Speaking to the broader economic strategy of his employer's site as foregrounding ideological perspective on the news over mere information, he went on to describe how even a "take" that doesn't take off, as it were, still contributes to the organization's bottom line: "They're also good for brand and for sort of signaling what the [site] stands for. . . . If a piece doesn't do well, it still has value because it shows that [the site] stands for something. If it does do well, then that's even better." In other words, the economic value of strongly argued "takes" on the news—pop culture news included—is understood in terms of the long-term brand positioning of partisan-leaning news sites as well as the more day-to-day quest for audience clicks.

As Ezra Klein (a cofounder of Vox) argues in the book *Why We're Polarized*, online news has developed into an industry of "identity journalism," as sophisticated digital analytics reveal audience profiles with newfound precision and create organizational incentives to reinforce the target audiences' social and political identities with coverage that flatters them.[12] Within this framework, opinion-driven "takes" on pop culture—a subject that is deeply tied to the defining of contemporary social identity—are tailor-made for serving the bottom-line needs of "identity journalism" outlets on both the right and the left. For instance, a journalist for a conservative entertainment-themed site noted that not only does he enjoy writing passionately argued opinion pieces on pop culture from a right-wing perspective more than simply reporting entertainment news, but "they get the most traffic from a pragmatic point of view."

It is important to note, however, that "takes" involving heated political opinion do not always amass more audience clicks than other kinds of commentary on entertainment. While pieces with a strong political point of view "tend to do fairly well, traffic-wise," as one entertainment journalist put it, a columnist who specializes in pop culture "takes" with a political bent stressed that the economic reality is often more complex than any simple formula might suggest:

> My colleagues in the newsroom who write more straightforward, "hey, the Grammys were a train wreck" . . . they're incredibly valuable to the organization as well. So I don't think that cultural journalism that's at the intersection of culture and politics is inherently more valuable or more profitable. But I think it was definitely something where there was a hunger for that.

In other words, politically oriented "takes" are not the only kinds of "takes" that succeed in the industry's push to capitalize on unique voice and perspective in the crowded digital news environment. Rather, the integration of political commentary into pop culture coverage is one key element of a larger industry trend of leveraging personal viewpoint to stand out from the competition.

Within the entertainment journalism field, the strategic shift toward political perspective is particularly conspicuous within the genre of the traditional critic's "straight review," which has always been opinion-driven by its very nature. As conventional reviews judging the aesthetic merits of a film or TV show have become increasingly commonplace in the digital attention economy, critics are under pressure to reinvent their approach to distinguish themselves in the intensive competition for online audiences. One film critic who often focuses on feminist perspectives in her work candidly noted this shift in the "straight review" genre, which, like straightforward reporting, risks commoditization in the crowded digital landscape: "To set yourself apart, you have to have a little bit of a different point of view from just 'this movie is good.' I think you have to inject more into it ... a review that is something a little bit more than just 'the explosions were good.'"

As she went on explain, incorporating a unique political perspective into reviews is one way of successfully answering the question of what will set one writer apart from another: "For the most part, I can only ever view movies through the lens of who I am . . . Iranian American, raised Muslim, first-generation immigrant, feminist. Those things are what shaped my perspective as a film critic. And so I think editors who are looking for pitches, if they hire you, they hire you based on your voice." Although she admitted that it is "honestly very cynical" to think of her social and political identity as a means of brand differentiation to make her film reviews stand out from the pack, she suggested that it is a reality of working in the industry at a time when news outlets are pressed to "set themselves apart from the onslaught of voices who are all seeing those same movies" and "want something different . . . you're always looking for a different angle on a movie to set you apart from other people, and if you have a specific point of view for how you view film, that's what people gravitate toward."

Furthermore, this critic described how entertainment news editors are often quite explicit in how they solicit reviews and commentary that align with the industry strategy of "standing out" through unique political perspective:

Editors who are looking for certain pitches . . . I mean, you can pretty much see this if you look on film Twitter when there's a big movie coming out, like "pitch me a different take on Rey and Kylo Ren [from *Star Wars*]," "pitch me a different take on the upcoming Marvel movie on Black Widow and what she represents as a female soldier." . . . I think sometimes editors have certain things in mind already, and they want to find the right writer who can bring that idea to life.

To thrive in this environment, she suggested, critics must adapt to an economic reality in which conventional reviews are a dime a dozen and unique political viewpoint has become one of the few available pathways for marketplace distinction. As another critic who primarily focuses on racial politics in her reviews put it, "you don't want to write the same article that everyone else is writing. . . . We're looking for ways to approach something that don't necessarily feel commonplace . . . like, what is the way that I can talk about this that doesn't necessarily feel like the same thing?"

Although politics may not be the only way to stand out from the crowd, many entertainment journalists emphasized how engaging with controversial issues in the news has become an increasingly common strategy for attracting audience attention and serving the economic demands of the industry. This has been especially true during the inflamed US political climate during the Trump presidency and its aftermath, where, as one entertainment critic put it, "so much has become politicized." She explained that the topics that "people are heated up about," such as the presidential election and Trump's impeachment as well as issues such as immigration that dominated his presidency, function as "triggers" for impassioned audience interest and response, and this pattern extends to the field of pop culture journalism: "I think it drives people more toward pieces that might address some of those things, but also loops in the pop culture part of it that they perhaps grew up on or were weaned on or enjoy." Along similar lines, a senior entertainment reporter commented:

In the era of the Trump administration, hitting on these sorts of hot-button issues and topics, even if it is through the Hollywood lens versus the political lens, is contributing to a bottom line. . . . For a website that thrives on ads that are sold against traffic numbers, you know, a strong, spicy, passionately argued thing that garners a lot of attention is going to garner a lot of clicks.

"I Wish This Happened All the Time": Identity Politics as an Uneven Market Trend

Among the hot-button topics that capture audience interest in this highly polarized climate, identity politics loom especially large. One reporter for a news and culture site aimed at female-identifying readers suggested how the site's frequent and widely viewed coverage of the #MeToo movement in Hollywood was driven at least in part by economic logics:

> It sort of pains me to say that I think there's a little bit of the business side of this, why this kind of reporting and writing is doing really well right now, because people want to click on the stuff. You know, putting "#MeToo" in a headline, I think, for some people does get them to click on it, because it's so on our minds. And I think people like that, sort of the controversy of it. . . . There is an unfortunate sort of business angle that it's good for business to write about this stuff, especially if you're a women's publication. So as much as I was writing about it before and was interested in these stories, I'm definitely getting assigned new stories way more than I ever was.

She went on to explain that while increased journalistic coverage of sexual harassment and assault in the entertainment industry was clearly a positive development in her view, such coverage was not as well supported by editors prior to #MeToo becoming a viral sensation and a proven magnet for audience attention. This fact was laid bare only when she began receiving these story assignments far more frequently after the initial wave of interest in #MeToo surged. Her account thus suggests how the economic realities of the digital news business can potentially limit entertainment journalism's political advocacy role as well as incentivize it, as editorial decision-making is inextricably tied to trend-watching organizational assessments of market viability. The fact that coverage of pop culture topics has been traditionally positioned in the industry as bottom-line-serving "soft news," in contrast to the "hard news" coverage of conventional politics that is seen as fulfilling the industry's public service mission, further contributes to this dynamic and makes it more difficult for entertainment journalism to transcend its commercial function and tackle key public issues even when they are not deemed to be financially advantageous.

A very similar pattern to the #MeToo coverage boom from around 2017 to 2018 was noted by several journalists who focus on issues of race in pop culture, which became an enormously hot topic in the news in the summer of 2020. As discussed in chapter 2, in the aftermath of George Floyd's killing by a white police officer which sparked intensive protests, a national "racial reckoning" emerged that led to a surge in journalistic coverage of anti-black racism in the entertainment industry. Within this environment, an African American freelance critic found that her work on racial issues in television was suddenly in high demand, yet this underscored for her how uneven such industry attention can be. As she commented during this period in 2020:

> This has always just been my area of interest. . . . If people weren't paying attention to the Black Lives Matter movement like they are now, I would still be writing about this stuff. . . . It just feels like when I sent that pitch [for a story on racism in reality TV], it got accepted literally five minutes after. I've never had a pitch picked up that quickly before, so that felt weird. . . . And then, basically off of a tweet about Tina Fey [wearing blackface in an episode of *30 Rock*], I immediately was asked to write about that. So just the responses that I've been getting and people's interest in me are definitely bittersweet, because I would like for people to have an interest in my opinions as a black writer all the time. But it's also exciting that I'm getting these opportunities. . . . I wish this happened all the time.

This "bittersweet" experience of being sought out by editors during a fleeting moment when Hollywood racism was a major trending news topic was echoed by a veteran African American pop culture critic who noted how quickly the fashion can change in the industry for this kind of work. Looking back at the "racial reckoning" coverage cycle of summer 2020, he noted:

> When George Floyd was killed, there was a week or two where people were really shocked. And when I say people, mostly I mean white people were shocked, and they were reacting to what happened, and they wanted to know more. They wanted to find out how extensive this problem was, and what exactly is systemic racism, and "what can I do to stop it?" . . . And so I think there was a two-week period where a lot of news outlets tried to provide that context and provide that material to people. . . . I had all these outlets sort of asking me for lists of movies that you could watch and things like that. And there was a huge hunger for that. and all these different places called me.

However, he went on to explain:

> By the time I got to that, I already had a sense that there was a cresting in
> the interest of this. . . . My sense now is that I think people are getting a little
> weary of the conversation already and kind of dropping off. And so I think
> the bubble of interest is already starting to wane. . . . You know, the thing
> that is sad and sometimes depressing about this situation is that the basic
> boundaries of what we're talking about have not changed that much.

As he suggested, editors' decisions to pursue critiques of anti-black racism in
Hollywood were shaped more by their estimations of audience interest than
by a sustained commitment to an advocacy journalism role, as they were all
too ready to move on to the next trending topic when that interest appeared to
flame out. In the chase for ephemeral clicks and advertising dollars, so it seems,
the industry's push for progress in pop culture can go in and out of style.

"To Get People Engaged, You Had to Get Them Mad": Crafting Coverage for Social Media Outrage

Another important way in which the economic concerns of the journalism
business shape news content centers on the need to garner not only audience
clicks but also social media shares. Chapter 5 will explore how journalists
who work at the intersection of entertainment and politics use social media
to inspire specific story ideas, get useful audience feedback, and contend with
the more aggressive and hyper-partisan reactions to their work. However, it
is important to also consider how this journalism is conceived at the outset
with social media circulation in mind, which is a front-line consideration for
any for-profit outlet in the digital news landscape. Although some journalists
noted that audience traffic from popular platforms such as Facebook and
Twitter has diminished in recent years and is often lower than commonly
assumed—a phenomenon attributed to changes in how these platforms algo-
rithmically construct their news feeds—social media success remains a major
priority in newsrooms across the industry. As many journalists emphasized,
this push for maximizing shares translates into a push for invoking strong
emotional reactions, which research has shown is especially effective in
driving audiences toward the "holy grail" of social media engagement.[13]

One reporter for several digital news sites described this as a quest for sparking "outrage or admiration" on the part of the audience, highlighting how both extreme positive and extreme negative emotions have become industry currency in the age of social news curation. As an example, she pointed to coverage of basketball superstar Kobe Bryant's death in 2020, which very quickly came to include commentaries addressing his past rape allegations and relationship to the ongoing #MeToo movement: "There have been really great pieces about 'how do we talk about this man who's so beloved by so many and these terrible actions that he's credibly being accused of?' But then there's also . . . it's easy to just read a headline and be really mad, and share it or demean it." While she stressed that there were legitimate non-economic reasons for addressing these hot-button issues in coverage, her comments also suggest that journalists are keenly aware of how controversy and provocation fit into the larger industry need for social media relevance.

A senior culture reporter who has worked in numerous digital newsrooms offered a historical perspective on how social media and its privileging of emotional intensity have profoundly influenced the day-to-day work of the field, pointing to the outsize impact of the Facebook newsfeed algorithm as a key traffic driver in the early 2010s:

> There were entire websites built around Facebook's algorithm. Facebook's algorithm was to get people engaged, and to get people engaged, you had to get them mad or get them happy or get them sad. And so it was almost like all the stories during that era were like "terrible things happening to black people," "some things that will change your faith in humanity." And that's what people shared. . . . Those habits have dictated how we interact with pieces today, and they kind of still inform how we write pieces today. . . . The whole idea of the way social media was back in the day, just like trying to get reactions, kind of trickled down into the way that we think about what we write now.

As he noted, after Facebook changed its newsfeed algorithm in 2018 to deprioritize news links in favor of more personal posts from friends and family,[14] the platform "doesn't promote them as much, and you don't see them popping up on timelines as much." Yet, even so, he argued that much of the contemporary work in the field stems from this legacy and represents "the eventual evolution" of journalism "that's meant to be shared."

Another veteran entertainment journalist gave a similar analysis of the industry's recent history, suggesting that the growth in the 2010s of pop culture criticism involving emotion-triggering political issues was directly tied to the rise of Facebook as a chief source of news discovery:

> When [traffic] was being driven by Facebook, a more identity-driven platform by definition, this was a thing, getting outraged. . . . Facebook drove people to anger and fear. . . . And that led to a world of, on the anger side, "look at all of these ways pop culture gets women wrong." But then, on the fear side, it was "look at all the ways that pop culture is trying to tell you that women are more powerful than men." There was a time when it was great economic strategy. It's less of one now, but you could still find good readership from that.

Here she evinced a palpable sense of cynicism regarding the industry's use of formulaic controversies to garner emotional reactions and achieve social media success, recalling familiar critiques of shameless "clickbait" on the part of digital news companies.

However, she also went on to suggest that entertainment journalists have learned to adapt to and work within this seemingly unavoidable industry reality in their day-to-day journalistic production. As she candidly remarked regarding her own pop culture criticism, "it's really hard for me to sell a piece that's like 'the finale of [TV sitcom] *The Good Place* in one perfect shot.' It's a lot easier for me to sell a piece that's like 'the finale of *The Good Place* let down bisexuals.'" In other words, pushing the right emotional buttons in the minds of the audience has become a core industry logic that journalists must internalize, and this often translates into work that focuses on the divisive social and political issues that audiences get the most vehemently passionate about.

"We Just Want You to Throw a Stick of Dynamite into This Conversation": Insincerity as Exploitation

Even as they accept this reality, however, journalists in the field often raise concerns about the excesses of pop culture "clickbait" that capitalizes on the emotional pull of partisanship. In particular, they tend to be wary of work that makes insincere arguments purely as a means of exploiting social media-fueled political controversy to get attention and shares. For instance, a staff entertainment writer commented:

> Sometimes you just have to look at something and say, 'No, this is just non-sense, and it's not something we need to cover.' [For example, there was] a mini controversy where people were saying that the [2019] movie *Harriet* played into a white savior trope. As far as our film critic could figure out, it was all driven by people who had not seen the movie complaining about something that hadn't actually happened in the movie. But it was a huge object of Twitter attention for days and days. And that was a case where we sort of had to look at it and say, "No, we're just going to sit this out and wait for that to pass."

As another staff critic suggested, such editorial restraint is a relative luxury for news outlets that can afford to sit out the latest attention-grabbing controversy on social media (a subject to which chapter 5 will return) in the service of upholding quality journalism standards:

> I try to reject any story idea or wading into a Twitter controversy just be-cause I think that it could get clicks. I'm lucky that I get to have that sort of discerning approach to the work, because I know a lot of people in my in-dustry don't have that. . . . When an editor might mention to me that he saw this controversy bubbling up on Twitter and ask me if I have a take on it or if there's something not right about it, and if I say, "No, I think it's a non-story that's being overblown" for whatever reason, they'll respect that, which I re-ally appreciate. But I recognize that I'm lucky that I have that, and not every publication that needs clicks to survive does have that.

As his remarks suggest, such concerns over insincerity and cynical audience exploitation in pop culture–politics coverage are heightened by the sense that it is a growing problem in the industry. Indeed, many entertainment journalists readily admit that facile and poor-quality arguments about the politics of entertainment and celebrity run rampant in many online outlets because of sheer market incentives. As one commentator put it, "a lot of po-litical viewpoints are capitalized upon . . . they can be exploited and harped upon" by news companies. As an example, she cited an article from a prom-inent news site in which "the point of view of the writer was that it's bad that there are no people of color in [the 2019 film adaptation] *Little Women*."

As she suggested, such an argument was designed to feed the appetite for "clickbait" around issues of racial representation and diversity, but in this case, the strategy backfired, as the piece "got bashed on social media, because first of all, *Little Women* was written [over a century] ago, and it's meant to be a white story. . . . People of color were saying, 'Why would you need a black actress in *Little Women*?'" In other words, audiences who would otherwise be sympathetic to such a perspective determined that the piece in question was cynically exploitative of identity politics rather than an authentic and meaningful contribution to the cause. However, the broader problem, she figured, is that news outlets are "trying to game" the audience to fall into familiar patterns of ideologically driven outrage that fuel social media circulation, regardless of whether this outrage is truly warranted.

This notion of cynical, market-driven overreach in coverage of the pop culture–politics nexus appears to be of particular concern to journalists on the left, who sense that criticism of identity representation can easily slip into inanity or absurdity if journalists do not handle it with appropriate care and are solely driven by the quest for online attention (indeed, they must constantly contend with these sorts of accusations from their colleagues on the right, as discussed in chapter 3). For instance, a veteran critic who often focuses on issues of LGBT media representation lamented:

> I've had editors propose a story to me where I thought, it's a really provocative argument or position that would not hold up past the third paragraph. It just doesn't make sense. And I said that. And they said, "Yeah, but we just want you to throw a stick of dynamite into this conversation." And I've been very, very fortunate to be able to say I don't want to do that. I'm not going be provocative just for the sake of being a provocateur. I want to write something that I can defend and believe in. But there are writers who are struggling, you know, who aren't in a position to be able to say no.

As he suggested here, there is a tendency in at least some corners of the industry to encourage journalists to cannily exploit audience passions around diversity and progressive representation regardless of the merit or substance of the critique. While editors are compelled by economic logics to "throw in a stick of dynamite" to maximize clicks and social media shares, some members of the field worry that doing so can lead to work that is devoid of actual political depth and meaning.

Along similar lines, another critic singled out a "take" cycle around the 2019 film *The Irishman* in which "there were a lot of stories that were like 'there are no women in this.' . . . It feels like low-hanging fruit, sort of like, 'Well, let's just look and see the very most obvious thing,' and there's not much more than that." Although this sort of feminist-inspired argument can often be appropriate, she figured, in this case, it was largely handled in a simplistic, knee-jerk manner that cynically catered to industry logics:

> It feels like there has to be more substance than just the headline "There's no women in here." There has to be more of a "and why that matters" aspect of it. Not just "hey, let's be angry about this together," or "let's all click on this and talk about this headline," which I do think is happening way too often. . . . I think that's a conversation to have, you know, an idea of a show not having enough representation, but I think it has to be done with a little more thoughtfulness than sometimes what we're doing.

As she suggested, rather than provide thoughtful arguments about how gender representation in pop culture can be improved, the *Irishman* "takes" exemplified an industry tendency to create "just a really great headline that we're all going to share on social media."

Part of the problem, so it seems, is that there is currently so much market demand for pop culture coverage involving identity politics that quality control becomes difficult, and any piece hitting the desired ideological notes can find publication and social media circulation regardless of its substance. One critic surmised:

> I think some of that comes from the fact that until recently, we weren't really seeing those stories, but now we're inundated with stories trying to talk about race and gender and kind of bungling it. . . . There's definitely a side to writing about identity politics that just takes a bit of a lazy approach and isn't really trying to do anything that hasn't already been done in terms of talking about identity. . . . There was a time when people were afraid to talk about identity politics and critique them at all. And now we're moving into this new era of "how do we talk about identity politics and make it good?"

The distinction that she draws here between quality, in-depth pop-cultural coverage and superficial content designed purely for online virality is similarly invoked by many journalists who seek to distance themselves from the latter as a means of upholding their professional reputation and status. As another journalist argued, not only does poor-quality, bottom-line-feeding work sully the overall image of the field, but it makes it more difficult for more substantive entertainment journalists to be taken seriously in a sea of "hot takes":

> I feel like when you say "hot take" now, even thoughtful criticism gets lumped into that, which is kind of the sad part about it. . . . Someone writes something substantial and good and really thought-provoking, and it's just like, "well, that's just a 'hot take,'" because of the many 'hot takes' that preceded it, even though it's not.

As he suggested, the industry-wide incentive to prioritize audience provocation at all costs has made it more difficult for quality entertainment journalism to stand out from the "clickbait" crowd. Buried under the weight of negative stereotypes that arise from industry logics, it seems as though pop culture commentators are subject to accusations of cynical insincerity and superficiality no matter what they do.

As noted above, this set of tensions appears to be far more pronounced in the entertainment journalism of the left, which is perceived—fairly or unfairly—to push political considerations of media representations and off-screen Hollywood activities to their very limit. Indeed, much of the concern about superficial and bad-faith pop culture criticism revolves around the notion of extending identity politics too far, to the point of absurdity or self-parody. On the right, these sorts of arguments become instant fodder for reactionary critiques, which, as chapter 3 showed, target both Hollywood and the mainstream news media for perceived left-wing dominance and overreach.

To this point, conservative criticism of excessive "wokeness" in left-wing cultural commentary neatly folds into a critique of the news business that is seen as being aligned with such agendas for financial as well as ideological gain. For instance, one right-wing critic complained that "there's a lot of crap out there" in terms of pop culture coverage that seeks to whip up political outrage:

> There's one little quote from a mainstream news outlet, and a million other websites will kind of jump on it, maybe torture it, maybe pull it apart, maybe reinterpret it, maybe read too much into it, [where] you don't know the context, you don't know the whole story. You get the quick "hot take," you get a lot of clicks for it, and you've got a wrong story.

As previous chapters have shown, the accusation that left-progressive journalistic criticism of pop culture amounts to "reading too much into things" is a frequent rhetorical tactic of the right, yet it is important to note here how such arguments graft easily onto critiques of broader news industry economics that view such coverage as shameless and disingenuous exploitation.

At the same time, chapter 3 has shown how some conservative entertainment journalists draw a distinction within their field between "nuanced" forms of pop culture commentary and more aggressive "red meat" coverage that is designed to spark passion and outrage, such as "quick hit" pieces on left-wing celebrities making derogatory statements about Donald Trump. However, the "red meat" side of the conservative news media is seen less as a problem of skewed industry incentives than as simply a pragmatic strategy for capturing certain segments of the audience who are on the far-right end of the spectrum. In contrast to their left-wing counterparts who often express worries about the negative impact of profit motives on journalistic quality, conservative entertainment journalists tend to be more forgiving of professional practices that are seen to successfully meet audience demand. For instance, even when distancing his own work from the "red meat" approach, one conservative film critic remarked, "I don't blame the 'clickbait' artists for doing what they do. It is a tough business. It is a tough industry."

Another right-wing commentator argued that while superficial and low-quality work may be a problem on both sides of the partisan news divide, it is simply an inevitable one:

> In a free system, in a capitalist system, it's a problem in every single form
> of communication, whether artistic or journalistic, whether left or right.
> There is always a temptation to play to the lowest common denominator.
> You know, because there's so much of the audience there, that's what makes
> it the lowest common denominator. . . . That's the way of the world.

As these remarks suggest, the right's broader ideological comfort with free-market capitalism tends to preclude serious criticism of its potential negative impact on journalistic practice, a pattern that extends to conservatives in the audience as well as in newsrooms.[15] While admitting that capitalistic profit motives may lessen the quality of coverage in some areas, entertainment included, conservative journalists appear to accept this as an unavoidable consequence of a system that they philosophically embrace with open arms. Conversely, commentators on the left, who tend to be more ideologically sympathetic to critiques of capitalism in general, are more likely to identify the threat posed by "clickbait" logics to their field of professional practice.[16] Whether they are able to take active steps to mitigate this threat, however, is far less certain.

Conclusion

As discussed in this chapter, reporters and critics who cover pop culture and its intersection with politics are operating in an industry that is under massive financial stress and in which reliable professional roles for entertainment journalism are shrinking, if not disappearing altogether. Within this strained economic context, journalistic strategies that prove successful from a bottom-line perspective are embraced, however hesitantly or begrudgingly, as a means of sheer professional survival. We have also seen, however, how the financial pressures of the news business are distributed quite unevenly, with those at the top of the hierarchy of prestige and brand viability in far better position to shrug them off in the name of journalistic quality than others lower down who must attract clicks and shares at all costs. As scholar Nikki Usher argues, quality journalism in the digital age has become something of a luxury for the kinds of affluent (and largely white) audiences who have the means to support elite, high-prestige journalism organizations, while other kinds of news outlets with lower status are left scrambling for crumbs by any means necessary.[17] For the latter, the incentive not only to cover but to potentially exploit political controversy in the world of entertainment is particularly acute, as it lands precisely at the cross section of some of the industry's most favored strategies for gaming the attention economy: the instant recognizability and allure of high-profile pop culture and celebrity topics, the emotional pull of identity-centered political debate and disagreement, and the provocative and opinionated tone of the cultural criticism format that melds easily with industry demands for unique viewpoint and distinctive "takes."

The poor industry reputation of this journalism as substandard, disposable, cynically hyper-commercial "hot takes" and "clickbait" stems directly from these alignments with key industry logics. However, the problems of the field, which are readily apparent to many of its own working members, are not necessarily inherent to the subject matter itself. Rather, they are at least partially the result of attitudes on the part of journalism industry decision-makers who position entertainment coverage as an easy way of shoring up the profits of news companies as opposed to a serious endeavor worth investing considerable organizational resources. Journalistic discussions of pop culture's political significance can, of course, meet the highest industry standards of quality—as well as the threshold of public relevance at a time when these two social spheres regularly intersect in consequential ways—yet this requires sustained commitment to professional talent and expertise, typically in the form of full-time dedicated staff roles.

The fact that these roles are being devalued by the industry at the same time as pop culture–politics news content is being prioritized as a major driver of internet traffic helps account for why so much of the output in this area falls short of professional standards and becomes the target of withering ridicule. To improve the quality and public value of the culture beat, the news business must reconceive it as an essential part of the newsroom's public mission and not just a quick way to garner clicks and shares. In addition to expanding staff positions and revaluing the contribution of cultural expertise in newsrooms, this would mean, for instance, commissioning journalism about topics such as Hollywood's relationship to racism and sexism above and beyond when they align with fleeting industry trends and ephemeral cycles of online attention.

Yet the pull of social media on the work of journalists at the pop culture–politics nexus is simply too big to ever ignore. Chapter 5 turns attention to how social media monitoring and feedback profoundly shape the day-to-day practices of entertainment news professionals, foregrounding the importance of being part of "the conversation" online while also highlighting further risks to the field in an age of intensive online hyper-partisanship.

5

Trending Outrage

How Social Media Impacts the Work of Journalists at the Pop Culture–Politics Nexus

Of all the common tropes of today's journalism at the pop culture–politics nexus, perhaps none is more dependable than the social media backlash story. Take, for instance, a sample of headlines concerning Gal Gadot, the outspoken Israeli actress who rose to fame portraying the superhero Wonder Woman: from the *New York Daily News*, "Gal Gadot's Plea for Peace in Israel Gets Social Media Backlash"; from the *Jerusalem Post*, "Gal Gadot's 'Imagine' Video Draws Snarky Social Media Backlash"; from *Maxim*, "Gal Gadot Faces Social Media Backlash for Starring in Upcoming 'Cleopatra' Movie." Each of these headlines refers to a major news cycle of pop culture controversy in its own right, the details of which are too complex to describe here. The point, rather, is that entertainment journalists have become accustomed to covering these controversies through the frame of the social media reaction, typically with a smattering of illustrative tweets that are used to make up the bulk of the reporting and serve as evidence of wider public trends.

This journalistic approach is clearly a sign of the times, as networked digital platforms such as Twitter have become the central clearinghouse for public expression and discursive activism regarding all sorts of issues and topics, Hollywood included. To cover anything political in the twenty-first century is to cover, among other things, what happens in the digital spaces of social media. Yet, from a professional news industry perspective, the social media reaction frame also provides a convenient and reliable way for journalists to remain close to the interests and passions of their audiences, who are also very often participants on these very same platforms. As social media has opened direct pathways of communication between news professionals and the public, it has been transforming the day-to-day work of journalists in significant ways. Those who cover the intersection of pop culture and politics have been experiencing this impact especially acutely— perhaps more so than in any other part of the newsroom—since the intensive

Pop Culture, Politics, and the News. Joel Penney, Oxford University Press. © Oxford University Press 2022.
DOI: 10.1093/oso/9780197557587.003.0006

online discussion around these accessible and emotionally engaging topics creates a social media noise that is far too loud to ignore. Yet, at the same time as social media has aided this journalism by providing up-to-the-minute material for reportage as well as real-time consumer feedback, it has also presented considerable new challenges.

This chapter explores both the benefits and the drawbacks of a media landscape in which news professionals now have direct digital lines of two-way communication with the public. As the discussion will show, the increasing reliance on social media as a gauge of public opinion and trending outrage has become a cause for concern among reporters and editors who are tasked with covering the latest pop culture controversy of the day, raising issues of skewed representation and the undue amplification of the most vocal extremes of contemporary online discourse. In addition, the chapter examines how digital feedback channels have become both a blessing and a curse to journalists at the pop culture–politics nexus, helping them to assess the performance and public impact of their work while also making them vulnerable to harassment and hate that is often politically motivated and disproportionately targets women and minority journalists who speak out against cultures of racism and sexism.

Generally speaking, social media is seen to be of considerable "market value" for self-branding in the journalism industry, and news professionals routinely use platforms such as Twitter to promote their work and careers and gain further visibility in the public eye.[1] When inserting themselves into the social media conversation, some journalists may be able to simply shrug off abusive comments and hideous death threats as just another part of being a public figure in the digital age. Yet others may be compelled to limit their professional social media presence as a matter of personal safety and survival and in some cases even pull back from certain kinds of reporting and commentary to avoid the wrath of vengeful online commenters.

To an extent, these journalists' experience mirrors that of Hollywood stars such as Kelly Marie Tran and Daisy Ridley of *Star Wars*, who both famously quit social media after being subjected to unrelenting sexist (and, in Tran's case, racist) abuse simply for appearing in franchise films that certain fans did not want to see them in.[2] For journalists who cover such controversies day after day and who frequently delve into hot-button topics such as identity politics in their reporting, these threats posed by social media are similarly inescapable. As will be discussed, the fact that pop culture news stories provoke such extreme online reactions, very often of a hyper-partisan nature, further attests to how the landscape of entertainment and celebrity has become a major battleground of contemporary political discourse.

"On Twitter People Are Mad a Lot": The Social Media Reaction Beat

As entertainment journalism has become increasingly interested in covering the political aspects of its Hollywood subject matter, the public conversation around pop culture has been elevated to a primary focal point of reportage. This is because quite often, it is the public reaction to a film, show, or celebrity remark—outrage being the most common—that drives politically inflected controversy and the news cycles and "take" cycles that follow. For this reason, journalists who cover entertainment are acutely aware of the importance of constantly monitoring social media to track these conversations in real time and find material for stories. One reporter explained:

> I look at my Twitter and Reddit at least every twenty minutes just to see what people are talking about, because if you see what people are talking about, then you want to write something in that same vein. Twitter and whatever are ways to find what people are interested in. And usually on Twitter people are mad a lot.

As he went on to note, this activity enables him to "write about a national outrage" that has built-in audience appeal.

This pattern of journalists' seeking out information about the interests of their audience to reach them more effectively is a relatively recent development in the profession. As Jacob L. Nelson discusses in his study of the journalist–audience relationship, there had been a long-standing resistance among journalists in decades past to affording any attention whatsoever to the audience, which was seen as irrelevant for their public service mission and threatened to conflict with their professional news judgment.[3] However, all of that has changed in the increasingly fractured digital information environment, which has left news outlets struggling for financial survival while also simultaneously within reach of a plethora of new kinds of data about audience news consumption and engagement. Although Nelson cautions that even precise digital metrics and analytics are unable to provide journalists with a clear-cut objective understanding of an audience whom they still must largely imagine subjectively,[4] the practice of monitoring social media for trending topics appears to give pop culture reporters a useful rubric for imagining what audiences will click on next.

As an example of this practice, the above-noted journalist referenced his reporting on the saga of Shane Gillis, a right-wing comedian who was briefly hired by *Saturday Night Live* as a cast member in 2019, only to be fired days later when past racist remarks caused an uproar on social media, complete with hashtagged calls for his sacking. This news cycle, which involved several days of intensive coverage and opinion pieces, is an archetypical example of how controversies at the pop culture–politics nexus flow through what media theorist Andrew Chadwick calls the hybrid media system. As Chadwick argues, the "new" world of amateur online communication and the "old" world of professional media have become closely interdependent as they interact regularly and adapt to each other's logics.[5]

One major development of the hybrid media system is that social media commenting now partially shapes the direction of professional news coverage (and vice versa), as journalists adapt to a newsgathering model that prioritizes the online conversation as a key signal of public opinion and a newsworthy beat in its own right. In the case of the Gillis controversy, initial news reports of his hiring by *SNL* sparked discussion and outrage on social media, as commenters surfaced and retweeted a video showing the comedian making racist comments about Asians. This then led to a hashtag activism campaign that fueled sympathetic news coverage of the public outcry, which in turn fueled more social media anger along with right-wing news media backlash, and so on. This back-and-forth between the "old" and "new" media worlds, referred to colloquially as the "social media outrage cycle," includes a significant role for professional journalists who actively search for, select, and spotlight online comments in their coverage as a means of constructing narratives about the salience of a given public controversy.

Although this dynamic is traceable in many areas of the contemporary news landscape, it is particularly pronounced in the field of entertainment journalism, which thrives on the emotional intensity of fandom and the willingness of audiences to both follow and participate in discussions around their objects of pop culture fascination. One entertainment journalist explained regarding the use of social media comments for generating so-called trend pieces:

> I think it's probably a little more valuable with pop culture journalism than
> with the kind of political journalism a lot of my colleagues at [the site] do, just
> because the kind of person who cares enough to read a really intense analysis
> of pop culture is more likely to be already talking about it on social media. . . .
> It can sometimes be a little bit more relevant to the conversation that way.

In other words, entertainment journalists imagine their audiences to be regularly engaged in social media discussions around such topics, which provides justification for using these discussions as a basis for news coverage which in turn targets these same audiences in a kind of feedback loop.

Entertainment reporters and critics are often quite forthright about how they shape journalistic output around their sense of "the conversation" on social media, with the intent of contributing to this very discourse. One critic, for instance, noted that "you see people talking about things online and being aware of that conversation, and that's something that sometimes inspires pieces or something you try to think about when you're writing pieces," while another commented that "Twitter's the place where I'm watching these conversations happen and getting an idea of the different viewpoints that people have . . . and I also find that when I take a break from Twitter and social media, I'm writing less, just because I'm out of the loop on the conversation."

Moreover, by assiduously tracking social media to gauge how audiences make sense of pop culture and its broader social and political significance, journalists uncover specific angles that they and their editors are compelled to integrate into coverage. For example, a film critic explained how her reporting on the 2019 film version of *Little Women* was molded via social media monitoring into a story about anti-feminist backlash:

> Before [*Little Women*] had even officially come out, there started to be
> this narrative building that men weren't seeing it. I think the various
> tweets . . . were a number of people asking questions about this, saying, "Are
> men really seeing it or not? And does it matter if they aren't?" Then, as this
> particular narrative started to pick up momentum, [my editors] came to me
> and said, "You know, this seems like something that we should maybe have
> coverage about."

Similarly, another film critic described how she reworked her review of the Harriet Tubman biopic *Harriet* around her editor's push to address the Twitter backlash to the film's star:

I went into *Harriet* knowing that the actress who had been cast in the role, Cynthia Erivo, had come under fire because when she was cast, people on Twitter found some tweets of hers where she mocked black Americans and she made fun of the black American accent. . . . The movie came out, and the news outlet assigned me to review it, and my review at first was mostly just an aesthetic consideration of the film and how I viewed it in the landscape of other films we've had recently about slavery. And then my editor came back and said, "What about the thing with Cynthia Erivo being cast and her Twitter issue?" So we then wove that into the review, because it's something that we knew people were looking for and probably would expect us to talk about.

As these accounts underline, tracking and reporting on the social media debate around pop culture have become an editorial priority, since this is seen to align with the interests of target audiences who are ostensibly participating in these very online discussions in the first place. As discussed in chapter 4, the economic incentive to cater to what audiences will react to and share on social media is especially heightened in the financially strained and highly competitive digital news landscape, and even more so in the subfield of entertainment coverage that is positioned as a commercialist attention-grabber for the industry. Thus, making the social media conversation part of pop culture coverage itself becomes a strategy to help break through and remain relevant in the crowded attention economy.

"Twitter Can Be Too Much of a Crutch": The Limits of Social Media Trend-Spotting

However, the process of translating a scattering of tweets and other online comments into a useful picture of how the public is responding to a given pop culture story or controversy is far from an exact science. Although sophisticated social media monitoring tools are in wide use across the industry, journalists tend to take a more impressionistic approach to assessing the scope and tenor of the social media discussion when they are constructing coverage (of course, news organizations regularly use these more quantitative tools to measure the online performance of their output for pragmatic economic reasons).[6] For instance, when one journalist was asked how the "social media conversation" is discerned for the purpose of reporting on it, she replied, "I don't think there's a quantitative answer to that question. I think it's a combination of how much people are talking about it and whether the conversation points to some larger cultural question that will be interesting to analyze." While the question of "how much people are talking about it" could feasibly be answered by diving into social media metrics, it seems many journalists working on deadline simply do not have time to conduct such fine-grained research. Rather, as her remarks suggest, they piece together an impression of the "social media conversation" by looking for overall trends, sometimes indicated by trending hashtags but also assessed by reportorial instinct alone.

For example, a staff entertainment reporter for a national news site described how her team conceived a piece about public backlash toward the Academy Awards for neglecting to nominate people of color in many categories:

> We do often look at reaction on social media, especially in big cases like that. . . . There's been a lot of dialogue around the lack of awards recognition of actors and actresses of color in the past. So when we looked at it, right away you could tell certain people parsed out exactly the way that the trajectory of that story was going to go. And then, sure enough, once you looked at the response on social media, it was clear that that was sort of the general consensus around it.

As she indicated in her comments, this impressionistic analysis is shaped by multiple factors, including a sense of previous established patterns as well as the voices of certain prominent figures who are perceived as key indicators of broader trends.

However, in seeking to gauge consensus from a crowded and chaotic sea of online comments, journalists risk flattening and overgeneralizing public opinion in ways that can skew coverage. Within the field, there is notable concern regarding the true representativeness of social media as an indicator of public opinion—an issue that has also dogged political journalism as industry commentators warn of overestimating the significance of vocal online activists who are often on the fringes of public debate.[7] Research conducted by scholar Shannon McGregor, which examines how political reporters use social media to represent public opinion, finds that journalists are "worried about an overreliance on social media to inform coverage," especially because of "social media users not reflecting the electorate."[8] In terms of the pop culture conversation, there is a similar sense that discussions on Twitter often operate in a bubble and are dominated by relatively small groups of highly engaged audiences. One entertainment reporter, for instance, noted, "sometimes I think Twitter can be too much of a crutch, because whenever I go home and talk to someone who's not extremely online about what's happening on Twitter, I realize how very little it matters to most people." Another surmised that "journalists can get very caught up on Twitter and assume that everybody knows everything that they do because they spend all day on Twitter. But people don't."

Although these sorts of concerns are sometimes raised by journalists on the left side of the partisan media divide, their right-wing counterparts tend to be especially skeptical of social media as a representation of public sentiment regarding cultural and political controversy. This is attributable to the perception that much social media outrage aimed at the world of entertainment and celebrity is a manifestation of an out-of-control leftist "cancel culture," which, as chapter 3 has shown, has become a chief preoccupation of contemporary right-wing discourse. As one conservative film critic lamented, "the dangerous thing about social media is the way that it makes a hundred angry people sound like a million angry people, when everybody in the group is spamming mentions and blowing up accounts and all that," while an entertainment editor for a right-wing news site explained, "I try really hard not to pay attention at all to what does well on Twitter, because I think that's like a really dangerous way to gauge your readership's interest. The Twitter bubble is just not at all representative." As she suggested, the target audiences of outlets like hers may not be as highly engaged in the "social media conversation" around pop culture which is perceived as tilted toward left-progressive activist concerns, therefore making it less relevant as a driver for conservative coverage (however, as chapter 6 will explore, conservatives are certainly active in these social media debates, if only to decry "cancel culture" in reactionary fashion). In any event, the warnings raised by entertainment journalists on the right further underscore the pitfalls of using online comments as a marker of consensus sentiment, especially considering how opinions on pop culture controversies are so fragmented along partisan lines.

An additional factor that may skew journalists' assessments of the "social media conversation" and its capacity to represent public opinion is the relative insularity of their own digital networks, which McGregor also notes in her research on "the highly curated Twitter feeds" of political reporters.[9] Many entertainment journalists described how they closely follow the accounts of their community of colleagues in the field, sometimes referred to by nicknames such as "media Twitter" or "film Twitter," to gain a sense of trends and patterns that then feed into their own coverage. For instance, when describing the process of crafting a piece on political backlash to the Academy Awards nominations, a journalist explained:

> When the news broke, people reacted, and the reaction seemed to be sort of consistent among a lot of the media types who were responding to it. So we would call it a trend feature, in the sense that "here's something that's trending and is becoming a larger portion of the dialogue around a specific news item, so therefore we're going to kind of take that into account."

In this case, the viewpoints expressed by the "media types" on Twitter— that is, other entertainment news professionals—were deemed important enough to build a trend feature around, seemingly irrespective of whether they comported with the full range of opinion across the social media landscape.

Although the assumption may be warranted that "media Twitter" is influential enough in the broader public discourse to justify attention and coverage, there is a risk that it can be overrepresented due to its heightened prominence in the newsfeeds of fellow journalists. As one entertainment journalist cautioned, "you can kind of be in your own bubble. If you're a critic or cultural writer, most of the people that you interact with online are also other critics and cultural writers, where you're, like, 'well, everybody knows this stuff, right?' And then you find out 'oh, no, everyone doesn't.'"

Certainly, social media "bubbles" and "echo chambers," created through a combination of homophilic self-selection and social and technological filtering processes,[10] are hardly unique to the journalistic profession. However, because journalists play such an outsize role in representing the "social media conversation" to the public, the potential blind spots that result from the insularity of their own social media usage can have significant repercussions for how such conversations filter into the broader discourse. At worst, the online discussions that occur within the community of pop culture reporters and critics run the risk of being overamplified in this discourse as they become fodder for one another's coverage in loops of mutual reinforcement.

"It's Hard to Know What Hits or Misses": Social Media as an Erratic Gauge of Success

Throughout the field of contemporary digital journalism, social media engagement (i.e., shares, comments, likes, and favorites) for individual pieces is used as a convenient barometer of success, although the interpretation of these metrics can vary widely. As noted above, some outlets and editors are broadly skeptical of platforms such as Twitter as a meaningful representation of their specific target audience and may therefore discount such data as offering only a limited and skewed perspective. On the other hand, many journalists pay very close attention to the social media engagement with their work, particularly since it is seen as an expression of what is perhaps the primary objective of today's digital news business: being a relevant part of the "conversation."

As one entertainment commentator noted in terms of assessing his own journalistic output, "on social media, I get a sense of what stories are not just getting retweeted or something like that, but getting people engaged in a debate, and whether it's positive or negative." For journalists who specialize in coverage of pop culture topics, this focus on tracking how they successfully catalyze audience discussion appears to be especially pertinent. As discussed in chapter 4, while traditional "hard news" politics coverage is typically perceived by industry managers as core to an outlet's public mission, the "soft news" side of the business, including most cultural coverage, must constantly prove its worth. Thus, having demonstrable evidence of impacting the public conversation helps entertainment journalists make the case to management that the issues that they cover and the ideas with which they engage resonate with audiences on a deep and substantive level.

Another reason many journalists closely track social media data is that it is the only form of audience measure to which they always have immediate and reliable access, regardless of their status as freelance or staff. Most, but not all, journalists in full-time staff positions are privy to internal site data from proprietary services such as Chartbeat, which show precise measures of "hits" and retention rates on individual pieces. As researcher Caitlin Petre finds, many rank-and-file staff journalists scrupulously follow these internal metrics through dashboards that feature a "habit-forming, game-like user interface."[11] Freelancers, on the other hand, are almost never given internal data from publishers on the performance of their individual contributions. As one freelance journalist explained, "every once in a while, [an editor] will say to me, 'Oh, that story that you wrote did really well,' or 'That got us a lot of traffic,'" but that is usually as far it goes in terms of direct feedback. In the absence of such data, as another freelancer noted, social media becomes "a very good proxy for how popular" a piece has become. Thus, freelance journalists—who make up an increasingly large share of the labor force for entertainment coverage and commentary—are particularly watchful of shares and comments on public social media platforms such as Twitter and Facebook to gauge whether their work is successful in reaching an audience.

As discussed in chapter 4, viral circulation is a core currency of the contemporary digital attention economy, and thus social media engagement looms large in any consideration of how journalists shape their work to meet industry demands. However, while making an impact on the digital conversation is always a goal, journalists are often hesitant to take past viral success as a straightforward directive for how to craft future work. This is because social media virality is perceived by journalists to be greatly unpredictable, even random. As one entertainment critic put it, "sometimes you can't make sense of the way your article is going to appear in other people's timelines. And the way it gets shared is so arbitrary, there isn't really a pattern to it." Another similarly asserted, "I try not to let [social media] completely dictate the way I approach the story or what kind of stories I am approaching, because you really can't totally control the way the internet will feel about a piece. You kind of have to do the best you can and then put it out there and hope for the best."

When they put out work that does attain viral status on social media, they are often mystified by its success and wary of drawing too many concrete conclusions. For instance, a conservative entertainment columnist recalled:

> I did a piece about [athlete] Ryan Lochte getting railroaded at the Olympics in Brazil and how he was really screwed over by the media . . . and that got an ungodly number of shares and hits and was huge for like two weeks. And then sometimes you just get something that's got forty shares, and you think, "Oh, I thought that the Oscars would be bigger than that." It's hard to know what hits or misses with audiences, because everybody in the audience is individual.

Another columnist likewise described social media as "a really weird hit-and-miss," explaining that when it comes to pop culture topics, "some things have real niche audience pockets, and it'll trigger them, so you just don't really know," such as a rabid fan base for a particular entertainment property (a topic to be discussed more later). This notion that social media engagement for entertainment news and commentary often hinges on the idiosyncratic dynamics of online fandom was also noted by a film critic who described getting online shares for pieces "just because of a personal passion for some director or author or something like that . . . social media is somewhat fickle." Furthermore, he stressed how the virality of this news content typically depends on the erratic gatekeeper participation of key influencers and opinion leaders, who can blow up a piece nearly instantaneously by sharing it with their large groups of followers.

Because of this unpredictability, entertainment journalists are typically wary of tailoring their work to simply mimic past social media successes. For instance, when a veteran pop culture critic was asked if she had learned what works well on social media based on past experience, she exclaimed, "God, if people knew that, they'd be gaming it left and right!" At the same time, however, journalists were able to identify some broad patterns about the nature of audience engagement on social media that meaningfully inform their creative process. At a very general level, one reporter offered that a pop culture event that "can intersect with the human-interest side, I think, always tends to do really, really well." A journalist who covers LGBT representation in the media, he noted that celebrity stories involving same-sex weddings, for instance, have been particularly good performers in terms of social sharing because of the emotional resonance and uplift of the storytelling. As discussed in chapter 4, news content that elicits strong emotional reactions from audiences tends to be shared online more often,[12] and while such impassioned responses can be difficult to predict, journalists are able to track when they do occur by carefully monitoring social media feedback.

At best, these insights drawn from social data can provide journalists and editors with broad strategies for how to proceed in the competitive attention economy, even if they cannot ensure the virality of any one individual piece. To this point, the strategy of leveraging outrage and passion around divisive social and political issues—discussed in chapter 4 as one of the major ways in which economic pressures shape entertainment news and commentary—is generally well supported by the social media feedback. As one critic underlined, "if you write about something in the culture that's become a flashpoint . . . then it's likely to be retweeted and to reach somebody who has influence online." Although the specifics may be tricky, tracking social media reactions to pieces helps entertainment journalists and editors affirm the value of political controversy as a reliable strategy for sparking audience emotion and discussion and achieving the elusive prize of virality.

"Thank You for Saying This": Meaningful Online Audience Feedback

Social media, along with other forms of online communication such as emails and article comments sections, enable journalists to have instantaneous audience feedback that is greatly helpful for assessing the reception of their work and the degree to which it is successful in the goal of driving the "conversation." However, when tapping into public passions with journalism at the pop culture–politics nexus, the question of what the subsequent online response actually represents in terms of the audience can be quite thorny. In general, topics such as racial and gender diversity in Hollywood are "hot issues," as one entertainment writer and editor put it, that inspire both extreme positive and extreme negative reactions online:

> By hot, I mean really likely to generate any number of impassioned responses across the spectrum, from supportive of the idea that there should be more diversity in pop culture, to angry that the topic is being brought up, to people who believe that diversity is the enemy of quality or a way of lowering standards. The opinions run the gamut, but it's something that people feel very eager to express their opinion about, no matter where they lie.

However, just as journalists are concerned with the degree to which social media may present a skewed image of public opinion when conducting research for stories, they are also mindful that the online feedback to their own work can be similarly unrepresentative of the true scope and diversity of the audience.

Many journalists have come to treat this online feedback somewhat skeptically, since it seems to come only from certain types of audience members who have a strong motivation to express feelings of either approval or disdain. As a conservative commentator noted, email responses to his opinion columns are driven by such emotional highs and lows: "Generally, if somebody takes the time to email, it is one of two extremes, 'I absolutely loved it' or 'I hated it.' The indifferent, the sort of middling comments . . . they don't email." Another journalist noted a very similar pattern in other types of on-line feedback: "When you're hearing on social media and in the comments section, it's from the people who are polarized. And I don't think that's rep-resentative of the average reader, although it is representative clearly of some portion of the readers." As she went on to suggest, the distorted image that emerges in online posts and comments can effectively hide those segments of the audience who do not fall into the most polarized camps: "I do think there's a silent majority of readers who appreciate nuanced coverage, but they're not going to go on social media or into the comments section and start yelling about how much they love nuance." The problem, she argued, is that using social media and online feedback as measures of audience sen-timent risks leading to coverage decisions that cater to only the most vocal and impassioned segments. Accounts such as these thus hint at a sense of frustration in the industry over how social media skews the relationship be-tween journalists and their audiences toward the most extreme—and often reactionary—segments.

Notably, this includes effusive praise as well as acrimonious scorn. While many journalists working at the intersection of pop culture and politics noted receiving angry responses on a regular basis, particularly from in-censed members of fan communities (a topic explored in more detail below), others tend to hear more from the opposite end of the spectrum. This ten-dency toward the extreme positive, in addition to the extreme negative, is attributable to the niche appeal of many forms of pop culture news and com-mentary, which, as discussed in previous chapters, are targeted with laser precision to like-minded audiences who seek identification and validation of their own perspectives. For instance, a staff journalist for a left-oriented news and culture site expressed that she has been surprised by the positive online feedback to her more opinionated articles, "especially if it's something that has a personal impact on people. I've written a lot about diversity and Asian American representation, and I find that people really respond to that be-cause they feel a lot of gratitude that there is more Asian American represen-tation and the fact that there's a lot of Asian American writers writing about Asian American representation." Here the appreciative online response signals her success in serving this specific role for an audience that is eager for such perspective and viewpoint and is likely seeking it out in deliberate fashion. A right-leaning columnist and film critic similarly noted receiving "overwhelmingly and almost entirely positive support" on social media for certain pieces that resonate strongly with a conservative readership, such as one mocking environmentalists and lauding their portrayal as villains in Hollywood films: "People were saying, 'Yes, this is exactly right, like I'm tired of having my straws taken away and my being told that I need to flush the toilet once every six days.'"

Beyond these "thumbs up" expressions of audience agreement and approval that are a predictable outgrowth of niche-targeted opinion and commentary, some journalists also noted getting more in-depth positive responses through online feedback channels that were singularly meaningful to them and even helped shore up their sense of professional purpose. For instance, a critic who covers LGBT representation in pop culture for a left-leaning news site told a story about getting an email from a man who said he was a pastor:

> He had stumbled upon a story that I had written. . . . [He] said that it sort of opened his mind to things he hadn't thought about before and that he appreciated it. And I thought that was a lovely email to receive. . . . It's rare to have someone reach out and say that they've had their mind changed about something, but it does happen. And every time it does, it sort of validates why writing about these things is important.

This idea of gaining a sense of professional fulfillment from receiving tangible evidence of influencing how an audience member thinks—as opposed to merely reflecting their views back to them—was echoed by a critic for another left-leaning site, who noted that when it comes to online feedback from audiences, "what I tend to mostly focus on is when individual people will respond to the piece of writing and say that it changed their minds." As an example, she cited responses to an article in which she laid out a detailed argument in favor of "canceling" Hollywood celebrities who had been targeted by the #MeToo movement over accusations of sexual misconduct: "People actually did respond to that and say, 'Oh, I had actually never thought of it that way, I had thought we were treating these people too severely, but now I've changed my mind.' . . . Whenever I get that response, I think, oh, that's good. That's the ideal." A film critic who focuses on feminist analysis likewise remarked, "I have had comments and feedback on pieces that are very explicitly political that are like, 'OK, I didn't think about it this way,' or 'You mentioned this one thing in your review, I'll research that and see what it's all about.' And so, I mean, that's really why you do it."

At one level, accounts such as these illuminate the professional aspirations of journalists who seek to advance political viewpoints in their pop culture coverage: although they largely serve a like-minded audience due to the segmented structure of the contemporary polarized news landscape, they strive to have an active role in shaping opinion and relish moments when their status as influential thought leaders can be confirmed and verified. At another level, their testimony sheds light on how social media posts and other forms of qualitative online feedback (emails, website comments, etc.) have become highly important for assessing the public impact of such journalism, far beyond the quantitative metrics of clicks and engagement that reveal only the broad contours of audience interest and popularity. By hearing authentic, in-depth stories of how audience members are affected by a given piece, journalists can reach a deeper understanding of what they are truly contributing to the public sphere and why it matters for them personally as well as professionally.

The value of this kind of intimate, individualized feedback is particularly well illustrated in the remarks of a senior writer and editor for a national news site who focuses on LGBT representation in his coverage. As he explained, "all I can hope as a journalist, if I write anything, is that it makes an impact with the readers who read it." Although he noted that one way to gauge this is by seeing one of his pieces "being circulated on social media or on the internet," a more meaningful representation of impact has come from certain kinds of audience emails:

> The most powerful thing you can receive by email sometimes was somebody just saying "thank you, I felt alone." . . . A common response when you write about LGBTQ issues is "Thank you for saying this, it's something that I feel myself. . . . I didn't feel that anyone was hearing me, and you vocalized something I wanted to say, and you've made me feel less alone, or less marginalized, or less attacked." And that's a very powerful thing, because I think sometimes members of minority groups can feel not only marginalized but also very isolated. So obviously, if any writing makes anybody feel less isolated, I think that's a very powerful response to receive.

His comments thus highlight how online audience feedback can make profound contributions to a sense of public mission and purpose for journalists who take on a social advocacy role in their work on entertainment topics and beyond.

"Why Are You Trying to Spoil My Fun?":
Angry Fans Unload

Heartfelt responses such as these represent perhaps the most valued and welcomed online feedback that journalists receive when they weigh in on hot-
button issues of politics and culture. However, negative, nasty, and decidedly
unwelcome online messages and posts are also highly common in this line of
work. Some of the most vehement online reactions to entertainment journalism arise when fans of a given pop culture text find their object of reverence under the microscope of ideological critique. While it is generally the
case that fans will go online to vocally disapprove of negative reviews and
commentary, there is something particularly triggering about criticism that
calls the politics of a beloved entertainment property into question (chapter 6
will offer firsthand responses from fans like these and explore how practices
of "hate clicks" and "hate shares" provide an avenue for social media activism
as well as contribute promotional labor, ironically, for their objects of journalistic scorn).

To give a sense of the sheer intensity of this response, one critic who
focuses on political analysis of entertainment noted numerous instances
when a low-scored review for a movie or video game with a large and impassioned following resulted in fans launching DDoS (distributed denial of
service) attacks that temporarily crashed his employer's website. In addition,
he explained that his ideological criticism of franchises such as *The Avengers*
and the *Red Dead Redemption* video games were met with "customary death
threats" from members of their respective fan communities, as he glibly put
it, along with "hateful comments" that were "implicitly political."

The journalists who frequently contend with this kind of audience backlash in their Twitter mentions, email inboxes, and comments sections tend to
understand it as a consequence of how pop culture fandom has become a key
source of identity for so many in the contemporary era. When this identity is
subjected to the ostensibly stern judgment of political critique, the response
can be belligerent to a degree that non-fans may find absurd. Indeed, some
journalists shared a sense of bewilderment about the ferocity with which
fans strike back in these scenarios. As one explained, "there are just certain
celebrities or personalities or moments that are triggers. I wrote a review on
this Mötley Crüe drama on Netflix that was really bad, and oh my God, you
would have thought I had killed the pope." Another critic similarly joked
about the confounding nature of these reactions:

The idea that somebody would feel so tied to a piece of cultural work that it
became a part of their identity so that if anybody said, "This has some issues
around x," they would say, "Oh, you have made an attack on me, madam,
and we will have pistols at dawn." It's so antithetical to the way that I think
about culture and the way that I think about criticism.

Despite being baffled by the animosity of this response, however, she went
on to offer a helpful insight about what it might represent: "I get it, people
love what they love, and they're insecure when what they love gets attacked,
especially when what they love gets attacked on what they believe are moral
grounds as opposed to aesthetic grounds." In other words, fans may feel
as though their own personal morality is being questioned when they so
strongly identify with a piece of pop culture that a critic labels as politically—
and thus morally—problematic. As another critic suggested, such a backlash
represents the flip side of how fans look for positive validation of their identities by engaging with pop culture analysis and commentary in the news:

> There's this push-pull between people wanting their entertainment to be
> taken seriously, but only if it makes them feel good about their preferences.
> And so when you praise a piece of really popular mass culture and find a
> deeper meaning in it, people love that. But if you take something where
> people have invested in it and don't want to look at it too closely, and ask
> them to do that, then all of a sudden, they don't want you to take it seriously
> anymore. . . . I get a lot of "Why are you trying to spoil my fun?"

This notion of fans feeling personally judged when the morality of their
deep-seated pop culture investments is called into question is particularly
helpful for making sense of reactionary responses to journalistic criticism
that addresses issues of representation along lines of race, gender, and sexuality. In many cases, progressive calls for change and increased diversity in
popular entertainment properties are taken as personal affronts by certain
fans who were already happy with the existing representations and whose
sense of identity is closely tied up with them. A journalist who frequently
writes about diversity in pop culture for a major national news outlet surmised that many of the angry online comments she receives are likely from
fans who are "possessive of some sort of piece of pop culture that they don't
want people who don't look like them to be the stars of, because they want
to relate to the person on-screen. And that has been a white man for all of

eternity." The word "possessive" here is key, as it suggests the degree to which some fans may view scrutiny of the politics of their objects of fandom as one and the same as scrutiny of their own identities.

To this point, a journalist for a feminist news and culture site pointed to the telling example of online reactions to her article criticizing the 2019 film *Star Wars: The Rise of Skywalker* for minimizing the role of Kelly Marie Tran, the Asian American actress who, as noted at the beginning of this chapter, had been a controversial presence in the franchise among some vocal segments of the fan base. The journalist explained:

> That Kelly Marie Tran piece got so much negative feedback from a group I call the "Star Boys," *Star Wars* fans who really don't want anybody outside the 1970s originals, like any representation beyond that. They just kind of come out en masse and find these pieces. And there were hundreds and hundreds of comments . . . people who are incensed that anybody would even suggest that Kelly Marie Tran's disappearance in the final film was a problem.

The fact that she had come up with a nickname for the "Star Boys" in the first place suggests the magnitude and consistency of this type of response, although it is certainly not exclusive to this specific fandom. Rather, the angry comments of the "Star Boys" typify a much broader pattern of reactionary online audience backlash to critical discourse on diversity and representation in entertainment journalism.

This pattern of response can be especially noticeable in the largest and most vocal online fan communities for those very reasons, but it is not limited to these groups or to the commonly understood universe of fandom more generally (e.g., science fiction and fantasy franchises such as *Star Wars*). According to journalists who produce this coverage, it is a dynamic that traverses many areas of pop culture, with a common theme of entertainment that is cherished by those most likely to feel personally attacked by diversity and inclusion discourse (read: straight, cis, white, and male). One commentator who focuses on this type of critique, citing the furious tweets he received in reaction to a piece criticizing comedian Dave Chappelle's jokes aimed at the LGBT community, suggested that "it shouldn't be surprising that the sort of stories that incite the most backlash are the ones that go after or sort of interrogate an entertainer who's very, very popular with a stereotypically straight male contingent."

Due to the anonymity of these angry online messages and social media comments, the journalists who regularly receive them are never quite sure who exactly is behind them. As one columnist joked, "They could be women living in coastal cities, who knows? You can't tell from a Twitter egg." However, she went on to suggest:

> A lot of these people, judging based on the emails I receive from them and the exchanges that I have with them, are older men. I think that it's really hard if you're a group in power to feel like there's any reason that you should give up even a tiny bit of that power and share it with any other type of person. And I think that's mostly what really gets them fired up.

Like the reactionary right-wing news commentary discussed in chapter 3, the audience backlash against progressive pop culture discourse in the news aligns closely with the broader opposition to identity politics that has dominated conservative rhetoric in the proverbial "culture wars" and animates the movement's pushback to calls for increased diversity. In this context, the loss of power and status may seem minor or slight—a small reduction in the on- and off-screen representation of men, whites, heterosexuals, and cisgendered people to make room for traditionally marginalized groups— yet this cultural symbolism is clearly meaningful to those who are motivated to go online and express their outrage at journalists who cover TV, movies, and celebrities. Moreover, as seen in chapter 3, the credo in conservatism that "politics are downstream from culture"—reinforced over and over in right-wing news commentary and pop culture analysis—lends an acute sense of urgency to battles over Hollywood that ideologically aligned audiences carry forward on social media and beyond.

To this point, some of the most aggrieved online reactions tend to come from those who deliberately seek out such coverage for the sole purpose of loudly objecting to it. As discussed in chapter 2, left-oriented pop culture commentary that focuses on identity and representation is typically aimed at an ideologically like-minded audience, and journalists often assume a level of mutual sympathy when making prescriptive claims about the need for progressive change in the entertainment industry. Yet, at the same time, this circle of ideological agreement and reinforcement is constantly disrupted by "trolls," as they are often characterized, who are looking for a fight. One staff journalist for a feminist news site noted being perplexed by this phenomenon:

It's bizarre. It's something that I wasn't expecting when I started working at [the site], just how many people take time out of their day to come to a website and tell us that racism and sexism and intersectionality of the two aren't real. . . . I've often wondered, where are these people coming from? Like, why are you looking at [this site] if this kind of news angers you?

A freelancer who writes for another feminist website, among other outlets, likewise remarked:

A lot of times when I would get someone writing me and saying, "This is bullshit, I don't believe any of this," it is someone I wonder about, I don't really know maybe how they found this, because they seem much more outside of the group. It seems like I imagine you might have gone there just to be angry about it, because I don't see it as being your place.

Chapter 6 will explore this question of the psychology of "hate clicks" and "hate shares," focusing on audience social media practices that use journalism at the pop culture–politics nexus as building blocks for personal political expression. Here it is important to note that such migrations of angry commenters are often attributable in part to the activities of oppositional news outlets, which typically link to progressive-oriented articles and news sources as a means of lambasting and shaming them. As chapter 3 showed, right-wing entertainment journalism frequently uses its left-wing counterpart as the basis for reactionary critiques that emphasize grievance over perceived bias in the news media as well as in Hollywood. When a piece gets "called out" on a conservative site, it becomes an instant target for online backlash from members of that site's audience. As one left-oriented journalist recounted, "I'll be on Twitter, and I will have linked a piece, and I'll get a kind of normal set of responses. And suddenly, I'll get like two hundred just eviscerating responses, and I'll think, 'Oh, OK, so I'm on Breitbart.' You can almost time it to the minute that it happens."

Another journalist noted how these hostile online comments from audiences tend to closely follow the arguments laid out by conservative news commentators: "When you get a big response, it gets posted somewhere on some site or blog with an agenda. And there will be talking points in that post, and that's the kind of feedback you get." As an example, she pointed to an article that criticized comedian Ricky Gervais for mocking left-wing activism in Hollywood while hosting the 2020 Golden Globes.

After being posted "on kind of an alt-right website," she noted, "the response was angry that I had somehow sided with elitist Hollywood. . . . It's almost taking the stance of the Fox News idea of 'we're liberal media, elite media,' that kind of thing."

As her account underscores, much of the negative online response to progressive pop culture journalism can be understood as a direct outgrowth of broader anti-media rhetoric within the conservative movement, which, she stressed, had been "ramped up with the Trump administration" and its labeling of the news media as the "enemy of the people."[13] In other words, political attacks on the press from right-wing politicians and news commentators establish a rhetorical script of sorts that like-minded audiences adopt in their personal emails, comments, and social media posts. Such a pattern cuts across the entirety of the journalistic field; this commentator, for instance, mentioned how she receives similarly negative online responses to political columns that discuss both pop-culture and non-pop-culture-related topics. However, it is important to note the degree to which entertainment journalism is now firmly entrenched in these broader partisan battles, waged at the citizen level of online expression and outrage as well as at the level of media institutions that provide the marching orders.

This dynamic of anti-news-media backlash, coupled with the backlash against identity politics discourse, is rather specific to audiences on the right. However, that is not to say that angry, politicized online reactions to entertainment journalism do not sometimes flow from the opposite direction. As noted in chapter 3, professionals at right-wing organizations tend to assume that they are speaking exclusively to their ideologically aligned target audience and that left-wing audiences (including those in the entertainment industry) are simply absent. However, when conservative criticism of pop culture appears in more mainstream news outlets that left-wing audiences are likely to encounter, the social media backlash can be similarly intense. For example, a conservative film critic who publishes in a national news outlet that is generally popular with a liberal demographic described how he has come to expect social media outrage from the left for his pieces. Highlighting one of his columns that mocked the Marxist-inspired satirical film *Sorry to Bother You*, he remarked: "I won't say it was intentionally and solely designed to annoy the 'Bernie Bro,' socialist 'rose Twitter' left, but it was very much written with that in mind. And I know how badly that annoyed a lot of people, because I heard from every single one of them about how I was a terrible tool of imperial aggression."

Clearly, heated online backlash against politically oriented pop culture coverage is a phenomenon that traverses partisan lines. Although left-leaning journalists may be subjected to it more regularly than their right-leaning counterparts, it remains unclear to what extent this represents is a substantive difference in the expression of left versus right partisan anger online or if it is instead a consequence of diverging audience consumption patterns for pop culture and politics coverage. However, the fact that conservative audiences seem more eager to seek out entertainment news and commentary from across the ideological divide as a basis for venting political frustration and grievance indicates something important about how this group approaches journalism itself, alongside Hollywood, as a "culture war" battlefield.[14] As we have seen, these expressions tend to closely track with broader conservative rhetoric that vilifies media and cultural institutions in the same breath for their perceived insurgent dominance and the threats that they are seen to pose to a traditional social order.

"Every Horrible Gendered Word That You Can Imagine": Contending with Online Hate and Harassment

Among more extremist segments of the reactionary right-wing audience, this acrimonious online response can resemble the very worst forms of online hate and harassment that have become all too common across the internet. As scholar Caitlin E. Lawson discusses in her study of racist and sexist attacks on actress Leslie Jones on Twitter, these patterns stem from the vulnerabilities of digital platforms as well as from "the alt-right's rise and the mainstreaming of explicitly racist, misogynistic behaviors."[15] It is alarming, if not altogether surprising, that journalists who discuss issues of racism, sexism, homophobia, transphobia, and more in their coverage of pop culture routinely become targets of this hate themselves.

To be clear, this kind of personal attack should be distinguished from even the most vociferous online backlash against journalistic commentary explored above, as it crosses a line into hate speech and in some cases threats of material harm that can have legal repercussions. However, such verbal abuse aimed at journalists appears to be rooted in the same emotional intensity around matters of identity and morality that inspires more seemingly benign forms of online outrage. As one journalist figured it, "when people like something and they see someone critique it, it feels like a personal attack to them. So they extend that feeling to you." Another similarly remarked that "you become the enemy" when making an argument in a work of journalism that directly challenges the beliefs of those "who feel very strongly and very emotional" about a certain celebrity or object of entertainment fandom.

It seems that anyone who steps into the contentious terrain of identity politics in pop culture coverage is likely to experience some form of online harassment and abuse. However, journalists who are members of marginalized groups are especially vulnerable. As journalism scholar Silvio Waisbord notes, "rising numbers of online attacks against journalists have been documented globally. Female, minority reporters and journalists who cover issues interwoven with right-wing identity anchors have been primary targets."[16] One progressive-leaning entertainment journalist who reported being the subject of doxing-style trolling campaigns, in which his personal information was posted online to encourage harassment en masse, described this as an "occupational hazard that didn't exist twenty five years ago . . . the price you pay for being able to have really instant feedback" on the internet. Yet he maintained that "women or people of color have it much, much worse than I've had it" as a white male journalist. To this point, a female film critic who frequently writes on gender issues explained:

> It sometimes feels like being a woman who expresses opinions on the internet means that you have entered into a war zone and are being attacked. There is a sort of barrage of abuse and anger that comes with doing this kind of writing. . . . You kind of can't write anything as a woman on the internet, especially anything about feminism, without people deciding that everything about you is fair game for criticism. And that can be really, really hard to deal with.

One reason journalists make such easy targets for online misogyny, racism, and other forms of hate is that they are public figures whose identities are on full display next to every byline. Sometimes merely publishing with a female name can trigger gender-based harassment from angry "troll" audiences, regardless of the content of a given piece. One female journalist lamented, "I've gotten really bizarre, politically tinged responses to writing about movies with no political interest, just like 'you're so dumb.' . . . There are definitely people who react because of their own political commitments to a woman who's a film critic. And I hate to think of it that way, but that's how it's kind of become."

When journalists from marginalized groups publicly voice opinions on hot-button issues of identity politics in their work, they become even more susceptible to hate-based online attacks from those who are enraged by such discourse. A freelance pop culture critic underscored this point:

> As a visible brown woman, it's just easier to attack me than it might be to attack other people. . . . I think a lot of it is that I'm writing about identity politics and I am a marginalized person, so that's not something that I've missed. . . . In the freelance community, my writer friends who get the most hate are the ones who are black, the ones who are trans.

Highlighting the extent to which this online abuse becomes hurtfully personal in nature, she noted responses to a piece criticizing the Netflix series *Insatiable* for its handling of body size issues: "A common theme in the fatphobia comments were like, 'This sounds like it was written by a bitter fat person' and stuff like that. So it's like more personal digs than it is talking about the subject matter itself."

When discussing her reaction to such vile comments, she stressed that it is "a given with anonymity on Twitter and social media" and that she has become used to it as a longtime internet user, to the point where "most of the comments don't really strike me as actually personally offensive." However, she pointed to one particularly chilling incident in which she received a rape threat on social media after publishing a piece that criticized a true-crime TV show for glorifying serial killers: "I think because there was a threat of violence, it kind of hit deeper. . . . That really just struck a chord of, like, wow, someone would actually do this, take the time to send me a message threatening rape because they didn't like something I wrote, and that's pretty scary." Another female journalist shared a similar story involving the online responses she received to an article praising the toy company Mattel for debuting a new gender-neutral doll: "Man, did I get so much nastiness. I got threats of rape. I got people calling me every horrible gendered word that you can imagine in the book."

Unfortunately, this experience of receiving threats of sexual violence has become all too common for women on the internet, as was dramatically demonstrated in the infamous #GamerGate campaign of 2014 that targeted feminist video games journalists, among other groups of women, with intensive abuse and harassment. Referring to #GamerGate as "emblematic of an ongoing backlash against women and their use of technology and participation in public life," scholar Adrienne Massanari draws attention to how the design of many social media platforms supports and encourages this kind of toxic behavior, not only in terms of user anonymity but also in terms of platform governance, content policies, and algorithmic systems that reward certain forms of attention-grabbing activity.[17] Although the #GamerGate controversy brought a wave of mainstream attention to the problem of online hate and harassment and spurred activism that pressured internet companies to combat it more stringently, years later it remains an everyday reality for women and members of minority groups who spend any amount of time communicating online.

Within this fraught digital landscape, journalists from marginalized groups whose work strikes at the very heart of the underlying issues of sexism and racism—and whose pop culture subject matter often seems to catalyze the most intensive forms of emotional response—find themselves on the front lines of what Massanari terms "toxic technocultures."[18] Having a professional need, as discussed above, to monitor social media and other online feedback channels to track cultural trends, find material for stories, and assess the performance and impact of their work, these journalists can hardly afford to avoid the source of the problem altogether. However, many have developed strategies to minimize the threat of online hate and harassment in their day-to-day lives as working journalists.[19]

In addition to forwarding particularly egregious cases of abuse to security teams or law enforcement, one popular option is the use of content filters that automatically block messages that are detected to be offensive. Another strategy, cited by a staff writer for a feminist blog site, is to foster community governance systems whereby audience members can actively participate in content monitoring within the news outlet itself: "We have a really great community of commenters who kind of self-police to keep the trolls out. . . . We have a whole separate folder of comments that are flagged as hate speech, and that folder has so many comments that are just flagged as upsetting or offensive by the other readers."

When it comes to the more chaotic world of social media platforms, it is a near mandate in the contemporary journalism industry to have an active presence for the purpose of strategic self-branding,[20] yet one journalist of color noted how he removed his Twitter account from his news site's author page, "just because people would be kind of racist" toward him on the platform upon seeing his photo. While this step alone may not prevent abusive tweets, it adds a buffer zone of sorts that can serve as a deterrent for quick-triggered trolling reactions from visitors to his employer's site.

Beyond these more logistical strategies, many journalists have simply learned over time to tune out hateful and offensive online comments as a means of self-preservation. An entertainment critic for a left-leaning news and culture site explained:

> At a certain point, you have to decide whose opinion you're going to care about and whose you're not, because it's just physically impossible to let everyone's opinion weigh the same when you're doing this kind of public writing on a regular basis. And I was able to decide pretty early on that I was not going to care too much what people on the far right and the alt-right thought about what I was writing. . . . The choice I've made has been to never engage with harassment that people send me.

Another remarked that while he is "always tempted to respond, I think it's just healthier not to. . . . I don't want to be goaded into an argument with some random fascist fan online." Although such dismissals may serve as a helpful means of self-care, researchers Seth C. Lewis, Rodrigo Zamith, and Mark Coddington point out that it can also have the effect of alienating targeted journalists from their audience and ultimately eroding the audience–journalist relationship in consequential ways.[21]

This strategy of conscious avoidance seems especially pertinent for left-oriented commentators who constantly contend with reactionary racist and sexist attacks associated with the online alt-right movement. However, some right-wing journalists also noted a degree of abstention from social media and other online feedback mechanisms, as they, too, can become targets of internet ire. As one conservative columnist bluntly put it:

> I'm sure there's shit out there that people bitch about me and think I'm history's greatest monster. I just couldn't care less. . . . As far as combing for emails or trolling for comments or surfing social media for mentions of myself, I just don't. I'm just generally comfortable enough that I don't care what other people think of me.

Of course, this more nonchalant kind of dismissal must be understood in context—as a white male, he is not nearly as vulnerable to the kind of identity-based attacks that industry colleagues from marginalized groups face on a routine basis.

Despite navigating a digital minefield of hate and harassment, female and minority journalists often stress that they are not dissuaded by this online abuse and remain committed to voicing their perspectives in public through their work, no matter how ugly the reaction can be. One female journalist commented that seeing hateful social media and email comments "doesn't discourage me because it's just kind of run-of-the-mill sexism. . . . There are some people you're never going to be able to convince, and that's fine." Another commentator who often addresses sexism in her pop culture coverage similarly maintained that "the flood of negative attention that comes in" as a consequence does not affect her resolve: "Being a woman on the internet, it's a rough place, so you just kind of have to ignore it and realize that you can't win them all, you can't change everybody's mind, and just keep on writing the things that feel important and that feel true." Accounts such as these suggest that although the problem of online harassment and abusive social media messages can be a source of frustration—and sometimes danger—for journalists on the front lines of the "culture wars," it does not necessarily pose an existential threat to their work. Rather, they appear to largely accept it as an unfortunate reality of the contemporary digital landscape and find ways to navigate around it while keeping their sanity in check.

"You Start Making Decisions That Are Somewhat Self-Protective": The Specter of Chilling Effects

However, one critic suggested that this constant barrage of hateful online backlash can compel journalists to deliberately avoid certain stories and topics to quell the tide of abuse. As an African American woman who directly confronts racism and sexism in her pop culture columns, she noted being especially susceptible to the very worst forms of online bigotry and harassment:

Eventually, I think doing this job and existing online long enough, particularly if you're a woman or a person of color, you start making decisions that are somewhat self-protective. Because you know the sorts of things that are going to end up putting you in a situation where you're asking your editor, "Hey, can you monitor my mentions just to make sure no one's trying to, like, publish my phone number or my social security number?" which is a pretty awful position to be in sometimes.

As an example of this self-protective practice, she pointed to a time when she was considering publishing a critical piece on the 2019 film *Joker*, which had become a lightning rod for political controversy even before its theatrical release due to its portrayal of masculine violence as well its vocal support from certain comic book fan communities. She explained part of the reason she didn't end up writing the article on *Joker*:

> I knew I was just going to be deluged with harassment if I did. And in fact, I made one tweet [about the film] and then spent the rest of the day basically asking one of my editors if they would just check on my mentions to make sure that no one was either threatening me or threatening to dox me or swat me, or any of the sort of extreme measures that folks will sometimes go to if you say something publicly that they disagree with.

It remains unclear exactly how common it is for a journalist to kill a piece in this fashion to evade online hate and harassment. Yet the story powerfully illustrates the negative impact such abuse can have on the production of journalism that tackles hot-button cultural issues in the age of social media and instant online audience feedback.

This potential for compelling self-censorship is ultimately the most significant problem that internet harassment poses for journalists, apart from the possibility of "trolls" actually following through on their odious threats of harm. Indeed, the issue has begun to receive a significant amount of attention in the field of journalism studies. As scholars Michelle Ferrier and Nisha Garud-Patkar argue, "when journalists are targets, the online harassment takes a toll on the news enterprise. The chilling effect on individual journalists and journalistic lines of inquiry can lead to the silencing of diverse voices in the media."[22] Similarly, Waisbord warns that these attacks amount to a form of "mob censorship," illustrating how "just as it multiplies opportunities for speech, [the] internet also expands censorship by offering platforms for ordinary citizens to police journalism through violent words and deeds."[23]

Although this problem is particularly acute for members of marginalized groups who become targets of racist and sexist extremism due to the nature of their identities as well as their journalism, the sense that social media animosity can create a chilling effect on the industry is shared by some conservatives as well. An entertainment reporter for a right-wing news site likened the situation to broader concerns within conservative circles over "cancel culture," in which speakers with controversial viewpoints are seen to be pressured into silence by the censure of the internet mob. As he explained regarding his own journalistic output:

> I do think that it has become much harder to express a more nuanced view. And I think cancel culture and the promulgation of social media have made that possible. . . . When there are more voices out there, that means there's going to be a lot of shouting and trying to tear other people down. . . . These are the kinds of things that drown out the nuance of the conversation.

Certainly, the kind of online backlash cited here is not nearly as severe as the threats of harm and hateful slurs that other journalists report receiving. Nevertheless, his comments further signal the concrete impact that online audience feedback channels can have on the work of journalists who enter the fray of today's heated "culture wars." As he suggested, the threat of being "canceled" on platforms such as Twitter—which, beyond critical and angry responses, can involve coordinated calls for a person to be fired from their job—can potentially pressure journalists into self-censoring and holding back from saying certain things that raise the audience's ire. At the same time, as seen in chapter 4, impassioned online reactions are the currency of today's digital news business, driving editorial interest in covering pop culture and its political controversies in the first place. It thus seems that industry professionals are tasked with striking a difficult balancing act, in which the goal is to get audiences emotionally worked up enough to engage and partic-ipate in online conversation but not so worked up to the point of becoming abusive or threatening. In rigorous pursuit of the former, journalists working in the impassioned spaces of the pop culture–politics nexus are fated to con-stantly contend with the latter.

Conclusion

This chapter has shown how social media and other online feedback mechanisms have become a constitutive—and at times destructive—force in the production of politically oriented entertainment journalism. Although this kind of reporting and commentary far predates the internet and social media (as discussed in the historical narrative of chapter 1), its current it-eration is a full-fledged product of the hybrid media system,[24] in which online discussion of pop culture trends and controversies becomes a major part of the story that professional journalists cover as well as a barometer of how that coverage is received as it filters back into the digital conversation. Industry members extract many useful and valuable things from monitoring social media and other forms of online feedback—not the least of which is an entire area of reportage stemming from the "outrage cycles" powered by impassioned amateur fans and online activists—yet these two-way digital communication channels also pose numerous risks. Among them is the problem of unrepresentativeness, as online commenting tends to skew toward the most vocal, and often the most extreme, segments of the audience and can thus distort journalists' perception of both public opinion and the public reception of their own work.

This tendency toward the extreme in digital communication also contributes to the problem of abuse and harassment toward industry professionals, which is at best a nuisance that must be navigated around and at worst a driver of journalistic self-censorship to avoid the wrath of the "trolls." The fact that hostile and threatening online speech is so often aimed at journalists who are women and people of color, as well as those who address issues of racism, sexism, and other forms of prejudice in their work, highlights the danger inherent in publicly challenging traditional social hierarchies at a time when hate has gained a powerful and vastly underregulated digital megaphone.

Although many of the dynamics explored in this chapter apply to the journalistic field as a whole, they are especially pertinent for understanding the professional practices of entertainment reporters and commentators who are tasked with covering some of the most passionately discussed subject matter on the internet. Indeed, many of the news cycles and politically charged controversies explored throughout this book would seemingly not exist apart from the "conversation" on social media and other networked digital discussion spaces, and the journalists who cover them are keenly aware of the need to keep constant watch on the latest fan community outrage or "cancel culture" debate that erupts online as well as the need to make an impact on these discussions through their work, all while navigating the potential minefields of "toxic technocultures." The fact that pop culture issues and controversies in the news catalyze some of the most heated—and hateful—forms of online political speech further demonstrates their key significance in today's public discourse, in which cleavages of social and cultural identity have risen to newfound prominence. Chapter 6 will examine how entertainment news content is used as raw material for personal political expression and activism as it is shared and discussed on social media platforms such as Twitter. As we shift focus from the perspectives of news professionals to those of engaged members of their audience, we will also have the opportunity to explore how journalism at the pop culture–politics nexus is made meaningful in the minds of the public.

6

Pop Culture News as a Bridge to Politics?

Exploring the Audience Perspective

This chapter turns attention to the perspectives of audiences who engage online with journalism at the intersection of pop culture and politics. Their firsthand accounts help illuminate not only how this news is consumed in day-to-day contexts but also how—and why—it is shared and discussed on social media as part of a broader online public discourse around these issues. As stressed in preceding chapters, social media is now deeply integrated into the logics of contemporary journalistic production, and news outlets are conscious of the need to be a part of the "conversation" on major digital platforms such as Twitter. Research has also found that news audiences are most likely to post comments in response to "controversial stories . . . about high-profile public affairs topics,"[1] which further suggests how news coverage of controversy in pop culture functions as a magnet for online interactivity and engagement. By examining the experiences of Twitter users who share and discuss entertainment news that addresses hot-button political issues, we can get a feel for the texture of the "conversation" around this type of journalism, which both supplements and expands on the observations of industry members who produce it.

To be clear, the Twitter users selected for the research spotlighted in this chapter are not meant to be representative of the entire spectrum of the audience for this news. Rather, they provide a small but valuable window into the thoughts and actions of some of the most highly engaged audience members who actively participate and help shape its circulation in the digital information landscape.[2] This audience-side perspective, albeit limited, is nonetheless useful for exploring one of the central questions that surrounds journalism at the pop culture–politics nexus: how it might provide audiences with an accessible gateway or bridge to the political sphere. Later in this chapter, this key question will be addressed in considerable detail, in the process sketching a "bridge to politics" theory that is more complex than such a simple formula might suggest. Before doing so, however, it is first necessary to gain a sense

Pop Culture, Politics, and the News. Joel Penney, Oxford University Press. © Oxford University Press 2022.
DOI: 10.1093/oso/9780197557587.003.0007

of how the engaged audience approaches the political content of entertainment journalism, as well as how the audience members situate it within the
context of their broader news consumption and sharing practices. As will be
explored, this journalism functions not only as a discursive link between the
cultural and political spheres but also as a springboard for personal political
expression and interaction online. The fact that engaged audiences experience and act upon pop culture news content as a "real" and consequential
form of political discourse—if not always one that is seen as wholly positive
for democracy—has important implications for understanding its complicated role in broader civic life.

"The Problem with the 'Hamilton' Movie"? Four Stories of Audience Engagement

To better understand how audiences use pop culture news content to communicate about political issues on social media, we begin with four stories
that illustrate the broad range of this activity, all stemming from the same
journalistic point of origin. In July 2020, CNN published "The Problem with
the 'Hamilton' Movie," an opinion piece written by contributor Ed Morales.[3]
In the article, Morales argues that the film, adapted from the hit stage musical
beloved by many for its ostensibly progressive multiculturalism, is in fact "at
odds with Black Lives Matter's strident call for radical change to an America
where the legacy of white supremacy lives on." Specifically, Morales criticizes
Hamilton for avoiding the portrayal of African slaves during the American
Revolutionary period, even while it features African American performers
in the roles of white politicians who were slaveholders. Published amid a
wave of antiracist activism sparked by George Floyd's notorious killing at the
hands of police, the article is one of many that sought to reassess the treatment of race in the entertainment industry as part of a "racial reckoning"
throughout American society. In this case, the CNN contributor's critique of
Hamilton's racial politics—published to coincide with the film's high-profile
debut on the Disney Plus streaming service—became a flashpoint for discussion and opinion expression on social media.

Grace (audience member names in this discussion are pseudonyms), one
of the audience members who linked to the article on Twitter, had been eagerly searching for something like it to appear online. She described how
"through Google News, I was kind of watching for some essay pieces on

Hamilton. . . . I was interested to see if someone was going to write about it." Prior to finding the CNN piece on Google News, Grace, who is an Asian American in her thirties, had posted her own criticism of the film's handling of race on her Facebook, Instagram, and Twitter accounts: "I just felt so unsettled by it because of *Hamilton*'s ideologies and how it felt to me like a really big mismatch for some of the social movements going on presently. So I was just interested in that, and I wanted to say something." However, she found it somewhat difficult to express her complicated views on the subject in her own words, since "*Hamilton* is kind of a puzzling experience to me. . . . I liked it as a work of art, but then I was so disturbed by it." Furthermore, she was concerned about how some of her online friends who were *Hamilton* fans were reacting to her posts, noting, "I'm pretty sure I alienated a lot of people by writing what I did," and "quite a few people deleted me on Facebook" as a result. She then decided to look online for a journalistic piece that could more effectively communicate her critical perspective and better situate the film "in the context of the current political moment" of ongoing Black Lives Matter protests.

As Grace figured it, the CNN piece was a useful, ready-made substitute for her own social media commentary, having the added advantage of being developed by a professional journalist: "I already kind of wrote my own mini op-ed through Twitter . . . [but] I thought, what if this were article length? But I guess I didn't have motivation enough to put in that time. But then somebody else did it, and I thought, 'Oh, great.' And then that's why I shared that." In addition to its longer length, Grace also valued the piece for its eloquence and thoughtfulness, which she felt captured her political viewpoints better than she could on her own: "I felt the article articulated some of the things that I had been thinking but wasn't able to express in the same way, or able to express it all. . . . I thought, yeah, that's kind of what I was trying to get at, but I didn't have the resources in my mind to be able to do it." By posting the article link on Twitter, Grace effectively outsourced the work of her personal political expression. Moreover, she hoped that by using the CNN journalist's "more intelligent" words in place of her own, she could better navigate the inevitable pushback from social media connections who disagreed with her views on both *Hamilton* and racial justice issues more broadly.

Grace's story has some striking parallels with that of Keisha, who also retweeted the CNN article in solidarity with its critical political message. However, Keisha, an African American in her twenties, found the piece not from online searches but rather from her father, who frequently emails news stories to her and other family members. The family had recently sat down together to watch *Hamilton* on Disney Plus, but opinions were split. Some enjoyed the film, but Keisha and her father found themselves "on the same page" in objecting to its uplifting message of American racial progress. After discussing their shared reactions, he sent her the CNN article shortly thereafter. She explained:

> I decided to post it on Twitter because I know a lot of people love the play, and it was a huge thing that everybody was talking about. I was really excited when I originally was going to finally watch [the film] for the first time. And because I was so disappointed, and I knew there were a lot of *Hamilton* fans, and just with the political climate and everything that's going on, I thought I'd just post a different perspective about the article, as an African American female, that kind of expressed and backed up some of my opinions.

Unlike Grace, Keisha declined to post her own social media comments on the subject, but she similarly used the CNN article link as a proxy for her own opinion expression:

> I didn't really want to post my opinion without an article that can kind of back up that other people feel this way, too, because there are a lot of internet trolls who will kind of come for your life. And I'm really not trying to deal with that. . . . I didn't want my opinion to be misconstrued or taken out of context because of the limited number of characters that I had. So I felt that posting the article, and the article addressing multiple points of how I felt, was a better way to kind of display my opinion.

Thus, sharing the professional commentary from CNN enabled Keisha not only to articulate her views in more depth but also to lend them a degree of credibility and legitimacy that comes from being validated or "backed up" by a high-profile news outlet.

After posting the link, she was mostly pleased with the resulting online conversations that she sparked with friends who were the targets of her efforts: "Two of them said, 'Wow, thank you for sharing your opinion. I never thought about [*Hamilton*] like that, you know, thank you for sharing. I didn't have that experience with the show.' And all the people who did respond were Caucasian females." This outcome fit well with the overall goals of her Twitter account, which she described as "to educate and to positively impact people who are on my social media." In this case, pointing her white friends to a journalistic critique of *Hamilton*'s racial politics helped them to consider the musical in a new light, as well as exposing them to a broader set of perspectives on US race relations that Keisha felt they would benefit from engaging with.

However, not everyone who retweeted the CNN piece agreed with the viewpoints of the author and wished to amplify and spread its message. While Keisha and Grace used it to stand in for their own opinion expression and fend off social media backlash, others linked to the piece as a means of directly challenging its content. Juan, a Hispanic male in his thirties, encountered the article while scrolling through the Microsoft News app on his phone and immediately sought to make his displeasure known: "I felt a strong reaction to it and decided to opine about it on Twitter, basically posting the initial article with the turn that said, 'this is why we can't have nice things.'" As he explained, the strong negative response that he had to the piece was born of his personal fandom for *Hamilton*:

> [*Hamilton* was] something that was a really neat musical achievement ... and I do enjoy history and thought it was a neat way to be able to express history and provide perspectives, and also to do different things in terms of the casting, you know, primarily minorities and people of color. So that was something where I probably have a soft spot in my heart for it.

In Juan's view, the critical commentary published by CNN "failed to acknowledge a lot of the good" that he himself saw in *Hamilton*, politically as well as aesthetically, and he remarked that "for [the author] to bring those kinds of political topics into it probably offended me more than it probably would have offended most."

By affixing his comment "this is why we can't have nice things" to the article link, Juan made clear that he was disparaging the author's views rather than endorsing them. Moreover, his comment expressed a "sense of cynicism," as he put it, about this type of journalistic commentary more broadly, which he characterized as "attempts to basically cast political aspersions against all aspects of life, including pop culture." He reasoned:

> I don't necessarily need a piece of art to reflect my own values. And it can still be a good piece of art that maybe conflicts with my own personal values, whether political values or social values. And so for me, I do find it

jarring when it seems that there's a continual attempt to draw a political line on that and to make sure that art needs to resonate with your values.

Here Juan's frustration with the perceived overpoliticization of entertainment by news commentators on the left dovetails with familiar arguments made by many on the right (discussed in chapter 3), even though his personal politics lean more Democratic. A bit later, this chapter will explore how the backlash against "cancel culture" animates pop culture news engagement on both sides of the partisan political divide.

For now, a more fundamental question remains: if Juan objected so strongly to CNN's critique of *Hamilton* as politically and racially problematic, why did he choose to draw attention to it by linking to it on his Twitter account? As he explained:

> I would say it's sharing it as a talking point in hopes to have a discussion about it. . . . It's for somebody who maybe follows me and has a different perspective from mine can also contribute to it, but also to see if it does resonate with people, you know. It helps me in processing the piece of content as well and trying to build perspective around that.

In other words, Juan sought to spark conversation about the broader controversy and hear a range of different reactions and opinions, not just for the sake of social interaction itself but also for his own personal sense-making around the issue.

From a civic perspective, we can identify this outcome as an example of deliberative discourse in the public sphere, which is frequently upheld by scholars as a valued democratic ideal.[4] From an economic perspective, however, such conversation holds a different kind of value. As discussed in chapter 4, news organizations operating in today's digital landscape have a strong financial incentive to shape journalistic content for maximum social media engagement, and journalists are keenly aware of the need for their work to be a relevant part of the "conversation" on platforms such as Twitter. Within this framework of the attention economy,[5] critical discussion of a piece on social media is just as beneficial for a news outlet's bottom line as positive praise. In Juan's story, we can observe the role of strong negative emotions such as outrage and offense in fueling audience shares and comments around works of news commentary,[6] all of which helps expand its reach and attending advertising revenue. Indeed, he noted that he is most

likely to retweet news articles that "resonate" with him, "in a positive or negative sense," signaling that sharing the CNN piece that he so emphatically
disagreed with is part of a broader pattern of engaging with journalism to
express indignation as well as appreciation. The fact that his offended feelings
stemmed from a deeply held fandom toward the object of critique is important to note, as it highlights the role of pop culture in arousing the passions
of news audiences and sparking engagement and conversation that serve the
industry's economic needs.

However, impassioned fandom is not the only source of strong emotional
response toward journalism at the intersection of entertainment and politics. Debra, a white woman in her sixties, admitted that she had not even
seen *Hamilton*, either the stage musical or the film, before retweeting the
CNN link. Unlike Juan's, her objection to the views expressed in the article
had nothing to do with a love of *Hamilton* or a defense of its racial politics
as being sufficiently progressive. Rather, as a conservative and enthusiastic
Trump supporter, Debra saw the piece as a prime example of the left's out-of-
control "cancel culture":

> [I shared it] as a way to illustrate, "see, these people are never going to be
> happy." . . . I just felt like, oh my God, I mean, so now *Hamilton* isn't good
> enough. It seemed to be celebrated before, now it is being condemned. And
> I'm not sure what happened exactly . . . it just seems like it's very strict about
> what is acceptable or what is to be criticized.

She went on to clarify that by linking to the article, she was "not necessarily
trying to make a point about *Hamilton*, but it just rubbed me the wrong way
that now the movies aren't even good enough for these people, these critics."
Her sense of aggravation thus had less to do with pop culture itself than with
how it is discussed and evaluated in the news media, with her antipathy
aimed squarely at left-oriented cultural critics whom she saw as redrawing
the lines of social and ideological acceptability in narrower and narrower
ways to the point where "it's getting to be ridiculous."

Like Juan's story, Debra's illustrates how online engagement with pop
culture news commentary can be catalyzed by negative as well as positive
reactions and among hostile as well as receptive audiences. As noted in
chapter 4, journalists in the field are well aware of the phenomena of "hate
clicks" and "hate shares" as a reality of today's digital news landscape, with
one even suggesting that the best way to ensure the popularity and profitably

of a piece is to enrage the audience, because "hate clicks are still clicks." Indeed, we can note the irony in the fact that by providing a data point of Twitter engagement, Debra effectively contributed to CNN's financial health as well as the journalist's industry standing, even though she strongly disapproved of both.

However, focusing on industry dynamics alone misses something important about the act of sharing journalism on social media as a means of chastising or ridiculing it. Debra, for one, characterized herself as "an advocate on Twitter for certain views," and unlike Juan, who emphasized the goal of sparking deliberative conversation with his peers, she was forthright in her motive of "using Twitter to shape opinion." Her retweet of the CNN article, framed in context as a kind of public shaming of the journalistic trend it is meant to symbolize, can thus be understood as a form of political advocacy and an attempt at peer persuasion. In making the argument "see, these people are never going to be happy," Debra sought to advance the conservative cause of countering the perceived "cancel culture" of the mainstream news media, along with the broader left-wing identity politics that typically fuels its cultural critiques. Underscoring the sizable political significance of this kind of right-wing backlash against progressive cultural discourse, she at one point remarked, "I voted for Donald Trump, and part of it was because I thought he would fight this politically correct culture." For Debra, attacking the "political correctness" of CNN journalists on social media was part of an influence campaign to promote her ideology as well as her favorite politician.

These four stories, taken together, signal the range and complexity of audience engagement with entertainment journalism that addresses political issues. Even though Grace, Keisha, Juan, and Debra all performed the exact same act of digital news sharing, they did so for a variety of reasons and from contrasting ideological perspectives. However, these stories all share one important common element: the audience's use of pop culture coverage as a starting point to engage in acts of political expression and interaction. We have already considered that from an industry perspective, such activity is highly desired and sought after, regardless of whether it springs from positive or negative emotion. Within this framework, sharing journalism as a proxy for one's own opinion expression, as in the case of Grace and Keisha, or as a means of critiquing it and pointing out its perceived flaws, as in the case of Juan and Debra, is equally valuable for the bottom line of for-profit digital news outlets that deliberately tailor coverage for social media attention. Yet beyond this crucial point, to which chapter 7 will return, what can the audience's online engagement with journalism at the pop culture–politics nexus tell us about its broader role in contemporary civic life?

Engaging with Entertainment News as Political News

To begin unpacking this question, it is important to reiterate how members of the engaged audience see coverage of entertainment as being a worthy basis for their own political expression and commentary. Whether they consume it sympathetically or resentfully, they take it seriously enough to act upon it as consequential political discourse. This is clear, for instance, in the pattern of linking to pop culture news articles as a means of highlighting disagreement and dissent. Such a practice can be considered one of the most intensive forms of what journalism scholar Jennifer Rauch terms "resisting the news," which describes how audiences absorb popular critiques of the mainstream news media and position themselves as "opposing it, withstanding the effect of it, refraining or abstaining from it," as they align themselves with alternative sources of news.[7] Moreover, by putting this journalism into the spotlight of ideological critique, audience members inherently make the case for its political importance.

This actively resistive practice appears to be especially common among conservative audiences, for whom vocal backlash against the perceived leftist biases of mainstream news media—and especially the "cancel culture" of identity-politics-infused cultural criticism—is a core animating practice. Notably, some self-identified liberals follow this pattern as well, such as one audience member who shared the above-noted CNN piece on *Hamilton* because "I'm very concerned about what I call illiberalism coming out of the left. . . . I kind of am in a group of people who consider ourselves very liberal, but we're very, very concerned with some things coming out of the left that you consider not liberal."

However, this sort of dissenting critique on the part of the audience can also come from other ideological directions. For example, a trans woman who frequently tweets about issues facing her community explained that she linked to an article about *Harry Potter* author J. K. Rowling's controversial public comments on trans rights because she felt it was dangerously charitable toward Rowling's views: "I read the article and I was extremely disappointed. . . . I then posted it with my own viewpoint about how the article was just rehashed anti-trans propaganda. . . . This article riled me up, so I was happy to post it with my opinion about how terrible it was and how harmful it was to my community." As she explained, this kind of resistant media activism via Twitter is a common routine: "I would say that how often I tweet articles like this comes down to how many transphobic articles are written in a month. If I read an anti-trans article that I know to contain falsehoods, I will definitely post that with my opinion." Crucially, she made no distinction between stories about pop culture celebrities such as Rowling and other types of news and commentary that she saw as being transphobic. In her view, both were politically problematic in terms of giving anti-trans views "an air of authenticity," as she put it, and she further suggested that Rowling's high-profile public status made news coverage of the comments especially dangerous for the broader transgender rights movement.

At the same time, when audience members share pop culture journalism that contains political views that they agree with, they often emphasize its potential power and influence in the public sphere. Returning to CNN's critical piece on *Hamilton*, one white male audience member in his sixties explained:

> [I shared it] because I am generally sympathetic with the Black Lives Matter movement, and like many people in America who kind of were sleepwalking before we watched George Floyd get tortured to death, it turned me into a believer. And I'm somewhat apologetic for not being more informed about it in the past and having kind of downplayed it in the past. And to try to make up some ground where I may have been lacking, I'm generally trying to support my point of view in the [2020] election by tweeting news articles that support my point of view and amplifying them with my comments.

The piece dissecting *Hamilton*'s racial politics was only one of many articles that he shared in solidarity with Black Lives Matter, but it was clearly meaningful for his online activism efforts. Again, no distinction was drawn in this context between journalism coming from the world of entertainment and journalism that covers political issues from more traditional angles. What mattered for him, rather, were the ideas and viewpoints expressed therein, which he sought to amplify on social media as means of advancing the cause of antiracism and even the electoral fortunes of the Democratic Party.

This notion of pop culture news and commentary being politically significant enough to affect the outcome of an election may seem rather far-fetched, but for some members of its audience, it is not so unreasonable. For instance, discussing a retweet of an opinion piece calling for Hollywood to confront its legacy of racial stereotyping in the wake of Black Lives Matter activism, one audience member commented: "I'm just trying to make sure that their message is spread far and wide, so that many people are made aware of what's actually going on and so that it will inspire them to go out and vote." In articulating his motive for sharing this article, he further reasoned that "pop culture tends to shape and reinforce a lot of people's views, which then goes on to reinforce how they vote."

In a parallel fashion, an audience member who shared a piece criticizing the public backlash against Rowling for her comments on trans rights commented that "as a passionate, lifelong leftie, I find cancel culture alarming and increasingly fascist. My worry is that if we start cannibalizing our own, we are going to scare away the biggest and arguably most important demographic in this country, the nonvoter. We need nonvoters if we're going to win the 2020 election." By spreading journalism that was critical of "cancel culture," she suggested, she could help counteract what she viewed as a threat to the campaign to unseat Trump, who had notably made the fight against "political correctness" into a signature issue.[8]

Of course, it is impossible to know if these particular news-sharing practices had any impact whatsoever on voting behavior in the 2020 US presidential election—or in any other context, for that matter. Moreover, the claims of these engaged audience members should be taken with a degree of caution, considering that they may feel pressure to publicly justify online actions that are often derided as ineffectual "slacktivism." Setting aside the question of the true impact of such retweeting behaviors, however, what is important to observe in these remarks is the shared belief that entertainment journalism is a legitimate and meaningful part of the broader political information environment. Whether it is used to spark two-way conversation about public issues or to attempt to influence the attitudes of peers, news at the intersection of pop culture and politics is often understood as being consequential for the latter as well as the former. The next section will further explore the audience's experience of entertainment journalism *as* political journalism by examining how audience members variably encounter it as part of their broader news consumption practices. While some find their way to news at the pop culture–politics nexus from a position of pop culture fandom, many others are drawn to it primarily out of their high level of political interest, suggesting that any firm distinction between these journalistic fields may be increasingly untenable in the minds of today's digital news audiences.

The Politics-First Audience

How, exactly, can we characterize the audience for pop culture news and commentary that address political issues? Considering the four diverging stories that opened this chapter, any broad generalization would be rather difficult to make. Moreover, the interview research presented here is not intended to be statistically representative and only includes audience members who had actively shared this news content on Twitter. Yet, even from these limited accounts, it is apparent that the audience can include people of varying ages, genders, racial and ethnic groups, and political identities. Furthermore, the most consistent shared attribute among the research participants was not any demographic characteristic at all but rather a high level of interest in politics. In fact, many of these audience members reported having a stronger interest in politics than in pop culture, with the former driving their news consumption more than the latter. This reveals an important clue about how journalism at the intersection of the two fields circulates in the broader public sphere.

For what we can call the politics-first segment of the audience, news that stems from the world of entertainment tends to have an appeal largely—and in some cases exclusively— when it overlaps with social and political issues of interest. As one audience member of this type put it:

I would say I'm not a pop culture follower purely for the entertainment value. I would say I'm specifically looking for where the political intersection happens with pop culture. . . . Pop culture in and of itself is not my interest so much as where there's a crossover or a broader impact on politics or society more broadly, that is where my interest lies.

Another, who described herself as a "ravening news junkie," explained that "with me, it's mostly politics. But I take a keen interest in anything having to do with misogyny or racism . . . so when a news story intersects with a pop culture story having to do with misogyny or racism, I'm in."

This pattern was also exhibited by some audience members on the right end of the ideological spectrum, who, as discussed in chapter 3, sometimes avoid much of contemporary pop culture altogether because of perceptions of left-wing bias. One such right-wing pop culture avoider, who had shared an opinion column from Breitbart that accused Hollywood of "reverse racism" against white male actors, remarked:

I don't have any particular preference [about Hollywood news]. If something relevant comes up, I'll tweet it, and maybe I'll include a statement like "Boycott Hollywood" or "Shun Hollywood." . . . I'm also concerned about progressivism in academia, progressivism in the arts. I mean, it's just all over the place, it cuts such a wide path of dominance. It's just so pervasive.

In other words, backlash against the entertainment industry is just one of many similar topics that he follows on right-wing sites such as Breitbart, with the overarching theme of decrying progressive identity politics serving as the connective tissue rather than any particular subject matter.

For these sorts of politics-first news audiences, coverage of the pop culture field presents opportunities to engage with perspectives on social and political issues that they also find in other forms of journalism. Because of this, the specific entertainment or celebrity subject matter is often viewed as of less interest or importance than the political issue that it touches upon. Toward the beginning of the chapter, we saw how Debra opted to share and comment on a CNN article discussing *Hamilton*'s treatment of race despite not having seen the play or the movie. What mattered for her, rather, was the how the article manifested the broader issue of "political correctness" that she believed to be of the utmost importance. In general, this pattern of engaging with pop culture journalism without having any prior familiarity or interest in the actual pop culture in question seems to be common among the politics-first audience segment.

To cite another instance, an audience member who jokingly described herself as "a snooty tooty NPR person" and "not a real consumer" of pop culture nevertheless found it worthwhile to retweet a news story about racism on the set of the reality TV series *Survivor*, a show that she admitted she "would never watch." In this case, she felt that the journalistic criticism of *Survivor* was more important than the TV show itself, in the sense that it drew attention to the broader issue of racism in society:

Racism for me is, I think, one of the most, if not the most pressing issue, not even in just the country but the world. So it's a big deal. And I think the pop culture aspect of it, that just seems like what's so pernicious about it, that it just seems like "oh, it's not that big a deal." But you know what? It is. . . . And so I think it's important to kind of call that stuff out.

In her view, *Survivor*'s status as high-profile, widely seen pop culture meant that its handling of race was important news to consume and share, regardless of whether she had any personal investment in the show.

Accounts such as hers thus underscore how many audience members are comfortable with taking entertainment journalism seriously as political journalism when it overlaps with an issue that they feel is deserving of added media attention. The very fact that this type of journalistic content attracts an audience of "news junkies" or "political junkies" who are not heavy pop culture consumers is as strong an indication as any of its functional status *as* political journalism.

The Pop-Culture-and-Politics Audience and Critically Engaged Fans

The politics-first crowd makes up only one element of the diverse audience for journalism at the pop culture–politics nexus. Other engaged audience members profess a love of both pop culture and politics as well as a fascination with their interrelationship, which is perhaps to be expected given the journalistic content in question. For instance, one discussed how his life experience as a gay man has continually brought him to this intersection:

> At the risk of a huge generalization, I think gay people enjoy pop culture even more sometimes than the average person. . . . In terms of the crossover between pop culture and political issues, I look at everything with just a little bit of a political or social justice perspective. You know, part of that is being a gay man for fifty years.

As he explained, this heightened sensitivity to both the political and the cultural spheres continues to shape his news engagement habits on Twitter: "I share the kinds of things that interest me, which is a mix of pop culture and political news and social justice."

Notably, this specific mix of interests tends to define the imagined target audience for certain news outlets that position their brand identity as spanning politics and culture. To return momentarily to the journalist interviews that formed the core of previous chapters, a veteran staff writer for a feminist-oriented news site explained that "from day one, [the site] was always a site about the intersection of politics and pop culture. It never was about anything else. So, you know, that's what we do, and that's what our readers expect us to do. . . . I would say that they like pop culture stories and political stories just about equally." This sort of industry-side perspective on the imagined audience tracks with some, although certainly not all, accounts of those who engage online with news that bridges these two spheres. One audience member offered a typical description of this sort of orientation to news: "I do tend to read things where politics and pop culture do intersect for sure. And I think that has been on the rise. . . . Like, is there a way anymore to separate politics from pop culture? . . . It kind of just all melds together." Another emphasized the role of social media in aggregating and intermixing news from the two fields and helping audience members like her follow their overlap:

> I just find that [Twitter is] such an accessible place to keep tabs on all of that, pop culture and politics. . . . Twitter's just a really rich resource for surfacing kind of where politics intersects with every aspect of pop culture, news, information. . . . Whether it's TV, movies, music, sports, general celebrity culture, influencers, there's such a powerful intersection between the pop culture worlds and the impact or the intersection that occurs with politics. And it's difficult at times to separate the two.

Within this broad chunk of the news audience whose interests traverse pop culture, politics, and everything in between, we can further identify a subgroup that can be characterized as the critically engaged fan. For these audience members, pop culture's role in the broader society is not just a category of news interest but a veritable obsession, even a lifestyle. Like other highly engaged, typically younger fans of pop culture in the digital age, they are active "prosumers" of online content involving their objects of veneration. These activities include not only consuming and sharing news of interest to the fandom but also engaging in relevant conversations on social media and various online fan forums as well as contributing creative "remix" works such as fan art and fan fiction.[9] To be certain, not all members of "prosumer" fan communities are interested in the social and political dimensions of their pop culture obsessions, and we can assume that some actively avoid such territory. Yet, as scholars Ioana Literat and Neta Kligler-Vilenchik have shown, pop culture content is significant for how it "functions as a shared symbolic resource that may prompt political expression and communication within and across political differences," especially among groups of young people online.[10] Although this phenomenon is far from universal, the critically engaged fans who readily participate in pop-culture-inspired political discourse can be understood as an important subset of the larger online fandom world—and one that also likely overlaps with the politically interested news audience.

For example, an audience member in their twenties who identifies as nonbinary explained that sharing an article on Twitter that critiqued the racial politics of TV cop shows was only a small part of their online participation in this kind of discourse:

> I grew up watching all three *CSIs*, *Criminal Minds*, all four *Law and Order* shows, and reading a lot of detective fiction.... I eventually joined the [*Law and Order*] *SVU* online fandom and read and wrote fanfic. . . . However, over time, I've come to notice the kinds of stories that get told in shows like this, and what ethnicities, sexualities, and gender identities get to be the heroes, and who gets to be a sympathetic victim the audience roots for . . . that's something I'm always discussing with other fans and trying to approach in my own fan works.

They went on to describe how their keen interest in the ideology of these programs, cultivated by engagement in fan community discussions and creative fan forums, led them to seek out professional journalism that also addressed such issues: "As I'd already been thinking about procedurals and how they affect us when the [2020 Black Lives Matter] protests first started and the police started reacting to protestors, I was very much interested in media criticism around cop shows and how many of them are going to move forward given recent events." Retweeting the specific article in question, which called for the cancellation of these programs as part of a broader "racial reckoning" in the entertainment industry, led to a conversation with a friend and fellow fan about how they've "both been grappling with our love of these shows."

This kind of ongoing critical engagement with the politics of pop culture, which draws from journalistic reports and commentary alongside more amateur sources of digital discourse, is a distinctive feature of the broader online fandom ecosystem. In another illustrative example, a member of the fan community for the Netflix drama series *The Bold Type* described how she sought out professional commentary on the show's handling of a controversial plot line due to conversations that she had already been having with other fans on Twitter. In brief, the controversy involved a sympathetically portrayed relationship between a queer black woman and a white conservative woman whose father ran a gay conversion therapy center. As she explained, "for a while, it was just folks within the fandom . . . who were pointing this [criticism] out, and it was a little frustrating that no media outlets were really saying anything about that. They were recapping the episodes, but no one was really talking about this weird, problematic thing that was going on." As a black queer woman herself, she felt that this storyline was "dangerous" and "a terrible message to be sending to queer people period, and black people period, and black queer people especially." After commiserating online with like-minded fellow fans and arguing back and forth with others who disagreed, she found an article on the Huffington Post that reflected her views and thus served as useful ammunition in her efforts to win other fans of *The Bold Type* to her side.

Similar to Grace's and Keisha's stories that opened this chapter, she described using the article as a stand-in to shore up her own opinion expression within the fan community:

> [Posting a critique] written by somebody who actually gets paid to do that and is not just some random fan on the internet I thought added credibility and also said what I was trying to get through a little bit more succinctly than I was able to do at that moment. . . . Nobody's paying me to spend time on writing a coherent argument about this, and I'm tired of saying the same points over and over again, so I can just post this now, and you can read that, and you can see what the issues are.

As her account underlines, journalistic pop culture criticism plays a significant role in the discourse of online fan communities as it is circulated, discussed, argued over, and used as a credibility-lending (and time-saving) proxy for personal political expression and advocacy. For fans who are critically engaged with the social and political dimensions of their favorite pop culture and who already participate in this sort of discourse online, relevant journalistic content serves as a useful resource for their ongoing discursive engagement.

This pattern represents perhaps the most intensive form of audience relationship with politically oriented entertainment journalism, as critically engaged fans track it closely and seek it out as fuel for their own digital activities.

However, it is unclear how common such a pattern may be among the overall audience for this journalism, and while pop culture fan communities are greatly widespread in the contemporary digital landscape, it remains uncertain how many of their members are critically engaged in the politics around their objects of fandom to the point of actively seeking out professional news and commentary of this type.

The Pop-Culture-First Audience

At the same time, the story of *The Bold Type* fandom suggests how this journalism can circulate within online fan communities at large due to the efforts of their most politically engaged members. More broadly, the notion that less politically minded fans of pop culture may be exposed to relevant political discourse—journalism included—because of their fan engagement is important to consider for the present discussion. We have already seen how a politics-first crowd makes up a sizable portion of the audience for journalism at the pop culture–politics nexus, but what about an audience that is pop-culture-first, or fandom-first?

Although the present data are limited in this area, there is some evidence to suggest that such an audience does, in fact, exist. Take, for instance, the account of an African American audience member who retweeted a news report about how Anthony Mackie, an African American costar of several Marvel superhero films, had publicly criticized the franchise for a lack of racial diversity in behind-the-scenes roles. As the audience member explained, "I was browsing YouTube for Storm [and] Black Panther clips and came across it, and I agreed . . . Mackie had a point. We deserve jobs on every set, as do white people on films like *Black Panther*." In other words, he encountered this coverage of racial representation in Hollywood not by searching for it directly but rather through seeking out unrelated content about Marvel superhero characters. While he clearly expressed an interest in the broader political issue of expanding racial diversity and combating anti-black racism, noting that "I'm a fan of [Mackie] picking this moment in time and our current troubles" to make the public comments, it is significant that this is not what initially led him to the news in question. Rather, his engagement as a Marvel fan is what provided the entry point, illustrating how an interest in pop culture can pull audience members toward journalism that focuses specifically on its political aspects.

In a similar fashion, some audience members who shared news about Rowling's controversial comments about the transgender community described how they had been following the story because they were longtime *Harry Potter* fans, while others noted they had encountered commentary about the racial politics of *Hamilton* because they were fans of the musical. In cases like these, pop culture fandom serves as the impetus for introducing news audiences to related journalism that crosses into political territory. However, whether they are already interested in the political content to begin with or if this interest is piqued because of consuming the pop culture content is a trickier question.

As discussed in chapter 1, one of the key issues surrounding cultural journalism is how it may or may not serve as a bridge to political engagement, particularly for audiences who are less likely to consume more traditional kinds of political information. The fact that pop culture has such a wide public appeal and strong emotional resonance suggests that it has the potential to grab the attention of news audiences and point it in new directions, including toward the sphere of civic issues and debates. As Lynn Schofield Clark and Regina Marchi argue, young people who tend be well versed in contemporary pop culture may find heightened value in news that situates public issues within the field of their impassioned interests,[11] yet our investigation is not limited to the youth demographic alone. The next section will interrogate the "bridge to politics" theory by examining how a range of audience members experience it in the context of their own pop culture news consumption, as well as draw upon it as inspiration for spreading this journalism to peers. As will be shown, the metaphor of the bridge is helpful for making sense of the civic value that audiences report gaining from journalism that traverses the entertainment and politics fields. However, the pathways of movement it provides appear to be far more complex, and at times more concerning, than would be suggested by a simple model of transporting a pop-culture-focused public into the domain of civic engagement.

A Bridge to Politics?

When considering the notion that entertainment journalism can serve as an accessible gateway to political issue discourse, it is important to first observe that this idea has been widely adopted among those who consume and share this journalism online. Audience members invoke it so frequently, in fact, that it can be understood as a kind of conventional wisdom or a popular lay theory of "how media works" in the contemporary digital landscape. As Rauch argues, "lay theories of news matter because they guide how people not only think about but also interact with media, as well as with society."[12] To articulate this lay theory, here are just some of the ways audience members described pop culture news stories that address political issues: "an approachable access point," "a way to make politics closer to home," "a filter that is more accessible to a lot of people than many of the other contexts," a way to "help make relevant societal issues like politics more relatable and easier to wrap one's head around," "a lens that makes it easier for people who are not inherently political or even versed in the subject to understand better."

As these characterizations suggest, such a theory is closely linked to the perception that for many, political news remains relatively inaccessible. Whether it is too difficult to understand, too dry or boring to hold one's attention, or too overwhelming or stressful to deal with, traditional political journalism is often conceived of in the public imagination as an obstacle to political engagement. Entertainment journalism, by contrast, tends to be framed by news audiences as the exact opposite: broadly appealing, fun to consume, and easy to comprehend. At the same time, some audience members believe that it is also civically valuable for its content and thus a helpful means of increasing the political interest of people who would otherwise be disengaged. In the words of one audience member, "I think a reason some people shrink away from politics is that they're intimidated by it, but I think that pop culture really breaks it down for people in a way that is understandable and simple." Another succinctly remarked that "politics is draining at times. . . . Some folks only suffer politics with a pop culture issue on top."

Although this line of thought often rests on assumptions about the news consumption habits of unknown and generalized others—a manifestation of the "third person effect" that Rauch finds is very prominent in lay theories of the news media's public impact more broadly[13]—some audience members point to how they use entertainment journalism as a personal tonic for their own political disengagement. For example, an African American woman in her twenties explained that while she feels the need to keep up with political issues that affect her life, consuming entertainment journalism on relevant topics helps her do so in a way that would otherwise prove difficult:

> Politics isn't something I like to read, and it's not particularly enjoyable. Getting into politics is more of a chore. . . . If I don't make it my business to study politics or to have an avid understanding of what's going on, I remain ignorant, and as an African American woman, I'm going to feel the repercussions of that. I have to advocate for myself, and the best way to do that is staying current. Adding pop culture into the conversation makes it more relatable and easier to consume. . . . Sometimes politics are super heavy to get into regularly, and having pop culture allows me to consume more information without feeling drained after.

Her remarks offer evidence, if anecdotal, that pop culture news *can* be used deliberately as a "bridge to politics" for those who are less inclined to follow traditional political journalism. In other words, it seems to be more than just wishful thinking on the part of pop culture news devotees, although exactly how much more remains unclear from the present data (furthermore, it should be kept in mind that these audience members may have felt the need to exaggerate the value of their online actions as a means of justifying them). Along similar lines, another audience member who could be classified as pop-culture-first according to the discussion above commented, "I know I spend much more time engaging with popular media and the arts than I do politics, so it can be helpful to use one as a tool to understand the other." Notably, remarks such as these stand in contrast to previous research suggesting that news audiences see entertainment and celebrity news content as being largely irrelevant to civic issues.[14]

Figuring that connections like these are quite common, many audience members who post links to politically oriented pop culture stories on social media explicitly cite the "bridge to politics" idea as a primary motivation. For instance, when asked why she retweeted a news story about the entertainment industry's "racial reckoning" in the summer of 2020, one audience member explained, "I think it's easier to digest for mainstream readers," while another described sharing a similarly themed article in the hopes that it "can reach a wider audience than a regular news story might." Another still noted that he retweeted an article about the popular music group the Dixie Chicks changing their name in the wake of antiracism protests because "I just appreciate the added weight and spread of information that celebrities can provide." At one level, these comments speak to a core motivation for citizens sharing news on social media more generally: to both educate and persuade their peers by aiding in the circulation of political information.[15] At another level, they under-score the popular perception that entertainment and celebrity topics have a wider public appeal than traditional political journalism and are there-fore valuable in efforts to expand the circle of civic engagement. Again, as Rauch stresses, popular lay theories about how journalism works have im-portant consequences for how audience members act upon it.[16]

In addition to reaching out to those who may be intimidated or exhausted by traditional political journalism, audiences who share politically oriented pop culture news on social media sometimes single out young people spe-cifically as targets of their efforts. This is closely connected to the perception that young people are both less interested in politics than older adults and more tuned into the world of pop culture and celebrity, making them seem-ingly ideal candidates for a "bridge to politics" effect. For example, a woman in her early twenties who closely follows both politics and entertainment news cited the latter as an important entry point for less politically minded members of her age cohort: "I believe that especially with young people, they don't feel that politics is something that they have to get involved with, and that it is not their fight or something like that. But you can see the way that a country or a group of people feel based on the [entertainment] media that is coming out." As she suggested, young people who feel alienated from pol-itics can nevertheless begin to make sense of it by following the conversa-tion around pop culture, which, in contrast to the traditional political sphere, they see as something of their own.

From a different vantage point, an audience member in her fifties pro-vided an up-close account of this dynamic when discussing the news con-sumption habits that she observes in her two teenage sons. Referring to the earlier-discussed CNN article on the racial politics of *Hamilton*, which she had shared with her family as well as her Twitter followers, she explained:

> When you're talking about pop culture or something that grabs your atten-tion . . . like *Hamilton*, it's about a musical, that's something that they can relate to. If that [news article] was about a statue in Manhattan solely, they would kind of glance over it and go "yeah, yeah, yeah." Would they read that article? No. But something on *Hamilton* . . . they read it, and that's a great starting point of discussion and for them to maybe think about and go "hmm, I never thought that." : . . If you told them that they had to be inter-ested in the topic or, you know, a policy, they could care less. They want to be entertained. . . . [Pop culture] is easier, it catches their attention, engages

them to read. When it does bring in more about the pop culture, it's not so heavy where they say, "Oh, it doesn't impact me."

Like many who share this sort of news on social media, she expressed a positive appreciation for how it can be used as a "bridge to politics": "I think that [pop culture news stories] are extremely important in the realm that they capture the attention of young people [and] adults, and that they get people interested in politics and the topic. . . . So I think there's good with it." At the same time, however, she also spoke of potentially negative consequences of what she characterized as the "politics fluff" that comes from entertainment and celebrity coverage, which is explored in detail in the next section.

A Bridge away from Politics?

Specifically, this audience member raised concerns that young people like her own teenage sons are too easily swayed by news reports about the public political stances of beloved pop culture figures, which she argued threaten to overshadow more civically valuable sources of political discourse:

> The media tends to promote and push out those messages because [celebrities] are famous, so they're more likely to see an article that has been quoted with, like, LeBron James about a social issue or a political opinion. That's going to be picked up, and that's what they're going to see. But there could be a very well-respected university professor who has information that is probably more factual. . . . They're not going to get a chance to see it, because it's written by a professor, and he doesn't have the following of pop culture. . . . So that's kind of where I'm thinking it's good and bad. It gets people to want to promote it and want to read it, but sometimes they might be missing out on the other end because [other sources] don't have the notoriety, and they don't have the followers, and they don't have the celebrity status.

As she emphasized, her more critical view of pop culture news as a questionable source of political content is born of her own experience as a parent, frustrated with how her sons seemingly adopt the political opinions of their favorite celebrities in the news:

I see [my children's] opinions being so narrow because of what they're getting. . . . What's more scary is that they're being influenced, they're making their own decisions based on that information. They don't know that, no, that celebrity, just because they are a director or a producer or someone that you love in a TV show, that doesn't mean that they're the expert. And that's the scary part . . . that we, society, my kids, become so reliant on the fluff pieces . . . that because we like to hear what [*Hamilton* star] Lin-Manuel [Miranda] and whoever we idolize at the time [has to say], that their opinion becomes what we believe.

Her comments, from a self-identified conservative, to an extent reflect the familiar right-wing critique of both the entertainment industry and mainstream journalism as being agents of left-wing bias and undue political influence—themes, as discussed in chapter 3, that also dominate the field of right-wing news commentary on pop culture. However, the broader concern that she touched upon here—that entertainment news, and celebrity coverage in particular, lacks the depth of traditional political journalism and is therefore a problematic starting point for political engagement—is also shared by some audience members on the other end of the ideological spectrum.

For example, one audience member who noted her support of the Black Lives Matter movement commented:

It's really great that so many people have jumped on board with raising awareness about Breonna Taylor and the fact that her murderers have not been arrested yet. But I don't want to read or see articles about all these celebrities who have jumped on board. . . . I find it distracting, because really, what any of us needs to know is what's really going on and how certain issues are being addressed. . . . I want to see what's happening to fix this issue. So I just feel like I'm a little bit exhausted from reading stories about what celebrities are doing what and who's saying what about certain issues, and I think we just need more information about those issues. . . . I don't want a Buzzfeed recap of different things that celebrities have said, you know. I want something real.

By contrast, she explained that she gears her own news-sharing practices toward coverage that she feels "actually addresses the situation," such as a long-form analysis from the *Atlantic* about how the J. K. Rowling controversy relates to broader trans issues. Clearly, she did not reject the idea that news stories covering the world of entertainment can be civically valuable. However, the concerns that she raised about the uneven quality of this journalism—with Buzzfeed singled out as a symbol of the perceived shallowness of celebrity "clickbait" coverage more generally—are important to consider when assessing its broader civic role.

As discussed in chapter 4, industry professionals often voice similar critiques about the weaknesses of the for-profit digital news landscape which seeks to maximize audience appeal at the cost of sacrificing substance and depth. While the public fascination with celebrity ensures that news of this type will circulate far and wide, there is a sense among both audiences and journalists that it can be a distraction from public affairs if the pop culture focus becomes too dominant.

Such concerns were also voiced by an audience member who, in a moment of candor, expressed regret that he pays more attention to celebrity news stories than he feels he should. As he commented regarding news coverage of various "cancel culture" controversies:

> I think the conversation should be squarely focused on the minority struggle to gain a seat in today's conversation, not necessarily about privileged artists and directors who feel like they're being stifled in terms of their voices. But as a result of their stature, I find myself sort of engaging with them informally through my research and thoughts. So that, in a way, to me it's a distraction. . . . I'm a little bit concerned at the fact that these very influential pop culture artists or directors or writers or whatnot may draw our attention away from something that is, in my opinion, more important at hand.

Specifically, he pointed to articles that he himself had shared on Twitter about the Rowling controversy, lamenting that "I should be reading more about social justice, not about J. K. Rowling's view on transgender [issues]." Here he highlighted how consuming political information through the diverting lens of entertainment and celebrity may leave some audience members feeling undernourished, echoing the concerns of journalism scholars who warn of the deficiency of news that is intended more to entertain than to inform.[17] Moreover, his account suggests how this type of news can feel like a seductive yet potentially worrisome temptation for those who seek to maintain a civically fulfilling news diet.

For others, resistance to pop culture news as source of political information can be much stronger. Another audience member who shared the article about Rowling's transgender comments controversy, for instance, was quick to dismiss the idea that it was anything more than a momentary diversion from her regular political news consumption: "Cultural effluvia can be interesting. But do pop culture news stories inform my political understanding? Not at all. News is news. Pop culture is pop culture." In insisting on a categorical separation between the two, her remarks to some extent recall the backlash against the perceived overpoliticization of pop culture, which, as explored in earlier chapters, has become a frequent complaint aimed at entertainment journalism of the left and its engagement with the identity politics of race, gender, and sexuality. However, while this may be an important factor in some audience members' aversion to viewing entertainment journalism as a valuable route to political engagement, the issue can be delineated in a sense from concerns over its relative depth and quality (even as the two may become intertwined in certain contexts). In her specific case, both sets of issues appeared to be salient, as she decried much of journalistic political criticism of entertainment as a worrisome extension of "cancel culture" while stressing the superior civic value of traditional political news.

Although such concerns about the value of entertainment journalism arise from multiple directions, taken together, they suggest a more complicated relationship between this journalism and its audiences than a wholly optimistic reading of the "bridge to politics" theory would suggest. Following from this point, we can expand on the theory by reframing the bridge metaphor as a two-way route of transition. In other words, we can conceive of pop culture news as providing audiences with opportunities to move both toward meaningful civic engagement and away from it, depending on the context. In some cases, the accessibility and appeal of entertainment-themed news content appears to bring audiences meaningfully closer to the political sphere when they experience barriers to consuming traditional political information. In other cases, focusing on this kind of journalism may leave audiences with a diminished, even ersatz form of political engagement—one in which, for instance, narratives around the celebrities who dominate public attention create a distracting simulacrum of political discourse that crowds out space for more substantive issue discussions.

The fact that some audience members express reservations about the civic value of their own personal pop culture news consumption, or that of close family members, suggests that the threats it poses can be very real. At the

same time, accounts of audience members affirming the value of this journalism in overcoming their own political disengagement signals that the
popular lay theory of it serving as a valuable "bridge to politics" also has a
degree of validity. Through this type of exploratory audience research, we
cannot know exactly what proportion of audience members move in one direction versus the other on the proverbial bridge, or, for that matter, which
groups of people are more or less likely to reap civic benefits from consuming
pop culture news and commentary. These are indeed important questions
for future research. However, what this firsthand testimony helps to clarify
is that this journalism makes a difference in the civic lives of its audiences
and has important consequences—both positive and negative—for how they
make sense of and approach the social and political world.

A Supplemental Resource for Political Engagement?

In terms of more positive audience outcomes, it is also important to note
that some who closely follow both political and pop culture journalism—a
considerable subset of the broader audience for news at their intersection,
as discussed above—point to instances where they gained something of
civic value by consuming news about Hollywood-themed subject matter.
Although their high level of political interest disqualifies them in a sense
from a "bridge to politics" effect as it is typically conceived—that is, they are
already solidly on the side of the politically engaged and thus do not need
to be transported, as it were—their accounts further illuminate the ways in
which pop culture news and commentary contribute meaningfully to the
civic lives of their audiences.

For instance, a white woman in her fifties explained that while she has
followed the issue of anti-black racism throughout her life and considers
it highly important, news reports of Hollywood's "racial reckoning" in the
summer of 2020 continued to add to her developing consciousness around
race. Explaining her reaction to an article she shared on Twitter about racism
in the television industry, she commented, "I don't want to say it's confirming
what I always knew. I think in some ways it gives me a better understanding
and kind of pisses me off even more, if that would be possible. . . . [It] gives
me a better idea of how to be an ally." In other words, despite consuming
other forms of political information regarding the broader issue of racism,

she found coverage of its prevalence in Hollywood valuable as part of her continuing education on the subject.

A white male in his sixties, meanwhile, described how his political thinking evolved as a result of consuming news coverage of the "take a knee" NFL football player protests related to Black Lives Matter activism:

> To be honest with you, I was one of the guys, when [NFL star Colin] Kaepernick started kneeling, who said, "Oh my God, it's disgraceful to the flag, this is un-American," you know, I really believed that. But I also believe in the perspective that people died to give him the right to do that. And I've kind of changed a little bit of my thinking along the way because of the articles that I've read. . . . It's kind of opened my eyes to "hey, there are different viewpoints, there are different perspectives."

As a self-described avid consumer of political journalism, he would certainly have read quite a bit about the Black Lives Matter movement and the debates over its protest tactics without checking the sports section of the news. Yet, because he also closely follows sports and entertainment news, he encountered the issue through an alternative narrative lens that clearly resonated with him. Whether or not he required this lens of pop culture and celebrity to access the broader political issue is perhaps beside the point. What matters, rather, is that this coverage ended up playing an important role in his political issue engagement, even to the point of changing his position.

In a parallel to how the high-profile news saga of Kaepernick brought added public attention to Black Lives Matter activism, some audience members pointed to the role of #MeToo Hollywood celebrity coverage in advancing broader public engagement around issues of sexual harassment and assault. For instance, a man who expressed concerns about the relative importance of celebrity news nevertheless cited #MeToo coverage as an example of how it can sometimes be useful for his personal engagement with the political sphere, which he characterized as high to begin with:

> The #MeToo movement, I think, is entirely born of artists and directors who are very vocal about the struggles of women artists in the entertainment industry. In that specific respect, I thought it was great that a lot of the struggles have surfaced over time and the perpetrators were given the right punishments that they deserve. That to me was not a distraction. And in

that specific sense, it actually gave me more awareness and attention toward the movement, and also the issue at hand.

Although he regularly consumes a large amount of traditional political news, this was a case in which such journalism had seemingly failed to put an appropriate spotlight on the pressing issue of gender-based sexual violence and harassment. By contrast, coverage of famous Hollywood actresses' stories of abuse at the hands of powerful men in the industry created an enormous wave of public attention around the issue, and he found this journalism to be helpful in raising his own awareness.

In addition to sometimes finding civic value in news coverage of celebrities, some audience members who reported high levels of both political interest and pop culture news consumption pointed to journalistic commentary on film and TV entertainment as playing a significant role in their understanding of specific issues. For example, a woman who closely follows discourse around intersectional identity politics in both pop culture and the traditional political sphere recalled a time when a TV critic's analysis of a new Netflix series opened her eyes to a set of issues that she had only rarely considered before:

> I remember reading an article that was a critique of *Never Have I Ever*, the Mindy Kaling show. And their critique of the show was highlighting the ways in which Indian communities, even in the United States, may still play into things like racism and colorism and the caste system, which are things that I know a little about but not very much. And [the article] was just sort of a jumping point for the way it was portrayed, but a lot of it was talking about the ways this exists within both Indian and Indian American culture. And I would have had no entry point to that had it not been like, "Oh, somebody posted this critique. Let me read what it has to say."

Furthermore, the fact that the piece in question had been written by an Indian American journalist who related the portrayals of the fictional series to their real-life experiences was crucial for how it helped this audience member gain a new perspective: "A lot of the people who are writing about these things are folks who are parts of those cultures. . . . Because these shows are bringing them up, it gives folks the opportunity to talk about how those things play out politically but also how the politics play out personally." As discussed in chapter 2, many journalists who produce this sort of progressive-minded pop culture commentary do so with the explicit intention of providing audiences with underrepresented perspectives that stem from their own social identities and standpoints. In the case of this particular audience member, such an exchange was apparently quite successful. And while she may have already been greatly sensitive to the broader issue of racism, the journalist's discussion of the specificity of the Indian cultural experience, using the jumping-off point of a Netflix sitcom, gave her a valuable new lens through which to understand it that she had little access to before.

Her use of the term "entry point" to describe this process is also worth pausing on, as it is identical to language that many use to describe the notion of a "bridge to politics" for those who are largely politically disengaged. The fact that some audience members who are highly engaged with politics nonetheless see entertainment journalism as a valuable route of access for new and underexplored civic territory suggests that this "bridge to politics" can be far more nuanced than a simple transfer from one distinct and separate sphere to another. We can thus conceive of the bridge as not only multidirectional (in terms of potentially leading audiences both toward and away from political engagement) but also multifaceted and multibranched in terms of the potential connections that it can provide. To continue the metaphor, we can envision an intricate network of mini-bridges woven across the news and information landscape, as opposed to a solitary passageway standing between the cultural and political spheres.

This reimagining of the bridge metaphor thus helps account for the experiences of audience members who find entertainment journalism to be a useful entry point for accessing specific political issues and perspectives even when they are highly engaged to start with and have other points of access available, including traditional political journalism. Crucially, this widens the scope of the "bridge to politics" effect to potentially include major segments of the audience for politically oriented pop culture news who have a strong interest in political discourse across the board. Indeed, the audience research presented in this chapter suggests that journalism at the pop culture–politics nexus is consumed by "political junkies" as well as pop culture aficionados, and it would therefore be a mistake to focus only on the latter when assessing its potential civic benefits—as well as its potential downsides. Although there is some evidence to suggest that the conventional wisdom of the "bridge to politics" holds true in some cases—nonpolitical people being drawn toward political things via the accessible gateway of pop culture news—pinning the question of this journalism's civic value to such a narrow formula misses something important about how it actually functions in the day-to-day lives of its most engaged consumers.

It appears that for some news audiences, the lens of entertainment and celebrity is not an alternative to or substitute for political journalism but rather simply one of its many parts. Even for the highly politically engaged, an article about the activities of a famous actress or athlete or a critical review of a movie or TV series can open the door to a meaningful new perspective on a relevant public issue. At the same time, this journalism also holds the risk of drawing the politically engaged—as well as the disengaged—into loops of distraction and shallow understanding. In bridging the cultural and political spheres through myriad points of contact, entertainment journalism can lead its audiences in all sorts of directions. What is clear, however, is that these metaphorical bridges of connection are very real, and of no small consequence, for news audiences' engagement with the political sphere.

Conclusion

The in-depth audience perspectives explored in this chapter, although limited in their generalizability, are useful for developing theory about the public circulation and impact of entertainment journalism that addresses political issues. This news is often consumed and engaged with by audience members as a consequential element of the broader political information environment, although some are resistant to the notion that it is always an appropriate part of a political news diet. Yet, despite such reservations among certain segments of the public, this news forms the basis for a wide range of citizen-level political expression, conversation, and online activism. These practices include opinion amplification and what Sharon Meraz and Zizi Papacharissi call networked gatekeeping and framing,[18] with some audience members using pop culture news content as convenient and credibility-boosting stand-ins to help amplify public awareness and support for favored issues and causes. In addition, this networked gatekeeping and framing can also include more critical and reactionary modes of engagement that set out to directly counter the viewpoints expressed in such journalism. In tracing both sympathetic and resistant forms of engaged social media response, we can glimpse how entertainment journalism has become a meaningful site of polyvalent civic discourse around some of the most contentious and impassioned issues of the day.

As we map the different types of audiences who engage online with news at the pop culture–politics nexus, it is significant that a considerable number have a high interest in political journalism and follow pop culture news only when it intersects with public issues of concern. Since these intersections are seemingly becoming increasingly commonplace in the broader information landscape, it follows that politically focused news audiences would increasingly come into contact with the terrain of entertainment journalism that they would otherwise ignore or avoid. Not only do politics-first audiences cross over into pop culture territory when they view it as relevant, but some see little distinction between news about the politics of Hollywood and news about the politics of society more broadly, especially when it comes to topics such as racism and sexism that are so amenable to symbolic cultural representation and critique.

Other members of the news audience, meanwhile, are fascinated equally with entertainment, politics, and the intersection of the two and thus resemble the typical imagined audience of news outlets that specialize in coverage at the pop culture–politics nexus. Notably, this group includes critically engaged pop culture fans who incorporate professional works of journalism into their participatory discursive practices around their objects of fandom. While not all members of fan communities may be interested in discussing the political meanings and dynamics of their favorite pop culture, those who do tend to be close followers of journalistic reporting and commentary that take entertainment seriously as worthy of political scrutiny and analysis. Whether or not this journalism has the capacity to raise the political interest of pop culture fans who are relatively disengaged from traditional political discourse, however, is far less certain, although anecdotal evidence suggests that entertainment journalism can be a useful tool for some news audience members who feel the need to keep up with public issues and debates yet desire a more accessible and pleasurable entry point.

This notion of journalism at the pop culture–politics nexus helping to move a relatively apolitical audience toward political engagement represents the core of the "bridge to politics" theory that is widespread among the public and is frequently cited as justification for spreading this journalism to peers online. Yet the experiences of news audiences suggest a more complex set of processes at play. Some of the most significant public impact of entertainment journalism appears to involve audience members who have already arrived at the sphere of political interest and engagement yet find supplemental value in news that uses the lens of pop culture to explore public issues from new angles and perspectives. Furthermore, the audience data presented in this chapter suggest that entertainment journalism can function as both a helpful gateway to politics and a concerning "clickbait" distraction that risks pulling news audiences away from civic discourse that they see as more valuable. Chapter 7 will continue to probe this threat of a commercially fueled ersatz political discourse—as well as the threat of suffocating hyperpartisanship—by squaring the accounts of engaged audience members with the industry-side perspectives of pop culture news professionals. This will offer the opportunity to further interrogate the broader question of entertainment journalism's public value that has encircled this book's investigation as a whole.

7

Assessing the Public Value of Journalism at the Pop Culture–Politics Nexus

For too long, entertainment journalism has been framed as a frivolous alternative to "real" journalism, offering audiences little else but a pleasurable reprieve from the weighty public issues of the day while enhancing the profit potential of commercial news outlets. The preceding chapters have made the case that rather than being a sideshow or an escape from public political discourse, news about the world of pop culture has become one of its many key elements. The hybridization of entertainment and political coverage is now a hallmark of a digital news ecosystem that is characterized by the blurring of traditional boundaries. However, the trend extends back decades, reflecting broader long-term shifts in US politics toward issues of social and cultural identity and their symbolic representation in the public sphere. With the ongoing resurgence of progressive identity politics and its vehement conservative backlash in the early twenty-first century, journalism addressing the cultural symbolism of Hollywood and celebrity has never been more politically engaged or potentially more politically consequential.

As seen throughout this book, this journalism is often deliberately produced by news professionals *as* political discourse, is often consciously consumed by news audiences *as* political discourse, and catalyzes citizen-level political discussion and expression—including politically motivated hate and harassment—on interactive digital platforms. It is thus necessary for journalism studies, as well as the academic and journalism communities more broadly, to come to terms with entertainment journalism's status as "real" public affairs discourse and take seriously its complex role in contemporary political life. The interviews presented in the previous chapters move this endeavor forward by highlighting how both the production and the reception of journalism at the pop culture–politics nexus connect to broader debates around visibility and inclusion, bias and systematic oppression, the pursuit of social justice, the defense of freedom of expression, and much more. Moreover, pop culture news is not only inextricable from

Pop Culture, Politics, and the News. Joel Penney, Oxford University Press. © Oxford University Press 2022.
DOI: 10.1093/oso/9780197557587.003.0008

contemporary political discourse, but its accessible appeal and strong emotional resonance position it as a significant access point for political issue engagement for audiences on both the left and the right.

At the same time, this journalism is also fraught with tensions that stem from both its commercial character and its role in broader ideological projects that can flatten as well as augment the public understanding of issues. These tensions are palpable not only to certain engaged audience members who consume this news critically (and in some cases antagonistically) but also to many members of newsrooms and culture departments themselves. One of the key benefits of examining the firsthand accounts of entertainment journalism professionals, as was done in earlier chapters, is that these journalists are closely attuned to the problems as well as the strengths of their field. Constantly subjected to criticism from online commenters as well as from many of their own journalistic colleagues from the opposing side of the partisan divide, they are acutely aware of the controversies that surround this area of professional practice and are thus uniquely helpful in bringing these concerns into focus.

This concluding chapter revisits and expands upon the critiques of journalism at the pop culture–politics nexus, building on the discussions of previous chapters that forefront the perspectives of working entertainment journalists and editors as well as the experiences and observations of some of their most engaged audience members. The goal is to explore the core question that has encircled this inquiry as a whole: what are the contours, and the potential limits, of the public value provided by entertainment journalism that intersects with political issues? To put it another way, as we recognize that pop culture news and commentary undoubtedly produce a form of public political discourse, what, ultimately, can we say about the quality of this discourse?

To investigate this question, the following sections examine two interrelated forces that complicate a wholly positive assessment of this journalism's public value—first, the commercial pressures that threaten to empty out its substance in favor of pure audience gratification and, second, the hyperpartisanship that threatens to flatten complex and nuanced discussions of cultural symbolism into purely instrumentalist propaganda. After elaborating these very real concerns and addressing how the journalism field can potentially take steps to mitigate them, the discussion closes by taking stock of the crucial contributions of the entertainment journalism field in expanding both the diversity and the scope of the public information landscape. As scholars Barbie Zelizer, Pablo J. Boczkowski, and C. W. Anderson argue in *The Journalism Manifesto*, the news business is in dire need of bold reform and must move toward "a renewed future in which journalism showcases the voices, perspectives and experiences of the many who have historically been subjugated to the narratives of the few."[1] Despite the considerable weaknesses of the entertainment beat as a conduit to public affairs, it arguably serves as an important signpost in the march toward this future, following in a long lineage of the pop culture sphere more generally as an alternative space in which to articulate political critique and voice the perspectives and interests of those who have historically been left out of political discourse as usual.

Hyper-Commercialism and the Threat of Ersatz Political Discourse

Although entertainment journalism can have significant public value in terms of serving as a "bridge to politics," the preceding chapters have shown how this value is complicated by the economic models of for-profit digital news outlets and the commercial social media platforms that increasingly serve news to publics. At their core, these models are constructed around the leveraging of emotional response to secure audience attention and interactivity. Although there is no perfect formula for gaming a system that is as unpredictable as the internet itself, coverage of political controversy in pop culture appears to be exceptionally useful for riling up audiences in ways that serve news industry needs. Appeals to partisan identity, including the cultivation of outrage when those identities are seen to be threatened, now drive entire segments of the news business, creating what Ezra Klein has termed the "identity media" industry.[2] When these appeals are combined with extraordinary passions of pop culture identification and fandom, the result can be proverbial rocket fuel for intensive, affectively charged audience engagement. Yet, while emotion is an essential component of public and civic life and arguably the basis for all political action[3]—a point returned to below—it is also unquestionably a breeding ground for commercial exploitation by the news media.

As we have seen, the exploitative potential of entertainment journalism that addresses hot-button political issues involves more than simply the churning out of quick, opportunistic "clickbait" to satisfy audience desires. Rather, industry professionals are quite candid about the sometimes perverse incentives within the business to work up the audience's emotions at all costs, including the push to produce overly provocative work in cynical fashion to induce "hate clicks" and "hate shares." Chapter 4 noted how some editors will commission pieces that are deliberately designed to "throw a stick of dynamite into the conversation," as one veteran journalist put it, regardless of whether the viewpoints or arguments are sincerely held or stand up to scrutiny. When making an impact on the online conversation becomes a top industry priority, even intentionally bad work attains a strategic value for organizational bottom lines. To this point, in chapter 6, we heard from news audience members who are compelled to share pop culture journalism that offends and enrages them as a form of online activism and public shaming, particularly within the context of "cancel culture" backlash that has increasingly moved to the center of partisan political debate. Yet, as long as eyeballs remain trained on the contentious journalism in question, in love or in hate, it has succeeded in its function from a purely financial standpoint.

Furthermore, all of the news industry dynamics that propel the most emotionally provocative journalism at the pop culture–politics nexus are reinforced and strengthened by the profit models of the big tech companies that run social media platforms, which have made emotional manipulation for profit into a precise algorithmic science.[4] According to Pew Research, commercial social media platforms now serve as a source of news for more than half of the US adult population.[5] As long as this trend continues, the most emotionally captivating and reaction-generating news content will be increasingly rewarded with heightened public visibility and circulation in users' newsfeeds.

To be clear, it is a fallacy to label emotion itself as an inherent problem for journalism or for civic engagement more broadly. Such a framework, associated with an old-fashioned rationalist conception of the public sphere, has been rightfully challenged by critics who point out how proscriptions on emotional appeals and rhetoric have been historically leveraged to exclude women and minority groups from participation in civic life while privileging the ostensible "neutrality" and "reason" of the white male status quo.[6] Later, this chapter will consider the immense value of entertainment journalism in providing spaces for members of marginalized groups to publicly articulate their viewpoints and concerns, often in ways that draw on the affective power of pop culture symbolism to resonate strongly and meaningfully with audiences. However, keeping this in mind, it is nonetheless important to interrogate how the industrial dynamics of the digital news landscape can take advantage of what Zizi Papacharissi terms "affective publics," that is, networked groups of citizens who use emotion as a primary means of connecting to politics and public affairs.[7]

In research that upholds the central role of emotion in online-based social movements and in contemporary political life more broadly, Papacharissi also warns that affective stimulation can trap citizens in "constantly regenerative feedback loops" that distract from substantive engagement with public issues even as they satisfy deep emotional needs.[8] In *The Citizen Marketer*, I expand on this argument to address the risks of citizen-level political expression that adopts the emotionally resonant language of pop culture, such as humorous memes that draw connections between real-life politicians and heroes and villains from fictional Hollywood franchises. The most serious threat posed by such an approach to political communication, I argue, is the possibility that emotionally accessible and fulfilling "images and signs will ultimately lose any connection they once may have had to material politics— that is, the on-the-ground distribution of resources—and become pure simulations of the political."[9] In other words, cultural symbols that provide pathways to the political sphere also run the risk of becoming dead ends, as it were, if those connections to political realities are attenuated or even severed altogether.

A very similar threat is embedded in commercially produced journalism that uses pop-cultural subject matter as an entry point into the material political world. By this, I mean that the cultural symbolism of Hollywood and celebrity, while undoubtedly useful for drawing public attention to social and political issues and providing pathways for meaning-making, can also be packaged and sold to news audiences as a gratifying end in itself—an endless cycle of affective stimulation that ultimately has little bearing on matters of public policy and on-the-ground politics. As commercial entities, for-profit journalism organizations are primarily concerned with keeping their target audiences at attention and emotionally engaged, and while journalists within these organizations may aspire to a higher public mission of moving their audience toward political knowledge and civic engagement, the day-to-day realities of the news business place far more emphasis on the former than on the latter. The result, as seen in chapter 4's discussion of the economic incentives of journalism at the pop culture–politics nexus, is a field that is ripe for exploitation in ways that are rather transparent to many professionals who work inside it. Yet, beyond the prospect of cynically cashing in on audience appetites for this emotionally stirring news content regardless of its quality or broader import, entertainment journalism ultimately risks promulgating a kind of ersatz simulation of political discourse that can actively detract from substantive involvement with public issues.

Chapter 6 showed how some members of the engaged news audience grow increasingly concerned about the amount of attention that they themselves, or close family members, give to pop culture stories as part of a broader news diet. It is not that they deny the potential value of politically oriented entertainment journalism as a public good but rather that they worry about what happens if too much focus is placed on the cultural symbols themselves in lieu of the material political issues that they are ostensibly meant to symbolize. As these critical news consumers tend to stress, this tension is especially heightened in coverage of celebrities, which by its very nature emphasizes the individual over the structural. Landmark events such as #MeToo have powerfully illustrated that Hollywood celebrity news can play a crucial role in raising public awareness about broader civic issues.[10] However, if journalism outlets become too fixated on attracting audience passions via the dramatic intrigue of certain famous individuals, the pathway to substantive issue discussion may become far more difficult. The notion that Hollywood-oriented news can act as a bridge both toward the political sphere and away from it— offering opportunities for public knowledge building as well as empty diversion and distraction—helps to articulate this threat while also not dismissing the "bridge to politics" effect that many news audience members recognize in their own experiences and observations. In the research presented in this book, both realities are salient.

The idea of pop culture discourse as a troublesome and artificial simulation of politics has come into sharper focus in the context of growing public concerns over the role of culture-based outrage in US conservative news media. Following Donald Trump's electoral defeat in 2020 and the crackdown on his supporters' attack on the US Capitol in 2021, right-wing news outlets were eager to find new ways of keeping their target audiences roused and engaged. Almost immediately, battles over pop culture symbolism emerged as a favored agenda for conservative outlets, including backlash against the perceived left-wing "canceling" of children's books by Dr. Seuss, the cartoon character Pepé Le Pew, and the popular toy Mr. Potato Head, among others. At one point, Fox News prime-time host Tucker Carlson even told his audience regarding the Dr. Seuss controversy that "if we lose this battle, America is lost,"[11] and over the course of several months, the Fox News website ran more than thirty different pieces of news content about it. Critics were quick to point out that much of this reporting was misleading or inaccurate; for instance, the decision of Dr. Seuss Enterprises to cease publication of several titles due to their inclusion of outdated racial caricatures was not made under pressure from any progressive activist group or campaign, as pundits such as Carlson had suggested.[12] The fact that pop culture grievance emerged in the post-Trump era as a centerpiece of right-wing news narratives, often under false or misleading pretenses (and in the middle of a deadly Covid-19 pandemic that posed urgent public policy challenges), suggested a worrisome new phase of entertainment news as an intentionally illusory and distractive form of political discourse.

From a sheer economic perspective, this shift in the conservative news media agenda toward pop culture outrage made perfect sense. As seen in previous chapters, backlash against the reshaping of entertainment media to advance progressive social values resonates powerfully with the emotions of right-leaning (and some left-leaning) audience members, catalyzing highly valued clicks, shares, and online comments. These sorts of "cancel culture" stories, wrought with feelings of resentment over a perceived loss of power and social status, are a runaway hit with target audiences of conservative news media companies. It is therefore no wonder that production was ramped up so heavily on these kinds of stories even when the facts did not always support them.

However, from a tactical political perspective, the value of "the Dr. Seuss approach," as Democratic House Speaker Nancy Pelosi once mockingly referred to it to reporters,[13] was less certain. On the one hand, many on the left ridiculed this latest round of pop culture warfare—buoyed by both right-wing news pundits and politicians in unison—over its ostensible absurdity, dubiousness, and disconnection from the pressing issues facing the country. While Democrats were busy tackling the Covid-19 pandemic and other gravely serious policy matters, Republicans, so it seemed, were being led astray into a ludicrous fantasy world of cultural grievance, centered this time on an impassioned defense of childhood nostalgia from the forces of "wokeness." On the other hand, some commentators warned that this new wave of "cancel culture" backlash could have very real political effects in terms of mobilizing the conservative base with a powerfully emotional call to arms. For instance, in a clip that was eagerly reported by right-wing news outlets, late-night TV comedy host Jimmy Kimmel remarked that "this is how Trump gets reelected, by the way. Cancel Dr. Seuss.... That is his path to victory the next time around."[14] According to this line of reasoning, even if these pop culture news stories are contrived in cynical fashion and bear little connection to reality, the intense affect that they catalyze among targeted segments of the public can be concretely and strategically valuable for future partisan political struggles.

As noted in chapter 1, critics of for-profit opinion journalism and punditry have raised important concerns about how well-funded news companies use their industry position and power to manipulate audiences and promote the elite-serving agendas of their owners.[15] Here we can connect this line of critique to the issue of news outlets manufacturing pop culture controversy out of whole cloth to keep their audiences enraged and engaged. Not only does this journalism serve the bottom line in the short term, but it can also help foster long-term public support for political institutions that represent the interests of managers (in this case, the Republican Party). To put it another way, the threat of entertainment news discourse as an empty simulation of politics is about far more than just mindless commercial exploitation of audience affect. Rather, it is also about the use of economic power in the information landscape to secure political power, as the fabrication of emotionally gripping pop culture–politics coverage becomes a way for news companies to lure in audiences and keep them in line with institutional interests.

The Dr. Seuss saga of 2021, in all its apparent cynicism and vacuity, dramatically highlights how the conservative news media exploits pop culture warfare as an ersatz form of politics for financial and strategic gain. However, it is also important to recognize a parallel threat regarding for-profit journalism of the left, which shares the same core business models as its right-wing counterpart. Although many applaud left-leaning news organizations for using pop culture discourse as a vehicle to advance the values of social justice, such a project is not immune from being corrupted by institutional and profit-making agendas. The close of chapter 2 showed how entertainment journalists on the left (as well as on the right) express concerns about how corporations like Disney can exploit the rhetoric of diversity and inclusion to garner favorable news coverage, boost their public reputations, and expand their capitalistic profit-making efforts to new market segments, all while making superficial and cosmetic changes that fall short of meaningful progress. To a degree, such concerns point to the possibility of a progressive public discourse around pop culture that is similarly detached from political reality and hollow in its substance—a mirror of the empty simulation of political discourse fomented by segments of the right.

As addressed in chapter 2, some skeptical commentators on the left take entertainment companies to task for surface-level diversity moves that are seemingly motivated by corporate self-interest rather than a sincere and deep commitment to advancing social change. However, in the process of courting diversity-minded target audiences, left-leaning entertainment journalists have afforded an enormous amount of positive attention to Hollywood's inclusion efforts around race, gender, and sexuality, to the point where some of them worry that they are being taken advantage of merely to secure sympathetic coverage for corporate entertainment products. Such a critique highlights the profit motives of the entertainment industry as a potentially corrupting force on diversity discourse, yet it also suggests how the commercial imperatives of the for-profit journalism that covers it can exacerbate this threat.

Following from this point, the news industry trend of market segmentation along the lines of social identity—including corporate offshoots and "verticals" aimed at news consumers who are LGBT, women, African Americans, and so on—signals how identity politics has become big business and is therefore becoming more vulnerable to calculated exploitation. As Klein stresses in his critique of for-profit "identity media," this kind of market segmentation incentivizes outlets to prioritize news content that affirms the identity of target audiences and keeps them engaged and wanting more, while potentially leaving other news values as secondary priorities.[16] Notably, these kinds of identity-centered segments in the for-profit journalism landscape—for instance, the Black, Latin, Asian, and Queer Voices sections of the Huffington Post (owned by Verizon, and later, Buzzfeed), as well as the African American–aimed Andscape, formerly the Undefeated, from ESPN (owned by Disney) and the LGBT-aimed Them (owned by Condé Nast)—regularly feature coverage of pop culture representation and controversy that pertains to the specific identities of their target audiences. This is not to say that entertainment journalism in outlets such as these is necessarily reductive or detached from broader political discourse simply because of how it fits within commercial agendas of audience segmentation. Rather, it is that such a risk is magnified when profit-making models increasingly focus on the monetization of identity.

Just as some critics point out how entertainment companies can superficially sell diversity and progressive identity politics to audiences as just another product, so, too, can the journalism organizations that champion the pop culture diversity cause (in fact, due to patterns of contemporary media conglomeration, these companies can sometimes be one and the same). It is true that for many, any discussion of race, gender, or sexuality within a commercial news media landscape that has historically sidelined such issues will be welcomed as a net positive. However, if these discussions are contrived to simply flatter the identities of target audience groups and ensure that they remain emotionally absorbed, there is a risk that such coverage will become facile, rote, and ultimately of disservice to the cause of progressive social transformation which demands thoughtful and in-depth journalism of the highest caliber. At worst, such profit-seeking journalism at the pop culture–politics nexus risks distracting from on-the-ground struggles for social justice, with the flashy minutia of Hollywood casting news or celebrity tweets, for instance, crowding out space for journalism that more meaningfully addresses the material political realities that face marginalized groups.

As explored in chapter 6, this threat of empty distraction is far from abstract or theoretical for some news audience members who grow concerned about the amount of time and attention given to consuming politics through the appealing lens of entertainment and celebrity. However, such a threat is less about the mere act of conjoining cultural symbolism with political issue discourse than about the substantive quality of these connections as they are forged by news professionals. In other words, if entertainment journalism is to serve more as a "bridge to politics" than a bridge away from it, it must meaningfully articulate the relationship between pop culture symbols and the broader social issues that they signify—for instance, by making clear and direct connections between the hardships facing individual celebrities from marginalized groups and the wider oppression facing these groups at a structural level, or by highlighting how issues of racism, sexism, homophobia, and transphobia in Hollywood narratives can alert audiences to the struggles of those whose lives are not dramatized on-screen.

How can such connections be potentially strengthened in the service of public value? As chapter 4's discussion of news economics showed, tensions between journalistic quality and hyper-commercialism are experienced highly unevenly in the entertainment journalism landscape, with only the most financially successful and prestigious outlets having the luxury of keeping commercial pressures at bay and investing in more in-depth cultural reporting and commentary. Thus, simply calling for increased quality in entertainment journalism without addressing the economic discrepancies and inequalities within it does little to attack the broader problem. Recent industry shifts toward subscription revenue over advertising may help to mitigate some of the worst excesses of attention-seeking "clickbait," but even so, the business models of commercial news organizations are still intertwined with the attention-for-profit schemes of social media companies that now serve as news distribution channels for a majority of the public. As long as the core profit models endure, the threats posed by hyper-commercialism will continue to vex at least some segments of the entertainment journalism field, particularly those outlets that are struggling to survive in a highly competitive attention economy that has room for only a small upper echelon of resource-rich prestige brands.

An alternative to all of this, of course, is publicly funded journalism, which represents only a tiny fraction of a US news landscape dominated by commercial enterprises. Sadly, the expansion of US public media appears to be a lost cause in a digital era marked by information abundance rather than scarcity, even though there is a compelling argument to be made that public funding of high-quality journalism is needed now more than ever to counteract the hyper-commercialism that has greatly intensified in the transition to online news production and distribution.[17] Here the Nordic media landscape, which includes a sizable role for both cultural affairs reporting and state intervention and funding,[18] can be viewed as an aspirational model. As discussed in chapter 1, the conceptual framework of cultural journalism serving a public value has emerged largely from the Nordic context, as scholars there have identified the important role that it has played in democratic discourse and societal debate.[19] Although recent economic and technological shifts have challenged the Nordic media model and introduced new problems related to commercialism, an enduring public service ethos continues to define its journalism landscape, which, along with its ongoing commitment to socially and politically engaged cultural affairs reporting, remains unique in a global context.[20] At the very least, the Nordic example helps us to imagine how high-quality journalism at the pop culture–politics nexus can thrive outside of the most acute pressures of hyper-commercialism and contribute to the public value of the news and information environment as a whole.

Hyper-Partisanship and the Threat of the Propaganda Funnel

In addition to problems stemming from commercial forces, a further issue that can complicate the public value of entertainment journalism in its engagement with politics stems from the dynamics of hyper-partisanship. Although the two sets of issues are clearly intertwined, with the profit models of digital news incentivizing the production of "red meat" coverage for polarized audiences, it would be a mistake to view the latter as simply an outgrowth of the former. Rather, previous chapters have shown how the interpretive communities of both right-wing and left-wing journalists are committed to broader projects of social and cultural transformation that are often propelled by more than the promise of short-term monetary rewards. Within these ideological projects, we can identify certain excesses in tactics and rhetoric that risk flattening the nuance of political discussion as well as providing grounds for backlash that may impede the long-term goals that they set out to achieve. While such excesses are certainly heightened by the economic pressures of the digital journalism industry, they also emerge from deeper intellectual fractures regarding the appropriate role of arts and entertainment in society and the potential limits of their politicization.

Specifically, a palpable tension has been noted in entertainment journalism between upholding cultural expression as a humanistic enterprise wrought with complexity and open-ended exploration of social issues and approaching it as a more straightforwardly functionalist vehicle for political messaging and influence. Of course, the entertainment industry itself has been grappling with this tension for quite a long time, and chapter 2 has shown how the journalistic apparatus surrounding it has become a key source of pressure on cultural producers to make entertainment serve a more conscious and deliberate ideological role. As argued throughout this book, there is undeniable value in entertainment journalists drawing public attention to the political dimensions of entertainment and advocating for cultural change as a pathway to broader social change. However, whether that mission can at times be extended too far or pursued too rigidly, to the point of crowding out space for cultural discourse that does not fit as neatly along the lines of today's partisan political battles, is a question that has come to preoccupy the field.

To be clear, many entertainment journalists see even their most politically engaged work as traversing aesthetic, humanistic, and ideological considerations and would maintain that they are not necessarily mutually exclusive. Still, there are clear apprehensions within this journalistic community—as well as among some members of their audience—that a tactical emphasis on the political function of pop culture can be taken to extremes and that something of value may be lost in the process. One way to conceive of this threat, as it were, is to imagine what we can term the *propaganda funnel*. Invoking a word as historically loaded as "propaganda" may be a peril unto itself, but in this context, it is helpful for signaling the feared endpoint of pressing all cultural expression and discourse into the service of po-litical ideology. As the metaphor suggests, there is a risk of funneling arts and entertainment—long recognized as serving a range of complex social functions—into the polarized containers of partisan politics, effectively re-ducing culture to a propaganda role. Although such a risk is inherent to the field of cultural production, it is perhaps even more acute for the discursive interpretation of pop culture in the public sphere, where cultural texts are assigned meanings and value judgments that frequently connect to social and political concerns.

Chapter 2 noted how the position that "all art is political" is widely ac-cepted as a guiding conceptual framework of left-progressive cultural anal-ysis in the news media, and there is undoubtedly a great deal to be gained by applying this framework to any number of pop culture phenomena. However, we have also seen how numerous journalists who engage in such work nevertheless raise concerns about the prospect of pop culture be-coming valued exclusively for its utility in political debate and how this could flatten the richness of the cultural discourse that they value as professional participants. While upholding the notion of using journalism to explore meaningful intersections between the political and cultural fields, they si-multaneously worry that cultural analysis in the news media will suffer if it is collapsed entirely into political punditry along a polarized left-right axis.

Indeed, many entertainment journalists who incorporate elements of left-progressive ideology into their work object to the idea that they are one and the same as partisan pundits and seek to secure a professional space for cul-tural coverage and commentary that can color outside the lines of "camp red" and "camp blue." In parallel fashion, chapter 6 has shown how a portion of the engaged news audience (including some who identify as left-wing) express frustration with what they see as a constant conflation of pop culture and partisan politics as well as with a journalistic climate that seemingly empties out all other dimensions—and pleasures—of the arts in favor of their value as political tools. Of course, such backlash on the part of the audience can be ideologically motivated as well, as critics are often quick to point out. Even so, when the theory of "all art is political" is put into assiduous practice in the form of daily, even hourly headlines across a multitude of news outlets, the field of entertainment journalism runs the risk of exhausting segments of the public and even potentially alienating them from the project of cultural transformation as a pathway to political progress.

The contemporary "cancel culture" debates have put a searing-hot spotlight, at times unfairly, on the threat of the propaganda funnel in entertainment journalism of the left. As seen in chapter 3, conservative commentators have increasingly embraced the argument that pop culture has become overly politicized by its progressive critics and that audiences just want to be left alone to enjoy entertainment without being subjected to perpetual ideological indoctrination. However, while staking out such a position may be rhetorically convenient for rebutting certain left-wing cultural criticism, it is hardly a consistent philosophical stance of right-wing journalism. Rather, the Andrew Breitbart model of partisan warfare that has come to dominate the conservative news media is entirely constructed around its own propaganda funnel, in which entertainment news, like all other forms of news, is strip mined for its ideological ammunition value.

Although the growing imposition of progressive values in the entertainment industry has put right-wing journalism in a more ostensibly fun-defending, "leave us alone" position than it has been in earlier decades, it still regularly engages in active pop culture politicization when it is seen to further conservative narratives and agendas—such as in ongoing negative coverage of Hollywood for including LGBT characters and themes in children's entertainment[21] or in discussions of banning cultural works such as African American author Toni Morrison's acclaimed novel *Beloved* in conjunction with attacks on the teaching of critical race theory in public schools.[22] Far from securing pop culture as an apolitical space for innocent audience pleasures, much of right-wing entertainment journalism has vigorously followed Breitbart's mantra that "politics are downstream from culture" by making arts and entertainment into one of its central battlegrounds. This partisan warfare includes tapping into audiences' fatigue with progressive messaging when it helps to vilify the left, as well as strategically and selectively appealing to freedom-of-expression values when it is useful for arousing "cancel culture" outrage.

However, while some conservative journalists may take these positions cynically and inconsistently, this does not mean that the arguments themselves are wholly devoid of substance. Rather, the tensions that the right-wing news media play upon regarding the potential overpoliticization of pop culture are also vexing for many journalists—and some audience members—across the ideological divide. As seen in previous chapters, the desire for a public cultural discourse that functions as more than the most reductive punditry and that upholds the social role of the arts as complicated and messy rather than neatly polarized is felt broadly and widely in the contemporary news landscape. Indeed, it is a concern that transcends today's "cancel culture" controversies and debates that are often prosecuted in bad faith as a means of fomenting the very hyper-partisanship that news commentators feign to repudiate.

Setting aside the divisive "cancel culture" discourse that tends to muddle rather than clarify the core issues at hand, what can be done to mitigate the threat of the propaganda funnel in journalism at the pop culture–politics nexus and strengthen its intellectual sophistication? Beyond the industry taking steps to address how its profit models incentivize hyper-partisanship, as discussed above, it also stands to benefit from reconsidering the role of professional expertise in coverage of cultural affairs. Such expertise is critical for navigating the complex terrain of today's cultural debates in a way that avoids the pitfalls of overly reductive and flattened discourse. However, as discussed in chapter 4, one of the key complaints of entertainment journalism professionals is how the industry has come to devalue expertise in pop culture analysis, even as it finds extraordinary value in pop culture content itself as a reliable attractor of audience attention.

The ongoing reduction of dedicated professional roles for pop culture reporting and commentary is obviously tied to the challenging economic realities of an industry in profound crisis and transition. However, this trend also reflects industry decision-makers' dismissive attitudes toward the importance of cultural journalism as part of newsrooms' broader public mission. While managers may prioritize the up-to-the-minute quantity of coverage that tackles hot-button controversies in Hollywood, they appear less willing to invest in the quality of this coverage by committing sustained resources to the sorts of experts who are best equipped to elevate audiences' understanding of these issues. The fact that the culture desk has long suffered the reputation of being inessential "soft news," existing solely to pad the pockets of news organizations and subsidize more crucial "hard news" political coverage, has undoubtedly contributed to its undeserved devaluation within the industry.

Furthermore, since pop culture is by its nature such a widely accessible topic, it has come to be considered "fair game" for any industry worker to weigh in on regardless of subject expertise or training. To this point, chapter 4 has shown how some career entertainment journalists grow frustrated with the trend of political pundits dabbling in pop culture analysis without having any prior background in cultural affairs, resulting in work that is knocked for being overly simplified and flattened along well-worn partisan fault lines. As professional experts in arts and entertainment often maintain, not all pop culture opinions are of equal public value or quality, even though nearly everyone seems to have them and desires to share them with the world (as demonstrated by the intensive social media conversation discussed in chapter 5). Considering how significant and consequential the world of pop culture has become for contemporary political discourse, the journalism industry would be wise to make firmer commitments to professional expertise in its analysis and interpretation. On a practical level, this means expanding rather than cutting dedicated staff roles for cultural coverage, as well as improving the treatment of regularly contributing freelancers rather than merely exploiting the freelance labor market for fast, cheap, and interchangeable "quick hit" content.

Another advantage of investing in dedicated expertise in entertainment reporting and commentary is that it can help forge closer ties between this journalism and the scholarly fields of communication, media, and cultural studies. In the same way that academic medical research deeply informs the practice of health journalism or climate science shapes the work of environmental journalism, the scholarship on pop culture and its political dimensions contributes important insights that can be highly valuable for popular journalism's explorations of these topics. However, while entertainment journalists sometimes cite this sort of research or reach out to academics for a quick sound bite—often to add a veneer of legitimacy to discussions that are otherwise assumed to be frivolous, as celebrity studies scholar Graeme Turner points out[23]—the bridge between these two worlds can be made far stronger. To do so, journalists would need to engage regularly with academic research and draw upon it as a resource to help lead and guide, rather than merely buttress, coverage and commentary at the pop culture–politics nexus.

Of course, such engagement requires an amount of time and effort that likely far exceeds the capacity of journalists who are tasked by their managers with playing more and more professional roles. Yet, by committing more substantively to the development of this subject expertise within its workforce, the industry can help foster a more intellectually sophisticated mode of entertainment journalism that marries academic insight to the day-to-day reporting and analysis of pop culture controversy. As stressed in chapter 1, one of the key public contributions of today's entertainment journalism is that it can provide audiences with a mass-market version of media and cultural studies discourse that engages with issues of power, identity, symbolic erasure, and much, much more. If this role is to grow rather than wither in the face of increasing economic pressures and the most reductive forms of hyper-partisanship, the news industry must treat the pop culture beat as the serious journalistic enterprise that the public needs it to be, now more than ever.

There are those on the right who would likely counter that incorporating academic theory into journalistic discourse would only serve to ratchet up the tensions of hyper-partisanship. It is certainly true that critical theory—especially that which addresses inequality along the axes of race, gender, and sexuality—has become a major source of partisan contention in recent years (with critical race theory in particular being singled out as the latest public enemy number one of the conservative news media).[24] However, the actual scholarship in these areas tends to be far more complex and nuanced than its caricature in hostile news commentaries, whose authors would likely benefit from engaging substantively with this literature and its arguments rather than using them merely as politically expedient punching bags.

The fields of media and communication studies have indeed made important contributions to our understanding of audience reception and interpretation which can provide much-needed nuance to the public conversation around the entertainment industry's political impact. Too often, "quit hit" coverage of such issues leans on highly simplified ideas about media effects that have been largely abandoned by scholars in favor of theories that address the complexities of the audience meaning-making process (such as Stuart Hall's famous "encoding/decoding" model, taught widely in media studies courses, which emphasizes the agency of audience members of different social positions to interpret media content from negotiated and resistant positions as well as in the manner intended by producers).[25] Although some experts in the entertainment journalism field would be quite familiar with this body of theory, it is too much to expect that anyone who is assigned a byline that touches on pop culture's political dimensions would be able to study up on this homework, especially under tight deadline. Again, the more subject-specific expertise is cultivated in entertainment journalism, the better positioned the field will be to expand public understanding of the knotty issues at hand and avoid slipping into the most reductive and diminishing clichés.

Expanding What Counts as Political Discourse:
A Cause for Celebration

At the same time as we consider the significant criticisms that surround entertainment journalism in its engagement with political issues, it is also important to take stock of its achievements at a time when this area of coverage has risen to newfound public prominence. The ongoing explosion of pop culture–politics discourse in the news—buoyed by the rise of progressive social movements such as #MeToo and Black Lives Matter as well as intensifying cultural backlash from the right—has certainly brought about plenty of exploitative "clickbait" and other journalism of negligible quality and value. Yet it has also afforded a platform for vital new voices to emerge in the public sphere, particularly from members of marginalized groups who have long struggled to gain a foothold in the news media conversation.

This trend in journalism can be seen as an outgrowth of a much broader historical dynamic in which pop culture has served as a crucial vehicle for marginalized groups to secure entrance into public discourse when excluded from the "official," rationalist political conversation controlled by traditional social elites. Such a pattern has been central to myriad academic analyses of arts and entertainment as alternative avenues of political communication and public sphere participation, such as Richard Iton's work on the role of African American musicians and actors in impacting post-civil-rights-era public policy,[26] Wendy Parkins's work on the use of fashion in the women's suffrage movement,[27] and Larry Gross's work on the role of film and television visibility in the advancement of gay and lesbian rights.[28] As this book has shown, a parallel story has been unfolding in the journalism world, as the culture desk has developed over time into an epicenter for underrepresented and minority perspectives that historically have had difficulty breaking into more traditional areas of politics coverage.

The fact that the entertainment world itself continues to make advances in expanding diversity and inclusion has created felicitous conditions for the journalism that covers it to follow suit. However, credit is also due to the reporters, commentators, and editors who have actively embraced the pop culture beat as a platform to popularize the concerns of social groups that have been left out of traditional political discourse. Although the diversification of the entertainment journalism workforce remains a far from complete project, as discussed in chapter 2, we can nonetheless applaud the considerable advances that journalists from marginalized groups have made in redirecting the cultural conversation toward issues of oppression and justice. Crucially, these voices not only expand the range of available opinion and viewpoint in the news but also expand the scope of what counts as political discourse and what kinds of issues are considered newsworthy and pertinent for journalistic scrutiny. As I write this, for instance, the news is full of articles addressing the lack of Afro-Latino representation in the Dominican-American-themed musical film *In the Heights*.[29] Where else in the US news media would we hear about the problem of colorism in Latin American communities other than from cultural journalists from these communities raising the issue in the context of a new Hollywood release?

As seen in chapter 5's discussion of social media, entertainment journalists from marginalized groups persist in this important work in the face of immense online harassment and hate that targets their very identities and at times even threatens to intimidate and frighten their public voices into silence. Although all sorts of journalists are now subjected to online public animus due to the two-way nature of social media communication, minority and women journalists bear the brunt of it, especially when commenting on matters of identity politics that evoke extraordinarily intense reactions from certain segments of the audience.[30] Despite death threats, rape threats, racial slurs, and more, these journalists display enormous bravery in entering into some of the most contentious areas of contemporary public debate which nearly guarantee an ugly backlash. The fact that they are routinely subjected to abuse and harassment when calling for increased media representation of their own identities, for instance, underscores the continuing need for such advocacy as well as its central significance for contemporary political struggle more broadly.

Yet not all public reaction to pop culture coverage aimed at advancing the cause of social progress is so negative and hostile (or frustrated and exhausted, for that matter). Rather, firsthand audience testimonies, as well as journalists' accounts of online responses to their work, have shown how some members of the public find immense meaning and significance in news that explores how identity politics manifest in the world of entertainment and celebrity. In particular, some audiences report gaining valuable new perspectives on the struggles of various marginalized groups from seeing and hearing how journalists who are themselves members of those groups interpret their symbolic representation in the world of entertainment. In addition, chapter 6 has shown that some audience members are not only supportive of such discussions but also spurred to participate in them in the highly interactive digital media environment. In many instances, this journalism is used as building blocks for individual and networked acts of online political expression and advocacy in struggles against white supremacy, misogyny, homophobia, and transphobia, further signaling its public value in contemporary circuits of political communication.

For those who are generally sympathetic to the cause of progressive social justice and sensitive to the politics of identity representation, it may be relatively easy to find value in mass-market journalism that adopts such discourse and serves it up for public consumption and engagement, as simplified and flawed as it sometimes can be. By contrast, it may be more difficult to recognize the public value of entertainment journalism on the right, especially when it is seen to foment the very same oppressive and reactionary ideologies that fuel the critiques of its progressive counterpart. Nevertheless, we can follow the lead of Dannagal Young in noting how conservative media can contribute to a vibrant public debate, in this case regarding the politics of pop culture, through the use of outrage-heavy rhetorical styles that may cause outside observers to bristle yet resonate strongly with like-minded audiences.[31] Although this debate can often turn heated and even ugly, there is value to be found in each ideological faction pointing out the excesses and flaws of the other, and this includes the right's salient (if at times disingenuous) appeals to freedom of expression and aestheticist values as a counterbalance to the push for social progress through tightened control of pop culture symbolism. This is not to argue that conservatives have the higher moral ground in these debates, but rather to recognize that deliberative encounters with an ideological opposition can alert citizens of various persuasions to the weaknesses of their own frameworks and arguments and ultimately strengthen the intellectual sophistication of their advocacy.

Unfortunately, much of the cross-cutting journalistic discourse that currently takes place between cultural commentators of the left and those on the right is more reactionary than deliberative in character, particularly as the latter have come to use the former as a springboard for launching sensationalized "cancel culture" attacks. Yet, as also seen in chapter 3, certain segments of the conservative news sphere are committed to engaging in nuanced discussion on the politics of pop culture and distancing themselves from a more hyper-partisan news model that focuses solely on "red meat" content as "culture war" ammunition. Although the hyper-partisan approach continues to flourish in a post-Trump right-wing media landscape that has taken pop culture battling to newfound levels of aggression and vitriol, it appears that there is also room within journalism—as well as audience appetite—for a more deliberative and open-minded cross-cutting discourse.

Such a prospect is buoyed by the fact that some "nuance" journalists on the right lay claim to a shared set of core values with their progressive colleagues regarding the importance of media diversity, seeking not to cut off this public conversation but rather to expand it to include underrepresented groups who lean conservative, such as rural dwellers and the religiously observant. Along these lines, it was heartening to learn that two of the entertainment journalists interviewed for this book, one known for right-wing film criticism and one for left-wing film criticism, had cohosted a podcast in which they debated the pop culture controversies of the day in the spirit of mutually respectful public dialogue. The podcast and others like it suggest a promising journalistic model for how these perspectives can benefit from being in conversation with each other, as opposed to merely talking past each other or having entirely different conversations altogether.

Yet, despite the possibility of carving out a more deliberative space for pop culture–politics discourse in the news media, it is naive to propose that the broader struggles over social and cultural identity that animate such debates can ever be "solved" by fostering just enough public dialogue. Certainly, there is no Hollywood ending to the ongoing "culture wars" discussed throughout this book. Rather, they have become as heated as ever in contemporary news media and in US political discourse more broadly, boiling up from historical struggles over racism and other forms of systematic oppression and marginalization that are far from being settled anytime soon. For entertainment journalism to provide value to the public, it must not only reference these struggles as a means of grabbing audience attention but also forge thoughtful and insightful connections between the accessible symbolism of pop culture and the material political realities facing everyday citizens. The very best professionals in the field are already engaged in such an endeavor. Yet the journalism industry as a whole—along with the academic communities surrounding it—still has a long way to go in reconceptualizing pop culture reporting and commentary as essential tools for making sense of our complex social and political realities.

Notes

Chapter 1

1. John Street, *Politics and Popular Culture* (Philadelphia: Temple University Press, 1997).
2. This body of academic theory is referred to as mediatization, which is broadly concerned with "the role of the media in the transformation of social and cultural affairs." Stig Hjarvard, *The Mediatization of Culture and Society* (New York: Routledge, 2013), 5.
3. Michael Schudson, *Why Journalism Still Matters* (Cambridge: Polity, 2018), 123.
4. Ibid., 123–24.
5. Robert McChesney, *Digital Disconnect: How Capitalism Is Turning the Internet against Democracy* (New York: New Press, 2013), 189.
6. Caitlin Petre, *All the News That's Fit to Click: How Metrics Are Transforming the Work of Journalists* (Princeton, NJ: Princeton University Press, 2021), 6.
7. Jacob L. Nelson, *Imagined Audiences: How Journalists Perceive and Pursue the Public* (New York: Oxford University Press, 2021), 16.
8. Pablo J. Boczkowski and Eugenia Mitchelstein, *The News Gap: When the Information Preferences of the Media and the Public Diverge* (Cambridge, MA: MIT Press, 2013), 2.
9. Ibid., 22.
10. Bruce Williams and Michael X. Delli Carpini, *After Broadcast News: Media Regimes, Democracy, and the New Information Environment* (New York: Cambridge University Press, 2011).
11. George Brock, *Out of Print: Journalism and the Business of News in the Digital Age* (London: Kogan Page, 2013), 233.
12. Ibid., 94.
13. Ronald N. Jacobs and Eleanor R. Townsley, *The Space of Opinion: Media Intellectuals and the Public Sphere* (New York: Oxford University Press, 2011).
14. Michael Serazio, *The Power of Sports: Media and Spectacle in American Culture* (New York: New York University Press, 2019), 84.
15. Ibid., 89–90.
16. Ibid., 228.
17. Sharon Meraz, "Using Time Series Analysis to Measure Intermedia Agenda-Setting Influence in Traditional Media and Political Blog Networks," *Journalism & Mass Communication Quarterly* 88, no. 1 (March 2011): 176–94, https://doi.org/10.1177/107769901108800110; Chris J. Vargo and Lei Guo, "Networks, Big Data, and Intermedia Agenda Setting: An Analysis of Traditional, Partisan, and Emerging

Online U.S. News," *Journalism & Mass Communication Quarterly* 94, no. 4 (December 2017): 1031–55, https://doi.org/10.1177/1077699016679976.

18. Schudson, *Why Journalism Still Matters*.

19. Ibid., 151.

20. Jacobs and Townsley, *The Space of Opinion*, 9.

21. Eric Alterman, *Sound and Fury: The Making of the Punditocracy* (Ithaca, NY: Cornell University Press, 1999).

22. Edward S. Herman and Noam Chomsky, *Manufacturing Consent: The Political Economy of the Mass Media* (New York: Pantheon, 2002).

23. Jacobs and Townsley, *The Space of Opinion*.

24. David McKnight, "A Change in the Climate? The Journalism of Opinion at News Corporation," *Journalism* 11, no. 6 (December 2010): 693–706, https://doi.org/10.1177/1464884910379704.

25. Dannagal G. Young, *Irony and Outrage: The Polarized Landscape of Rage, Fear, and Laughter in the United States* (New York: Oxford University Press, 2020), 6.

26. McKnight, "A Change in the Climate?," 704.

27. Folker Hanusch, "Broadening the Focus: The Case for Lifestyle Journalism as a Field of Scholarly Inquiry," *Journalism Practice* 6, no. 1 (February 2012): 2, https://doi.org/10.1080/17512786.2011.622895.

28. Fritz Plasser, "From Hard to Soft News Standards? How Political Journalists in Different Media Systems Evaluate the Shifting Quality of News," *Harvard International Journal of Press/Politics* 10, no. 2 (April 2005): 47, https://doi.org/10.1177/1081180X0 5277746.

29. Howard Kurtz, *Media Circus: The Trouble with America's Newspapers* (New York: Times Books, 1994).

30. Hanusch, "Broadening the Focus," 2–11.

31. Elfriede Fürsich, "Lifestyle Journalism as Popular Journalism: Strategies for Evaluating Its Public Role," *Journalism Practice* 6, no. 1 (February 2012): 12–25, https://doi.org/10.1080/17512786.2011.622894.

32. Ibid., 22.

33. See Brian Kellow, *Pauline Kael: A Life in the Dark* (New York: Penguin, 2012).

34. Nete Norgaard Kristensen and Anna Roosvall, "Cultural Communication as Political Communication," in *Power, Communication, and Politics in the Nordic Countries*, ed. Eli Skogerbo et al. (Gothenburg: Nordicom, 2021), 177.

35. John Hartley, "Journalism as a Human Right: The Cultural Approach to Journalism," in *Global Journalism Research: Theories, Methods, Findings, Future*, ed. Martin Loffelholz and David Weaver (Oxford: Wiley-Blackwell, 2008), 44.

36. Marguerite J. Moritz, "How U.S. News Media Represent Sexual Minorities," in *Journalism and Popular Culture*, ed. Peter Dahlgren and Colin Sparks (London: Sage, 1992), 154–70.

37. Matthew A. Baum, "Sex, Lies, and War: How Soft News Brings Foreign Policy to the Inattentive Public," *American Political Science Review* 96, no. 1 (March 2002): 91–109, https://doi.org/10.1017/S0003055402004252.

38. Markus Prior, "Any Good News in Soft News? The Impact of Soft News Preference on Political Knowledge," *Political Communication* 20, no. 2 (April 2003): 149–71, https://doi.org/10.1080/10584600390211172.

39. Nick Couldry and Tim Markham, "Celebrity Culture and Public Connection: Bridge or Chasm?," *International Journal of Cultural Studies* 10, no. 4 (December 2007): 419, https://doi.org/10.1177/1367877907083077.

40. Ibid., 418.

41. Lynn Schofield Clark and Regina M. Marchi, *Young People and the Future of News: Social Media and the Rise of Connective Journalism* (New York: Cambridge University Press, 2017), 94.

42. Ibid., 95.

43. Jacobs and Townsley, *The Space of Opinion*, 5.

44. Ibid., 25.

45. Barbie Zelizer, "Journalists as Interpretive Communities," *Critical Studies in Mass Communication* 10, no. 3 (September 1993): 219–37, https://doi.org/10.1080/152950 39309366865.

46. Stanley Fish, *Is There a Text in This Class? The Authority of Interpretive Communities* (Cambridge, MA: Harvard University Press, 2000).

47. Zelizer, "Journalists as Interpretive Communities," 219.

48. Michael Brüggemann and Sven Engesser, "Between Consensus and Denial: Climate Journalists as Interpretive Community," *Science Communication* 36, no. 4 (August 2014): 399–427, https://doi.org/10.1177/1075547014533662.

49. John Fiske, *Media Matters: Race and Gender in U.S. Politics* (Minneapolis: University of Minnesota Press, 1996).

50. Brüggemann and Engesser, "Between Consensus and Denial," 422.

51. For a comprehensive recounting of the public controversy over *The Birth of a Nation*, see Melvyn Stokes, *D. W. Griffith's* The Birth of a Nation: *A History of "the Most Controversial Motion Picture of All Time"* (New York: Oxford University Press, 2007).

52. Michael Oriard, *King Football: Sport and Spectacle in the Golden Age of Radio and Newsreels, Movies and Magazines, the Weekly and the Daily Press* (Chapel Hill: University of North Carolina Press, 2004), 311.

53. It is worth noting that a tradition of explicitly leftist film criticism flourished in certain cinema journals such as the Communist *Nuestra Cinema* in Spain, yet such activity lay firmly outside the mainstream, at least in the United States. See Fernando Ramos Arenas, "Film Criticism as a Political Weapon: Theory, Ideology and Film Activism in *Nuestro Cinema* (1932–1935)," *Historical Journal of Film, Radio and Television* 36, no. 2 (April 2016): 214–31, https://doi.org/10.1080/01439685.2016.1167466.

54. For a discussion of the Arbuckle trial and the involvement of news media, see Gary Alan Fine, "Scandal, Social Conditions, and the Creation of Public Attention: Fatty Arbuckle and the 'Problem of Hollywood,'" *Social Problems* 44, no. 3 (August 1997): 297–323, https://doi.org/10.2307/3097179.

55. Jennifer Frost, *Hedda Hopper's Hollywood: Celebrity Gossip and American Conservatism* (New York: New York University Press, 2011), 114.

56. Kat Eschner, "The Columnist Who Shaped Hollywood's Most Destructive Witch Hunt," *Smithsonian*, July 28, 2017, https://www.smithsonianmag.com/smart-news/hollywood-columnist-who-shaped-its-most-destructive-witch-hunt-180964208/.

57. Bryan Curtis, "How Muhammad Ali Woke Up Sportswriters," *Ringer*, June 4, 2016, https://www.theringer.com/2016/6/4/16046290/muhammad-ali-sportwriters-rip-477fd1721947.

58. Harry Edwards, *The Revolt of the Black Athlete, 50th Anniversary Edition* (Urbana: University of Illinois Press, 2017), 36.

59. Ibid., 31.

60. Serazio, *The Power of Sports*.

61. See Lynn Spigel and Michael Curtin, eds., *The Revolution Wasn't Televised: Sixties Television and Social Conflict* (New York: Routledge, 1997).

62. Laura Mulvey, "Visual Pleasure and Narrative Cinema," in *Visual and Other Pleasures*, by Laura Mulvey (London: Palgrave Macmillan, 1989), 14–26, https://doi.org/10.1007/978-1-349-19798-9_3.

63. Katie Kilkenny, "How a Magazine Cover from the '70s Helped Wonder Woman Win Over Feminists," *Pacific Standard*, June 21, 2017, https://psmag.com/social-justice/ms-magazine-helped-make-wonder-woman-a-feminist-icon.

64. For a comprehensive history of the struggle over gay visibility in the media, see Larry P. Gross, *Up from Invisibility: Lesbians, Gay Men, and the Media in America* (New York: Columbia University Press, 2001).

65. Shanto Iyengar and Sean J. Westwood, "Fear and Loathing across Party Lines: New Evidence on Group Polarization" *American Journal of Political Science* 59, no. 3 (July 2015): 690–707, https://doi.org/10.1111/ajps.12152.

66. Lilliana Mason, *Uncivil Agreement: How Politics Became Our Identity* (Chicago: University of Chicago Press, 2018).

67. Anthony Giddens, *Modernity and Self-Identity: Self and Society in the Late Modern Age* (Stanford, CA: Stanford University Press, 1991).

68. Clark and Marchi, *Young People and the Future of News*.

Chapter 2

1. In total, thirty three entertainment journalists and editors were interviewed, representing a wide variety of legacy and digital-only publications. This chapter focuses on the testimonies of twenty four left-oriented news professionals, while those on the right are discussed mainly in the following chapter.

2. Moritz, "How U.S. News Media Represent Sexual Minorities."

3. See James Davison Hunter, *Culture Wars: The Struggle to Define America* (New York: Basic Books, 1991).

4. For an extended discussion of #GamerGate, see Shira Chess and Adrienne Shaw, "A Conspiracy of Fishes, or, How We Learned to Stop Worrying about #GamerGate and Embrace Hegemonic Masculinity," *Journal of Broadcasting & Electronic Media* 59, no. 1 (January 2015): 208–20, https://doi.org/10.1080/08838151.2014.999917.

5. Alice Marwick and Rebecca Lewis, "Media Manipulation and Disinformation Online," Data&Society, May 15, 2017, https://datasociety.net/wp-content/uploads/2017/05/DataAndSociety_MediaManipulationAndDisinformationOnline-1.pdf.

6. For a discussion of #MeToo and online activism, see Kaitlynn Mendes, Jessica Ringrose, and Jessalynn Keller, "#MeToo and the Promise and Pitfalls of Challenging Rape Culture through Digital Feminist Activism," *European Journal of Women's Studies* 25, no. 2 (May 2018): 236–46, https://doi.org/10.1177/1350506818765318.

7. For further discussion of how #MeToo news coverage illustrates the key political role of cultural journalism, see Kristensen and Roosvall, "Cultural Communication."

8. Maegan Clearwood and Hannah L. Jones, "Subjectivity, Identity, and Intersectionality in Arts Journalism: An Interview with Diep Tran," *Journal of Dramatic Theory and Criticism* 33, no. 2 (2019): 45–60, https://doi.org/10.1353/dtc.2019.0003.

9. For an overview of Gramscian theory, see Thomas R. Bates, "Gramsci and the Theory of Hegemony," *Journal of the History of Ideas* 36, no. 2 (April 1975): 351–66, https://doi.org/10.2307/2708933.

10. Theodor W. Adorno and Max Horkheimer, "The Culture Industry: Enlightenment as Mass Deception," in *Philosophers on Film from Bergson to Badiou*, ed. Christopher Kul-Want (New York: Columbia University Press, 2019), 80–96, https://doi.org/10.7312/kul-17602-005.

11. Stuart Hall, ed., *Representation: Cultural Representations and Signifying Practices* (London: Sage, 1997).

12. Isabel Molina-Guzmán, "#OscarsSoWhite: How Stuart Hall Explains Why Nothing Changes in Hollywood and Everything Is Changing," *Critical Studies in Media Communication* 33, no. 5 (October 2016): 438, https://doi.org/10.1080/15295036.2016.1227864.

13. Isabel Molina-Guzmán, "Why Hollywood Remains 'SoWhite' and a Note on How to Change It." In *The Myth of Colorblindness*, ed. Sarah E. Turner and Sarah Nilsen (Cham, Germany: Springer, 2019), 35–57, https://doi.org/10.1007/978-3-030-17447-7_3.

14. See, e.g., Stacy L. Smith, Marc Choueiti, and Katherine Pieper, "Inequality in 1,300 Popular Films: Examining Portrayals of Gender, Race/Ethnicity, LGBTQ & Disability from 2007 to 2019" Annenberg Inclusion Initiative, 2020, https://assets.uscannenberg.org/docs/aii-inequality_1300_popular_films_09-08-2020.pdf.

15. Andrew Breitbart, *Righteous Indignation: Excuse Me While I Save the World* (New York: Grand Central, 2012), 148.

16. For an overview of the #OscarsSoWhite campaign, see Reggie Ugwu, "The Hashtag That Changed the Oscars: An Oral History," *New York Times*, February 6, 2020, https://www.nytimes.com/2020/02/06/movies/oscarssowhite-history.html.

17. Andrew Chadwick, *The Hybrid Media System: Politics and Power* (New York: Oxford University Press, 2013).

18. Sarah J. Jackson, Moya Bailey, and Brooke Foucault Welles, *#HashtagActivism: Networks of Race and Gender Justice* (Cambridge, MA: MIT Press, 2020), 186.

19. See Julianne Schultz, *Reviving the Fourth Estate* (Cambridge: Cambridge University Press, 1998).

20. Nikki Usher, *News for the Rich, White, and Blue: How Place and Power Distort American Journalism* (New York: Columbia University Press, 2021).

21. See, e.g., Anne Johnston and Dolores Flamiano, "Diversity in Mainstream Newspapers from the Standpoint of Journalists of Color," *Howard Journal of Communications* 18, no. 2 (May 2007): 111–31, https://doi.org/10.1080/10646170701309999; Katsuo A. Nishikawa et al., "Interviewing the Interviewers: Journalistic Norms and Racial Diversity in the Newsroom," *Howard Journal of Communications* 20, no. 3 (July 2009): 242–59, https://doi.org/10.1080/10646170903070175.

Chapter 3

1. Breitbart, *Righteous Indignation*, 97.

2. Young, *Irony and Outrage*.

3. See, e.g., Robby Soave and Jane Coaston, "The State of Free Speech on Campus," *Cato Policy Report* 41, no. 5 (September/October 2019), https://www.cato.org/policy-report/september/october-2019/state-free-speech-campus.

4. As Alvarez and Kemmelmeier discuss, "in the United States, the belief in the constitutionally enshrined right to freedom of expression is a cornerstone of American ideology," although this belief is moderated by cultural context. Mauricio J. Alvarez and Markus Kemmelmeier, "Free Speech as a Cultural Value in the United States," *Journal of Social and Political Psychology* 5, no. 2 (February 2018): 708, https://doi.org/10.5964/jspp.v5i2.590.

5. For a discussion of Gramsci's influence on academic theories of cultural hegemony, see T. J. Jackson Lears, "The Concept of Cultural Hegemony: Problems and Possibilities," *American Historical Review* 90, no. 3 (June 1985): 567–93, https://doi.org/10.2307/1860957.

6. "Avengers: Endgame Overtakes Avatar as Top Box Office Movie of All Time," BBC News, July 22, 2019, https://www.bbc.com/news/entertainment-arts-49069432.

7. Pippa Norris and Ronald Inglehart, *Cultural Backlash: Trump, Brexit, and the Rise of Authoritarian-Populism* (New York: Cambridge University Press, 2018).

8. See David A. Neiwert, *Alt-America: The Rise of the Radical Right in the Age of Trump* (London: Verso, 2017).

9. See, e.g., George Leef, "Where Can You Find Diversity on College Campuses?," *National Review*, August 14, 2019, https://www.nationalreview.com/corner/where-can-you-find-diversity-on-college-campuses/.

10. "Understanding QAnon's Connection to American Politics, Religion, and Media Consumption," Public Religion Research Institute, May 27, 2021, https://www.prri.org/research/qanon-conspiracy-american-politics-report/.

Chapter 4

1. David Schilling, "How to Write a Think Piece," *Vice*, December 22, 2013, https://www.vice.com/en/article/9bzyj3/how-to-write-a-think-piece.

2. John Herrman, "Take Time," Awl, September 3, 2014, https://www.theawl.com/2014/09/take-time/.

3. Emily St. James, "Why Cultural Criticism Matters," Vox, December 31, 2018, https://www.vox.com/culture/2018/12/31/18152275/criticism-explained-cultural-writing.

4. Paul S. Moore, "Subscribing to Publicity: Syndicated Newspaper Features for Moviegoing in North America, 1911–15," *Early Popular Visual Culture* 12, no. 2 (April 2014): 260–73, https://doi.org/10.1080/17460654.2014.925252.

5. George Brock, *Out of Print: Journalism and the Business of News in the Digital Age* (London: Kogan Page, 2013).

6. St. James, "Why Cultural Criticism Matters."

7. Michael Barthel and Galen Stocking, "Key Facts about Digital-Native News Outlets amid Staff Cuts, Revenue Losses," Pew Research Center, July 14, 2020, https://www.pewresearch.org/fact-tank/2020/07/14/key-facts-about-digital-native-news-outlets-amid-staff-cuts-revenue-losses/.

8. For a detailed discussion of the uneven financial strains of the news business, see Usher, *News for the Rich, White, and Blue.*

9. See Hanusch, "Broadening the Focus."

10. Williams and Delli Carpini, *After Broadcast News.*

11. Serazio, *The Power of Sports*, 84.

12. Ezra Klein, *Why We're Polarized* (New York: Avid Reader, 2020).

13. Ariel Hasell, "Shared Emotion: The Social Amplification of Partisan News on Twitter," *Digital Journalism* 9, no. 8 (2021): 1085–102 https://doi.org/10.1080/21670811.2020.1831937.

14. For a discussion of Facebook's changes to its algorithm and its impact on journalism, see Jennifer Grygiel, "Facebook Algorithm Changes Suppressed Journalism and Meddled with Democracy," Conversation, July 24, 2019, http://theconversation.com/facebook-algorithm-changes-suppressed-journalism-and-meddled-with-democracy-119446.

15. See Jennifer Rauch, *Resisting the News: Engaged Audiences, Alternative Media, and Popular Critique of Journalism* (New York: Routledge, 2021).

16. Ibid. Rauch's research finds that those on the left focus more on structural critiques of news industry economics, while those on the left gravitate more to critiques of ideological bias in journalism.

17. Usher, *News for the Rich, White, and Blue.*

Chapter 5

1. For a detailed discussion of journalists' self-branding practices on social media, see Cara Brems et al., "Personal Branding on Twitter: How Employed and Freelance Journalists Stage Themselves on Social Media," *Digital Journalism* 5, no. 4 (April 2017): 443–59, https://doi.org/10.1080/21670811.2016.1176534.

2. See Rebecca Harrison, "Gender, Race and Representation in the Star Wars Franchise: An Introduction," *Media Education Journal* 65, no. 2 (2019): 16–19.

3. Nelson, *Imagined Audiences*, 15–16.

4. Ibid., 5.

5. Chadwick, *The Hybrid Media System*.

6. For a detailed discussion of news organizations' use of digital metrics, see Nelson, *Imagined Audiences*, 65–84.

7. Nate Cohn and Kevin Quealy, "The Democratic Electorate on Twitter Is Not the Actual Democratic Electorate," *New York Times*, April 9, 2019, https://www.nytimes.com/interactive/2019/04/08/upshot/democratic-electorate-twitter-real-life.html.

8. Shannon C. McGregor, "Social Media as Public Opinion: How Journalists Use Social Media to Represent Public Opinion," *Journalism* 20, no. 8 (August 2019): 1070, https://doi.org/10.1177/1464884919845458.

9. Ibid.

10. Daniel Geschke, Jan Lorenz, and Peter Holtz, "The Triple-Filter Bubble: Using Agent-Based Modelling to Test a Meta-Theoretical Framework for the Emergence of Filter Bubbles and Echo Chambers," *British Journal of Social Psychology* 58, no. 1 (January 2019): 129–49, https://doi.org/10.1111/bjso.12286.

11. Petre, *All the News That's Fit to Click*, 6.

12. See also Jonah Berger and Katherine L. Milkman, "What Makes Online Content Viral?," *Journal of Marketing Research* 49, no. 2 (April 2012): 192–205, https://doi.org/10.1509/jmr.10.0353.

13. For a discussion of anti-media rhetoric in the Trump era, see Lindsey Meeks, "Defining the Enemy: How Donald Trump Frames the News Media," *Journalism & Mass Communication Quarterly* 97, no. 1 (March 2020): 211–34, https://doi.org/10.1177/1077699019857676.

14. For further discussion of right-wing audiences' politicized resistance to mainstream news media, see *Rauch, Resisting the News*.

15. Caitlin E. Lawson, "Platform Vulnerabilities: Harassment and Misogynoir in the Digital Attack on Leslie Jones," *Information, Communication & Society* 21, no. 6 (June 2018): 819, https://doi.org/10.1080/1369118X.2018.1437203.

16. Silvio Waisbord, "Mob Censorship: Online Harassment of US Journalists in Times of Digital Hate and Populism," *Digital Journalism* 8, no. 8 (September 2020): 1030–46, https://doi.org/10.1080/21670811.2020.1818111.

17. Adrienne Massanari, "#Gamergate and the Fappening: How Reddit's Algorithm, Governance, and Culture Support Toxic Technocultures," *New Media & Society* 19, no. 3 (March 2017): 330, https://doi.org/10.1177/1461444815608807.

18. Ibid.

19. For a detailed discussion of the tactics used to combat online harassment of female journalists more generally, see Michelle Ferrier and Nisha Garud-Patkar, "TrollBusters: Fighting Online Harassment of Women Journalists," in *Mediating Misogyny*, ed. Jacqueline Ryan Vickery and Tracy Everbach (Cham, Germany: Springer, 2018), 311–32, https://doi.org/10.1007/978-3-319-72917-6_16.

20. Brems et al., "Personal Branding on Twitter."

21. Seth C. Lewis, Rodrigo Zamith, and Mark Coddington, "Online Harassment and Its Implications for the Journalist–Audience Relationship," *Digital Journalism* 8, no. 8 (September 2020): 1047–67, https://doi.org/10.1080/21670811.2020.1811743.
22. Ferrier and Garud-Patkar, "TrollBusters," 319.
23. Waisbord, "Mob Censorship," 1045.
24. Chadwick, *The Hybrid Media System*.

Chapter 6

1. Boczkowski and Mitchelstein, *The News Gap*, 19.
2. In total, thirty-five participant interviews were collected for the audience study during the summer of 2020, eighteen of which were conducted via phone (lasting approximately thirty minutes each) and seventeen via back-and-forth written email responses. The participants represent a broad age range, with six participants between eighteen and twenty-nine years old, seven between thirty and thirty-nine, seven between forty and forty-nine, nine between fifty and fifty-nine, and six between sixty and seventy. Regarding racial identity, there was relatively robust diversity, with forty percent of the participants identifying as nonwhite: twenty-one white, seven black, five Asian, and two Hispanic. Gender diversity was also present, with eighteen participants identifying as male, sixteen identifying as female (including two who are transgender), and one identifying as gender nonbinary. To recruit participants, the researcher first identified digital news content that fit the criteria of explicitly addressing both entertainment and political subject matter—Google News searches for "movies *and* political," "TV *and* political," and so on, were used to find relevant news articles that had been published online in the previous week by major commercial US news outlets (these included CNN, the *New York Times*, the *Washington Post*, the *Atlantic*, NBC News, the Huffington Post, Fox News, and Breitbart). Next, the researcher conducted URL searches for these articles on Twitter to identify accounts that had shared links to them. These accounts were then sent messages on Twitter inviting them to volunteer for the study and to begin an institutional-review-board-approved informed consent process.
3. Ed Morales, "The Problem with the 'Hamilton' Movie," CNN, July 7, 2020, https://www.cnn.com/2020/07/05/opinions/hamilton-movie-mixed-messages-black-lives-matter-morales/index.html.
4. See, e.g., Antje Gimmler, "Deliberative Democracy, the Public Sphere and the Internet," *Philosophy & Social Criticism* 27, no. 4 (July 2001): 21–39, https://doi.org/10.1177/019145370102700402.
5. See Brice Nixon, "The Business of News in the Attention Economy: Audience Labor and MediaNews Group's Efforts to Capitalize on News Consumption," *Journalism* 21, no. 1 (January 2020): 73–94, https://doi.org/10.1177/1464884917719145.
6. See also Hasell, "Shared Emotion."
7. Rauch, *Resisting the News*, p. 13.

8. For a detailed discussion of Trump's anti-political-correctness rhetoric, see Jessica Gantt-Shafer, "Donald Trump's 'Political Incorrectness': Neoliberalism as Frontstage Racism on Social Media," *Social Media + Society* 3, no. 3 (July 2017), https://doi.org/ 10.1177/2056305117733226.

9. See Rahma Sugihartati, "Youth Fans of Global Popular Culture: Between Prosumer and Free Digital Labourer," *Journal of Consumer Culture* 20, no. 3 (August 2020): 305– 23, https://doi.org/10.1177/1469540517736522.

10. Ioana Literat and Neta Kligler-Vilenchik, "How Popular Culture Prompts Youth Collective Political Expression and Cross-Cutting Political Talk on Social Media: A Cross-Platform Analysis," *Social Media + Society* 7, no. 2 (April 2021): 10, https://doi. org/10.1177/20563051211008821.

11. Clark and Marchi, *Young People and the Future of News*.

12. Rauch, *Resisting the News*, p. 14.

13. Ibid.

14. Couldry and Markham, "Celebrity Culture and Public Connection."

15. See Joel Penney, *The Citizen Marketer: Promoting Political Opinion in the Social Media Age* (New York: Oxford University Press, 2017), 143–50.

16. Rauch, *Resisting the News*.

17. Boczkowski and Mitchelstein, *The News Gap*, 22.

18. Sharon Meraz and Zizi Papacharissi, "Networked Gatekeeping and Networked Framing on #Egypt," *International Journal of Press/Politics* 18, no. 2 (April 2013): 138– 66, https://doi.org/10.1177/1940161212474472.

Chapter 7

1. Barbie Zelizer, Pablo J. Boczkowski, and C. W. Anderson, *The Journalism Manifesto* (Medford, MA: Polity, 2021).

2. Klein, *Why We're Polarized*.

3. See George E. Marcus, *The Sentimental Citizen: Emotion in Democratic Politics* (University Park: Pennsylvania State University Press, 2002).

4. For a comprehensive discussion of social media platforms as technologies of public exploitation, see José van Dijck, *The Culture of Connectivity: A Critical History of Social Media* (New York: Oxford University Press, 2013).

5. Elisa Shearer and Amy Mitchell, "News Use across Social Media Platforms in 2020," Pew Research Center, January 12, 2021, https://www.journalism.org/2021/01/12/ news-use-across-social-media-platforms-in-2020/.

6. See Karin Wahl-Jorgensen, "Questioning the Ideal of the Public Sphere: The Emotional Turn," *Social Media + Society* 5, no. 3 (April 2019), https://doi.org/10.1177/ 2056305119852175.

7. Zizi Papacharissi, *Affective Publics: Sentiment, Technology, and Politics* (New York: Oxford University Press, 2015).

8. Ibid., 120.

9. Penney, *The Citizen Marketer*, 173.

10. See also Kristensen and Roosvall, "Cultural Communication as Political Communication."

11. Yael Halon, "Tucker Calls for Preserving Legacy of Dr. Seuss: 'If We Lose This Battle, America Is Lost,'" Fox News, March 2, 2021, https://www.foxnews.com/media/tuc ker-carlson-dr-seuss-not-racist.

12. See, e.g., Akin Olla, "No, Dr Seuss and Mr Potato Head Haven't Been 'Cancelled': Here's the Difference," *Guardian*, March 6, 2021, http://www.theguardian.com/commentisf ree/2021/mar/06/dr-seuss-mr-potato-head-cancel-culture.

13. Tyler Olson, "Pelosi Slams GOP for Emphasizing Border Issues: 'I Guess Their Dr. Seuss Approach Didn't Work for Them,'" Fox News, March 11, 2021, https://www. foxnews.com/politics/pelosi-slams-gop-for-emphasizing-border-issues-i-guess-their-dr-seuss-approach-didnt-work-for-them.

14. Joseph Wulfsohn, "Kimmel Warns 'Canceling' Dr. Seuss Is 'How Trump Gets Reelected': Cancel Culture Is 'His Path to Victory,'" Fox News, March 3, 2021, https://www.foxnews.com/entertainment/jimmy-kimmel-dr-seuss-cancel-cult ure-trump.

15. McKnight, "A Change in the Climate?"

16. Klein, *Why We're Polarized*.

17. See McChesney, *Digital Disconnect*.

18. Nete Norgaard Kristensen and Kristina Riegert, "Why Cultural Journalism in the Nordic Countries?," in *Cultural Journalism in the Nordic Countries*, ed. Nete Norgaard Kristensen and Kristina Riegert (Gothenburg: Nordicom, 2017), 9–23.

19. Kristina Riegert and Anna Roosvall, "Cultural Journalism as a Contribution to Democratic Discourse in Sweden," in *Cultural Journalism in the Nordic Countries*, ed. Nete Norgaard Kristensen and Kristina Riegert (Gothenburg: Nordicom, 2017), 89–108.

20. Kristensen and Riegert, "Why Cultural Journalism in the Nordic Countries?"

21. See, e.g., Warner Todd Huston, "13 TV Shows and Characters Pushing the LGBTQ Agenda on Children," Breitbart, June 1, 2021, https://www.breitbart.com/entert ainment/2021/06/01/13-tv-shows-and-characters-pushing-the-lgbtq-agenda-on-children/.

22. See, e.g., Howard Kurtz, "Culture Wars Roaring Back with Virginia's Toni Morrison Book Battle," Fox News, October 28, 2021, https://www.foxnews.com/media/culture-wars-virginia-toni-morrison-book-battle-media-buzz-kurtz.

23. Graeme Turner, "Approaching Celebrity Studies," *Celebrity Studies* 1, no. 1 (March 2010): 11–20, https://doi.org/10.1080/19392390903519024.

24. For example, critical race theory was mentioned more than two thousand times on Fox News during the first half of 2021, in overwhelmingly negative fashion. See Jeremy Barr, "Critical Race Theory Is the Hottest Topic on Fox News. And It's Only Getting Hotter," *Washington Post*, June 24, 2021, https://www.washingtonpost.com/media/2021/06/24/critical-race-theory-fox-news/.

25. Stuart Hall, "Encoding/Decoding," in *Culture, Media, Language*, ed. Stuart Hall et al. (London: Hutchinson, 1980), 128–38.

26. Richard Iton, *In Search of the Black Fantastic: Politics and Popular Culture in the Post–Civil Rights Era* (Oxford: Oxford University Press, 2010).
27. Wendy Parkins, "Protesting Like a Girl: Embodiment, Dissent and Feminist Agency," *Feminist Theory* 1, no. 1 (April 2000): 59–78, https://doi.org/10.1177/1464700002 2229065.
28. Gross, *Up from Invisibility*.
29. See, e.g., Jasmine Haywood, "In the Heights Exemplified the Ugly Colorism I've Experienced in Latinx Communities," Vox, June 18, 2021, https://www.vox.com/first-person/2021/6/18/22537351/in-the-heights-lin-manuel-miranda-colorism.
30. Waisbord, "Mob Censorship."
31. Young, *Irony and Outrage*.

References

Adorno, Theodor W., and Max Horkheimer. "The Culture Industry: Enlightenment as Mass Deception." In *Philosophers on Film from Bergson to Badiou*, edited by Christopher Kul-Want, 80–96. New York: Columbia University Press, 2019. https://doi.org/10.7312/kul-17602-005.

Alterman, Eric. *Sound and Fury: The Making of the Punditocracy*. Ithaca, NY: Cornell University Press, 1999.

Alvarez, Mauricio J., and Markus Kemmelmeier. "Free Speech as a Cultural Value in the United States." *Journal of Social and Political Psychology* 5, no. 2 (February 2018): 707–35. https://doi.org/10.5964/jspp.v5i2.590.

"Avengers: Endgame Overtakes Avatar as Top Box Office Movie of All Time." BBC News, July 22, 2019. https://www.bbc.com/news/entertainment-arts-49069432.

Barr, Jeremy. "Critical Race Theory Is the Hottest Topic on Fox News. And It's Only Getting Hotter." *Washington Post*, June 24, 2021. https://www.washingtonpost.com/media/2021/06/24/critical-race-theory-fox-news/.

Barthel, Michael, and Galen Stocking. "Key Facts about Digital-Native News Outlets amid Staff Cuts, Revenue Losses." Pew Research Center, July 14, 2020. https://www.pewresearch.org/fact-tank/2020/07/14/key-facts-about-digital-native-news-outlets-amid-staff-cuts-revenue-losses/.

Bates, Thomas R. "Gramsci and the Theory of Hegemony." *Journal of the History of Ideas* 36, no. 2 (April 1975): 351–66. https://doi.org/10.2307/2708933.

Baum, Matthew A. "Sex, Lies, and War: How Soft News Brings Foreign Policy to the Inattentive Public." *American Political Science Review* 96, no. 1 (March 2002): 91–109. https://doi.org/10.1017/S0003055402004252.

Berger, Jonah, and Katherine L. Milkman. "What Makes Online Content Viral?" *Journal of Marketing Research* 49, no. 2 (April 2012): 192–205. https://doi.org/10.1509/jmr.10.0353.

Boczkowski, Pablo J., and Eugenia Mitchelstein. *The News Gap: When the Information Preferences of the Media and the Public Diverge*. Cambridge, MA: MIT Press, 2013.

Breitbart, Andrew. *Righteous Indignation: Excuse Me While I Save the World*. New York: Grand Central, 2012.

Brems, Cara, Martina Temmerman, Todd Graham, and Marcel Broersma. "Personal Branding on Twitter: How Employed and Freelance Journalists Stage Themselves on Social Media." *Digital Journalism* 5, no. 4 (April 2017): 443–59. https://doi.org/10.1080/21670811.2016.1176534.

Brock, George. *Out of Print: Journalism and the Business of News in the Digital Age*. London: Kogan Page, 2013.

Brüggemann, Michael, and Sven Engesser. "Between Consensus and Denial: Climate Journalists as Interpretive Community." *Science Communication* 36, no. 4 (August 2014): 399–427. https://doi.org/10.1177/1075547014533662.

Chadwick, Andrew. *The Hybrid Media System: Politics and Power.* Oxford Studies in Digital Politics. New York: Oxford University Press, 2013.

Chess, Shira, and Adrienne Shaw. "A Conspiracy of Fishes, or, How We Learned to Stop Worrying about #GamerGate and Embrace Hegemonic Masculinity." *Journal of Broadcasting & Electronic Media* 59, no. 1 (January 2015): 208–20. https://doi.org/10.1080/08838151.2014.999917.

Clark, Lynn Schofield, and Regina M. Marchi. *Young People and the Future of News: Social Media and the Rise of Connective Journalism.* New York: Cambridge University Press, 2017.

Clearwood, Maegan, and Hannah L. Jones. "Subjectivity, Identity, and Intersectionality in Arts Journalism: An Interview with Diep Tran." *Journal of Dramatic Theory and Criticism* 33, no. 2 (2019): 45–60. https://doi.org/10.1353/dtc.2019.0003.

Cohn, Nate, and Kevin Quealy. "The Democratic Electorate on Twitter Is Not the Actual Democratic Electorate." *New York Times*, April 9, 2019. https://www.nytimes.com/interactive/2019/04/08/upshot/democratic-electorate-twitter-real-life.html.

Couldry, Nick, and Tim Markham. "Celebrity Culture and Public Connection: Bridge or Chasm?" *International Journal of Cultural Studies* 10, no. 4 (December 2007): 403–21. https://doi.org/10.1177/1367877907083077.

Curtis, Bryan. "How Muhammad Ali Woke Up Sportswriters." *Ringer*, June 4, 2016. https://www.theringer.com/2016/6/4/16046290/muhammad-ali-sportwriters-rip-477fd1721947.

Edwards, Harry. *The Revolt of the Black Athlete, 50th Anniversary Edition.* Urbana: University of Illinois Press, 2017.

Eschner, Kat. "The Columnist Who Shaped Hollywood's Most Destructive Witch Hunt." *Smithsonian*, July 28, 2017. https://www.smithsonianmag.com/smart-news/hollywood-columnist-who-shaped-its-most-destructive-witch-hunt-180964208/.

Ferrier, Michelle, and Nisha Garud-Patkar. "TrollBusters: Fighting Online Harassment of Women Journalists." In *Mediating Misogyny*, edited by Jacqueline Ryan Vickery and Tracy Everbach, 311–32. Cham, Germany: Springer, 2018. https://doi.org/10.1007/978-3-319-72917-6_16.

Fine, Gary Alan. "Scandal, Social Conditions, and the Creation of Public Attention: Fatty Arbuckle and the 'Problem of Hollywood.'" *Social Problems* 44, no. 3 (August 1997): 297–323. https://doi.org/10.2307/3097179.

Fish, Stanley Eugene. *Is There a Text in This Class? The Authority of Interpretive Communities.* Cambridge, MA: Harvard University Press, 2000.

Fiske, John. *Media Matters: Race and Gender in U.S. Politics.* Minneapolis: University of Minnesota Press, 1996.

Frost, Jennifer. *Hedda Hopper's Hollywood: Celebrity Gossip and American Conservatism.* New York: New York University Press, 2011.

Fürsich, Elfriede. "Lifestyle Journalism as Popular Journalism: Strategies for Evaluating Its Public Role." *Journalism Practice* 6, no. 1 (February 2012): 12–25. https://doi.org/10.1080/17512786.2011.622894.

Gantt-Shafer, Jessica. "Donald Trump's 'Political Incorrectness': Neoliberalism as Frontstage Racism on Social Media." *Social Media + Society* 3, no. 3 (July 2017). https://doi.org/10.1177/2056305117733226.

Geschke, Daniel, Jan Lorenz, and Peter Holtz. "The Triple-Filter Bubble: Using Agent-Based Modelling to Test a Meta-Theoretical Framework for the Emergence of Filter Bubbles and Echo Chambers." *British Journal of Social Psychology* 58, no. 1 (January 2019): 129–49. https://doi.org/10.1111/bjso.12286.

Giddens, Anthony. *Modernity and Self-Identity: Self and Society in the Late Modern Age.* Stanford, CA: Stanford University Press, 1991.

Gimmler, Antje. "Deliberative Democracy, the Public Sphere and the Internet." *Philosophy & Social Criticism* 27, no. 4 (July 2001): 21–39. https://doi.org/10.1177/01914537010 2700402.

Gross, Larry P. *Up from Invisibility: Lesbians, Gay Men, and the Media in America.* New York: Columbia University Press, 2001.

Grygiel, Jennifer. "Facebook Algorithm Changes Suppressed Journalism and Meddled with Democracy." Conversation, July 24, 2019. http://theconversation.com/facebook-algorithm-changes-suppressed-journalism-and-meddled-with-democracy-119446.

Hall, Stuart. "Encoding/Decoding." In *Culture, Media, Language,* edited by Stuart Hall, Dorothy Hobson, Andrew Lowe, and Paul Willis, 128–38. London: Hutchinson, 1980.

Hall, Stuart, ed. *Representation: Cultural Representations and Signifying Practices.* London: Sage, 1997.

Halon, Yael. "Tucker Calls for Preserving Legacy of Dr. Scuss: 'If We Lose This Battle, America Is Lost.'" Fox News, March 2, 2021. https://www.foxnews.com/media/tucker-carlson-dr-seuss-not-racist.

Hanusch, Folker. "Broadening the Focus: The Case for Lifestyle Journalism as a Field of Scholarly Inquiry." *Journalism Practice* 6, no. 1 (February 2012): 2–11. https://doi.org/10.1080/17512786.2011.622895.

Harrison, Rebecca. "Gender, Race and Representation in the Star Wars Franchise: An Introduction." *Media Education Journal* 65, no. 2 (2019): 16–19.

Hartley, John. "Journalism as a Human Right: The Cultural Approach to Journalism." In *Global Journalism Research: Theories, Methods, Findings, Future,* edited by Martin Loffelholz and David Weaver, 39–51. Oxford: Wiley-Blackwell, 2008.

Hasell, Ariel. "Shared Emotion: The Social Amplification of Partisan News on Twitter." *Digital Journalism* 9, no. 8 (2021): 1085–1102. https://doi.org/10.1080/21670 811.2020.1831937.

Haywood, Jasmine. "In the Heights Exemplified the Ugly Colorism I've Experienced in Latinx Communities." Vox, June 18, 2021. https://www.vox.com/first-person/2021/6/18/22537351/in-the-heights-lin-manuel-miranda-colorism.

Herman, Edward S., and Noam Chomsky. *Manufacturing Consent: The Political Economy of the Mass Media.* New York: Pantheon, 2002.

Herrman, John. "Take Time." Awl, September 3, 2014. https://www.theawl.com/2014/09/take-time/.

Hjarvard, Stig. *The Mediatization of Culture and Society.* New York: Routledge, 2013.

Hunter, James Davison. *Culture Wars: The Struggle to Define America.* New York: Basic Books, 1991.

Huston, Warner Todd. "13 TV Shows and Characters Pushing the LGBTQ Agenda on Children." Breitbart, June 1, 2021. https://www.breitbart.com/entertainment/2021/06/01/13-tv-shows-and-characters-pushing-the-lgbtq-agenda-on-children/.

Iton, Richard. *In Search of the Black Fantastic: Politics and Popular Culture in the Post–Civil Rights Era.* Oxford: Oxford University Press, 2010.

Iyengar, Shanto, and Sean J. Westwood. "Fear and Loathing across Party Lines: New Evidence on Group Polarization." *American Journal of Political Science* 59, no. 3 (July 2015): 690–707. https://doi.org/10.1111/ajps.12152.

Jackson, Sarah J., Moya Bailey, and Brooke Foucault Welles. *#HashtagActivism: Networks of Race and Gender Justice.* Cambridge, MA: MIT Press, 2020.

Jacobs, Ronald N., and Eleanor R. Townsley. *The Space of Opinion: Media Intellectuals and the Public Sphere.* New York: Oxford University Press, 2011.

Johnston, Anne, and Dolores Flamiano. "Diversity in Mainstream Newspapers from the Standpoint of Journalists of Color." *Howard Journal of Communications* 18, no. 2 (May 2007): 111–31. https://doi.org/10.1080/10646170701309999.

Kellow, Brian. *Pauline Kael: A Life in the Dark.* New York: Penguin, 2012.

Kilkenny, Katie. "How a Magazine Cover from the '70s Helped Wonder Woman Win over Feminists." *Pacific Standard,* June 21, 2017. https://psmag.com/social-justice/ms-magazine-helped-make-wonder-woman-a-feminist-icon.

Klein, Ezra. *Why We're Polarized.* New York: Avid Reader, 2020.

Kristensen, Nete Norgaard, and Kristina Riegert. "Why Cultural Journalism in the Nordic Countries?" In *Cultural Journalism in the Nordic Countries,* edited by Nete Norgaard Kristensen and Kristina Riegert, 9–23. Gothenburg: Nordicom, 2017.

Kristensen, Nete Norgaard, and Anna Roosvall. "Cultural Communication as Political Communication." In *Power, Communication, and Politics in the Nordic Countries,* edited by Eli Skogerbo, Oyvind Ihlen, Nete Norgaard Kristensen, and Lars Nord, 177–96. Gothenburg: Nordicom, 2021.

Kurtz, Howard. "Culture Wars Roaring Back with Virginia's Toni Morrison Book Battle." Fox News, October 28, 2021. https://www.foxnews.com/media/culture-wars-virginia-toni-morrison-book-battle-media-buzz-kurtz.

Kurtz, Howard. *Media Circus: The Trouble with America's Newspapers.* New York: Times Books, 1994.

Lawson, Caitlin E. "Platform Vulnerabilities: Harassment and Misogynoir in the Digital Attack on Leslie Jones." *Information, Communication & Society* 21, no. 6 (June 2018): 818–33. https://doi.org/10.1080/1369118X.2018.1437203.

Lears, T. J. Jackson. "The Concept of Cultural Hegemony: Problems and Possibilities." *American Historical Review* 90, no. 3 (June 1985): 567–93. https://doi.org/10.2307/1860957.

Leef, George. "Where Can You Find Diversity on College Campuses?" *National Review,* August 14, 2019. https://www.nationalreview.com/corner/where-can-you-find-diversity-on-college-campuses/.

Lewis, Seth C., Rodrigo Zamith, and Mark Coddington. "Online Harassment and Its Implications for the Journalist–Audience Relationship." *Digital Journalism* 8, no. 8 (September 2020): 1047–67. https://doi.org/10.1080/21670811.2020.1811743.

Literat, Ioana, and Neta Kligler-Vilenchik. "How Popular Culture Prompts Youth Collective Political Expression and Cross-Cutting Political Talk on Social Media: A Cross-Platform Analysis." *Social Media + Society* 7, no. 2 (April 2021). https://doi.org/10.1177/20563051211008821.

Marcus, George E. *The Sentimental Citizen: Emotion in Democratic Politics.* University Park: Pennsylvania State University Press, 2002.

Marwick, Alice, and Rebecca Lewis. "Media Manipulation and Disinformation Online." Data & Society, May 15, 2017. https://datasociety.net/wp-content/uploads/2017/05/DataAndSociety_MediaManipulationAndDisinformationOnline-1.pdf.

Mason, Lilliana. *Uncivil Agreement: How Politics Became Our Identity.* Chicago: University of Chicago Press, 2018.

Massanari, Adrienne. "#Gamergate and the Fappening: How Reddit's Algorithm, Governance, and Culture Support Toxic Technocultures." *New Media & Society* 19, no. 3 (March 2017): 329–46. https://doi.org/10.1177/1461444815608807.

McChesney, Robert. *Digital Disconnect: How Capitalism Is Turning the Internet against Democracy*. New York: New Press, 2013.

McGregor, Shannon C. "Social Media as Public Opinion: How Journalists Use Social Media to Represent Public Opinion." *Journalism* 20, no. 8 (August 2019): 1070–86. https://doi.org/10.1177/1464884919845458.

McKnight, David. "A Change in the Climate? The Journalism of Opinion at News Corporation." *Journalism* 11, no. 6 (December 2010): 693–706. https://doi.org/10.1177/1464884910379704.

Meeks, Lindsey. "Defining the Enemy: How Donald Trump Frames the News Media." *Journalism & Mass Communication Quarterly* 97, no. 1 (March 2020): 211–34. https://doi.org/10.1177/1077699019857676.

Mendes, Kaitlynn, Jessica Ringrose, and Jessalynn Keller. "#MeToo and the Promise and Pitfalls of Challenging Rape Culture through Digital Feminist Activism." *European Journal of Women's Studies* 25, no. 2 (May 2018): 236–46. https://doi.org/10.1177/1350506818765318.

Meraz, Sharon. "Using Time Series Analysis to Measure Intermedia Agenda-Setting Influence in Traditional Media and Political Blog Networks." *Journalism & Mass Communication Quarterly* 88, no. 1 (March 2011): 176–94. https://doi.org/10.1177/107769901108800110.

Meraz, Sharon, and Zizi Papacharissi. "Networked Gatekeeping and Networked Framing on #Egypt." *International Journal of Press/Politics* 18, no. 2 (April 2013): 138–66. https://doi.org/10.1177/1940161212474472.

Molina-Guzmán, Isabel. "#OscarsSoWhite: How Stuart Hall Explains Why Nothing Changes in Hollywood and Everything Is Changing." *Critical Studies in Media Communication* 33, no. 5 (October 2016): 438–54. https://doi.org/10.1080/15295036.2016.1227864.

Molina-Guzmán, Isabel. "Why Hollywood Remains 'SoWhite' and a Note on How to Change It." In *The Myth of Colorblindness*, edited by Sarah E. Turner and Sarah Nilsen, 35–57. Cham, Germany: Springer, 2019. https://doi.org/10.1007/978-3-030-17447-7_3.

Moore, Paul S. "Subscribing to Publicity: Syndicated Newspaper Features for Moviegoing in North America, 1911–15." *Early Popular Visual Culture* 12, no. 2 (April 2014): 260–73. https://doi.org/10.1080/17460654.2014.925252.

Morales, Ed. "The Problem with the 'Hamilton' Movie." CNN, July 7, 2020. https://www.cnn.com/2020/07/05/opinions/hamilton-movie-mixed-messages-black-lives-matter-morales/index.html.

Moritz, Marguerite J. "How U.S. News Media Represent Sexual Minorities." In *Journalism and Popular Culture*, edited by Peter Dahlgren and Colin Sparks, 154–70. London: Sage, 1992.

Mulvey, Laura. "Visual Pleasure and Narrative Cinema." In *Visual and Other Pleasures*, by Laura Mulvey, 14–26. London: Palgrave Macmillan, 1989. https://doi.org/10.1007/978-1-349-19798-9_3.

Neiwert, David A. *Alt-America: The Rise of the Radical Right in the Age of Trump*. London: Verso, 2017.

Nelson, Jacob L. *Imagined Audiences: How Journalists Perceive and Pursue the Public*. New York: Oxford University Press, 2021.

Nishikawa, Katsuo A., Terri L. Towner, Rosalee A. Clawson, and Eric N. Waltenburg. "Interviewing the Interviewers: Journalistic Norms and Racial Diversity in the

Newsroom." *Howard Journal of Communications* 20, no. 3 (July 2009): 242–59. https://doi.org/10.1080/10646170903070175.

Nixon, Brice. "The Business of News in the Attention Economy: Audience Labor and MediaNews Group's Efforts to Capitalize on News Consumption." *Journalism* 21, no. 1 (January 2020): 73–94. https://doi.org/10.1177/1464884917719145.

Norris, Pippa, and Ronald Inglehart. *Cultural Backlash: Trump, Brexit, and the Rise of Authoritarian-Populism*. New York: Cambridge University Press, 2018.

Olla, Akin. "No, Dr Seuss and Mr Potato Head Haven't Been 'Cancelled': Here's the Difference." *Guardian*, March 6, 2021. http://www.theguardian.com/commentisfree/2021/mar/06/dr-seuss-mr-potato-head-cancel-culture.

Olson, Tyler. "Pelosi Slams GOP for Emphasizing Border Issues: 'I Guess Their Dr. Seuss Approach Didn't Work for Them.'" Fox News, March 11, 2021. https://www.foxnews.com/politics/pelosi-slams-gop-for-emphasizing-border-issues-i-guess-their-dr-seuss-approach-didnt-work-for-them.

Oriard, Michael. *King Football: Sport and Spectacle in the Golden Age of Radio and Newsreels, Movies and Magazines, the Weekly and the Daily Press*. Chapel Hill: University of North Carolina Press, 2004.

Papacharissi, Zizi. *Affective Publics: Sentiment, Technology, and Politics*. New York: Oxford University Press, 2015.

Parkins, Wendy. "Protesting Like a Girl: Embodiment, Dissent and Feminist Agency." *Feminist Theory* 1, no. 1 (April 2000): 59–78. https://doi.org/10.1177/1464700002 2229065.

Penney, Joel. *The Citizen Marketer: Promoting Political Opinion in the Social Media Age*. New York: Oxford University Press, 2017.

Petre, Caitlin. *All the News That's Fit to Click: How Metrics Are Transforming the Work of Journalists*. Princeton, NJ: Princeton University Press, 2021.

Plasser, Fritz. "From Hard to Soft News Standards? How Political Journalists in Different Media Systems Evaluate the Shifting Quality of News." *Harvard International Journal of Press/Politics* 10, no. 2 (April 2005): 47–68. https://doi.org/10.1177/1081180X0 5277746.

Prior, Markus. "Any Good News in Soft News? The Impact of Soft News Preference on Political Knowledge." *Political Communication* 20, no. 2 (April 2003): 149–71. https://doi.org/10.1080/10584600390211172.

Ramos Arenas, Fernando. "Film Criticism as a Political Weapon: Theory, Ideology and Film Activism in *Nuestro Cinema* (1932–1935)." *Historical Journal of Film, Radio and Television* 36, no. 2 (April 2016): 214–31. https://doi.org/10.1080/01439 685.2016.1167466.

Rauch, Jennifer. *Resisting the News: Engaged Audiences, Alternative Media, and Popular Critique of Journalism*. New York: Routledge, 2021.

Riegert, Kristina, and Anna Roosvall. "Cultural Journalism as a Contribution to Democratic Discourse in Sweden." In *Cultural Journalism in the Nordic Countries*, edited by Nete Norgaard Kristensen and Kristina Riegert, 89–108. Gothenburg: Nordicom, 2017.

Schilling, David. "How to Write a Think Piece." *Vice*, December 22, 2013. https://www.vice.com/en/article/9bzyj3/how-to-write-a-think-piece.

Schudson, Michael. *Why Journalism Still Matters*. Medford, MA: Polity, 2018.

Schultz, Julianne. *Reviving the Fourth Estate*. Cambridge: Cambridge University Press, 1998.

Serazio, Michael. *The Power of Sports: Media and Spectacle in American Culture.* New York: New York University Press, 2019.

Shearer, Elisa, and Amy Mitchell. "News Use across Social Media Platforms in 2020." Pew Research Center, January 12, 2021. https://www.journalism.org/2021/01/12/news-use-across-social-media-platforms-in-2020/.

Smith, Stacy L., Marc Choueiti, and Katherine Pieper. "Inequality in 1,300 Popular Films: Examining Portrayals of Gender, Race/Ethnicity, LGBTQ & Disability from 2007 to 2019." Annenberg Inclusion Initiative, 2020. https://assets.uscannenberg.org/docs/aii-inequality_1300_popular_films_09-08-2020.pdf.

Soave, Roby, and Jane Coaston. "The State of Free Speech on Campus." *Cato Policy Report* 41, no. 5 (September/October 2019). https://www.cato.org/policy-report/september/october-2019/state-free-speech-campus.

Spigel, Lynn, and Michael Curtin, eds. *The Revolution Wasn't Televised: Sixties Television and Social Conflict.* New York: Routledge, 1997.

St. James, Emily. "Why Cultural Criticism Matters." Vox, December 31, 2018. https://www.vox.com/culture/2018/12/31/18152275/criticism-explained-cultural-writing.

Stokes, Melvyn. *D. W. Griffith's* The Birth of a Nation: *A History of "the Most Controversial Motion Picture of All Time."* New York: Oxford University Press, 2007.

Street, John. *Politics and Popular Culture.* Philadelphia: Temple University Press, 1997.

Sugihartati, Rahma. "Youth Fans of Global Popular Culture: Between Prosumer and Free Digital Labourer." *Journal of Consumer Culture* 20, no. 3 (August 2020): 305–23. https://doi.org/10.1177/1469540517736522.

Turner, Graeme. "Approaching Celebrity Studies." *Celebrity Studies* 1, no. 1 (March 2010): 11–20. https://doi.org/10.1080/19392390903519024.

Ugwu, Reggie. "The Hashtag That Changed the Oscars: An Oral History." *New York Times,* February 6, 2020. https://www.nytimes.com/2020/02/06/movies/oscarssowhite-history.html.

"Understanding QAnon's Connection to American Politics, Religion, and Media Consumption." Public Religion Research Institute, May 27, 2021. https://www.prri.org/research/qanon-conspiracy-american-politics-report/.

Usher, Nikki. *News for the Rich, White, and Blue: How Place and Power Distort American Journalism.* New York: Columbia University Press, 2021.

Van Dijck, José. *The Culture of Connectivity: A Critical History of Social Media.* New York: Oxford University Press, 2013.

Vargo, Chris J., and Lei Guo. "Networks, Big Data, and Intermedia Agenda Setting: An Analysis of Traditional, Partisan, and Emerging Online U.S. News." *Journalism & Mass Communication Quarterly* 94, no. 4 (December 2017): 1031–55. https://doi.org/10.1177/1077699016679976.

Wahl-Jorgensen, Karin. "Questioning the Ideal of the Public Sphere: The Emotional Turn." *Social Media + Society* 5, no. 3 (April 2019). https://doi.org/10.1177/2056305119852175.

Waisbord, Silvio. "Mob Censorship: Online Harassment of US Journalists in Times of Digital Hate and Populism." *Digital Journalism* 8, no. 8 (September 2020): 1030–46. https://doi.org/10.1080/21670811.2020.1818111.

Williams, Bruce Alan, and Michael X. Delli Carpini. *After Broadcast News: Media Regimes, Democracy, and the New Information Environment.* New York: Cambridge University Press, 2011.

Wulfsohn, Joseph. "Kimmel Warns 'Canceling' Dr. Seuss Is 'How Trump Gets Reelected': Cancel Culture Is 'His Path to Victory.'" Fox News, March 3, 2021. https://www.foxnews.com/entertainment/jimmy-kimmel-dr-seuss-cancel-culture-trump.

Young, Dannagal G. *Irony and Outrage: The Polarized Landscape of Rage, Fear, and Laughter in the United States.* New York: Oxford University Press, 2020.

Zelizer, Barbie. "Journalists as Interpretive Communities." *Critical Studies in Mass Communication* 10, no. 3 (September 1993): 219–37. https://doi.org/10.1080/152950 39309366865.

Zelizer, Barbie, Pablo J. Boczkowski, and C. W. Anderson. *The Journalism Manifesto.* Medford, MA: Polity, 2021.

Index

For the benefit of digital users, indexed terms that span two pages (e.g., 52–53) may, on occasion, appear on only one of those pages.